ANTHROPOLOGY AND AI

Anthropology and AI explores the complex intersection of artificial intelligence and human society through a diverse collection of anthropological and social scientific perspectives.

Artificial intelligence is rapidly accelerating and permeating the everyday lives of people around the world in ways that are full of promise, perils, and potentials. How does anthropology respond to this? This timely volume brings together twelve chapters examining AI's many manifestations—from machine listening and engineers' philosophies to large language models and conversational agents. Curated with a broad humanistic and social scientific audience in mind but firmly rooted within broader anthropological and STS conversations about humanity and technology, the contributions are situated on a broad spectrum of approaches to artificial intelligence, spanning theoretical, empirical, and applied social scientific research.

Anthropology and AI will appeal to students and researchers across anthropology, science and technology studies, digital humanities, and computer science who are interested in critical perspectives on emerging technologies.

Lora Koycheva is founder of Robots, actually! and Assistant Professor at the Chair of Technoscience Studies in Brandenburg Technical University, Germany.

Angela K. VandenBroek is Assistant Professor of Anthropology at Texas State University, USA.

Matt Artz is the founder of Azimuth Labs and an Adjunct Professor at the University of Pennsylvania, USA.

ANTHROPOLOGY OF NOW

Series Editor: Jack David Eller

Dispossession
Anthropological Perspectives on Russia's War Against Ukraine
Edited by Catherine Wanner

Gun Rights Activists and the US Culture War
Embodied Fantasies of the Ethical Warrior in Contemporary Gun Culture
Joe Anderson

Anthropology of Ascendant China
Histories, Attainments, and Tribulations
Edited by Mayfair Yang

Culture and Diversity in the United States
So Many Ways to Be American
2nd Edition
Jack David Eller

What Brexit Means
An Anthropology of Polarization and Cultural Change in Britain
Max Horder

Exploring Ethnography of Outer Space
Methods and Perspectives
Edited by Jenia Gorbanenko, David (Jeeva) Jeevendrampillai, and Adryon Kozel

Anthropology and AI
Edited by Lora Koycheva, Angela K. VandenBroek, and Matt Artz

https://www.routledge.com/Anthropology-of-Now/book-series/ANTHNOW

ANTHROPOLOGY AND AI

Edited by Lora Koycheva, Angela K. VandenBroek and Matt Artz

Routledge
Taylor & Francis Group
NEW YORK AND LONDON

Designed cover image: AF-studio, Getty Images

First published 2026
by Routledge
605 Third Avenue, New York, NY 10158

and by Routledge
4 Park Square, Milton Park, Abingdon, Oxon OX14 4RN

Routledge is an imprint of the Taylor & Francis Group, an informa business

Library of Congress Cataloging-in-Publication Data
A catalog record for this title has been requested

ISBN: 978-1-032-87464-7 (hbk)
ISBN: 978-1-032-86619-2 (pbk)
ISBN: 978-1-003-53275-0 (ebk)

DOI: 10.4324/9781003532750

Typeset in Sabon
by Taylor & Francis Books

CONTENTS

ILLUSTRATIONS

Figures

Table

CONTRIBUTORS

Matt Artz is an anthropologist, designer, and technologist specializing in AI product development. He is the founder of Azimuth Labs, host of the Anthropology in Business and Anthro to UX podcasts, and co-editor of *EmTech Anthropology* (Routledge, 2024). His work has been featured on TED, UNESCO, South by Southwest, and Apple's Planet of the Apps.

Juana Becerra is a historian of science and technology, and Staff Research Scientist in the Responsible Tech group at IBM Research. Their research examines histories of the body, subjectivity, automation, and artificial intelligence in the twentieth and twenty-first centuries.

John N. A. Brown is a Lecturer at Robert Gordon University in Scotland, and former consulting UX researcher in Silicon Valley. He specializes in human interaction with technology and the environment, focusing on the evolutionary neuropsychology of learning in humans and AIs.

Rebecca Carlson is Project Coordinator for the SAFIRE programme at the University of Oulu, Finland. She was previously Associate Professor in Media and Culture at Toyo University. As a cultural and visual anthropologist, her research examines the production of subjectivity, knowledge, and power in the transnational circulation of science, technology, and media.

Edward Kang is a scholar of science and technology, and Assistant Professor in the Department of Media, Culture, and Communication at New York University, USA. His book project *Machine Voices* parses how human voices are rendered measurable, analyzable, and replicable mechanisms in voice AI systems.

Lora Koycheva is Assistant Professor at the Chair of Technoscience Studies, Brandenburg Technical University, Germany and founder of Robots, actually!—an initiative to rebuild the human condition with robots. She works at the intersection of anthropology, innovation, entrepreneurship, and robotics and is co-editor of *EmTech Anthropology* (Routledge, 2024).

Larry Sommer McGrath is a research leader at technology firms. He has published about the history and anthropology of science in Aeon, Human-Computer Interaction, and Journal of the History of Ideas. Larry's first book is *Making Spirit Matter: Neurology, Psychology, and Selfhood in Modern France* (2020).

Andrés Pachón is a researcher and visual artist based in Portugal. He holds a PhD in Social and Cultural Anthropology from the University of Coimbra, funded by the Portuguese Foundation for Science and Technology. With a background in Fine Arts, his practice intersects experimental ethnography and visual art, advancing an anthropology of AI.

Elizabeth Rodwell is an Associate Professor of Digital Media and the founding director of the User Experience (UX) Lab at the University of Houston, USA. Her current research examines conversational artificial intelligence and user experience. Her book, *Push the Button: Interactive Television and Collaborative Journalism in Japan*, was published in 2024.

Kate Sieck is Director at Harmonious Communities, Toyota Research Institute, USA. She is an anthropologist and writer exploring the intersections of culture, technology, and ethics. Her work bridges academic insight and practical innovation, with a focus on generative AI. She advocates for human-centered design and cultural understanding in the development and deployment of emerging technologies.

Angela K. VandenBroek is an Assistant Professor of Anthropology at Texas State University, USA, where she combines her research on innovation and entrepreneurship with her nearly two decades of experience in information technologies, design, marketing, and organizational strategy. Her work sits at the intersection of business and design anthropology and feminist science and technology studies.

Libuše Hannah Vepřek is a Postdoctoral Researcher at the Ludwig Uhland Institute for Historical and Cultural Anthropology at the University of Tübingen, Germany. Trained in cultural anthropology and computer science, her main research areas are digital anthropology, anthropology of technology, science and technology studies, moral anthropology, and digital methods.

Sydney Yeager is a digital anthropologist, accessibility advocate, and design researcher. Drawing on her experience with dyslexia, she advocates for accessibility in education and the workplace. She is convenor of the Digital Anthropology Interest Group (DANG), and head of workplace experience research for Walmart's new global headquarters.

ACKNOWLEDGEMENTS

The co-editors would like to extend their gratitude to David Eller for inviting us on this editorial journey and introducing us to the work of several authors featured here. At Routledge, we are thankful for the support of a number of staff members throughout the process and want to extend heartfelt appreciation for the spirit of intellectual encouragement and operational efficiency consistently afforded to us by Meagan Simpson. We also would like to thank several anonymous peer reviewers for their thoughtful and engaged reading of our book proposal, as well as chapters within the book.

Lora Koycheva would like to thank her co-editors and the authors, without whose dedication this project would not be possible. She wants to thank Rafael Hostettler and Alona Kharchenko; as well as colleagues at the Chair of Technoscience Studies at the Brandenburg Technical University, and Prof. Dr. Astrid Schwarz in particular, for their intellectual companionship in all topics of technology, environment, and society. She is forever grateful to Robert Launay, Helen Schwarzman, Bill Murphy, Andrew Causey, and the late Joan Erdman for teaching her about interpreting the world professionally. Finally, she is also in debt to her husband and toddler for their patience in waiting for her to finish yet another "just one more sentence."

Angela K. VandenBroek is grateful to the authors and her co-editors for their collaboration and for pushing one another toward deeper thinking throughout this project. At Texas State University, she wishes to thank her colleagues and students—especially Nicole Taylor and the graduate students in her Innovative Anthropologies Lab workgroup (Manar Naser, Sameeha Vardhan, Anna Huntington, Ian Whitehead, Annemarie Teagle, and Rhiannon Nelson)—for their inspiration, energy, and encouragement. Finally, many thanks to her partner Nick VandenBroek, whose companionship and support made this work possible.

Matt Artz would like to thank Lora, Angela and all of the authors for making this book possible. And he is grateful to Carolina, who patiently endures his creative pursuits while somehow still tolerating the chaos that comes with that.

John Brown would like to thank Jamie Sundance - for helping when it was needed.

Rebecca Carlson's project was funded by the Japan Society for the Promotion of Science's Grant-in-Aid for Scientific Research (C) 20K01188. She would like to thank all the bioscientists who participated in this research.

Edward Kang and Juana Becerra would like to thank the editors and our anonymous reviewers for their generous feedback, as well as Felicia Jing and Stacy Hobson for their support and early comments on this research.

Larry McGrath would like to thank Lora Koycheva and Matt Artz for their editorial guidance; as well as his doctoral advisor, Ruth Leys, for teaching him about the critical practice of interpretation.

Andres Pachon would like to thank Dr. Luís Quintais, University of Coimbra (Portugal). His work was supported by FCT Portugal—Fundação para a Ciência e a Tecnologia: Andrés Pachón Arrones [grant number 2020.04554.BD].

Elizabeth Rodwell gratefully acknowledges financial support for this research by the Fulbright U.S. Scholar Program and the Notre Dame-IBM Technology Ethics Lab. She is also extremely grateful to her hosts at "OratioNet", who allow her to ask constant questions and camp out in their lab for months on end.

Kate Sieck would like to thank David Zeitlyn, Prof of Anthropology, Oxford University; Charlene Wu, PhD, VP, Human-Centered AI at Toyota Research Institute; and Lora Koycheva and Matt Artz for the invitation.

Libuše Vepřek's research was funded as part of the research project "Playing in the Loop: New Human-Software Relations in Human Computation Systems and their Impacts on the Spheres of Everyday Life" funded by the German Research Foundation (DFG 464513114). Parts of the field research were funded by the DAAD program "IFI—Internationale Forschungsaufenthalte für Informatikerinnen und Informatiker (Doktoranden), 20192022 (57515303)". She would like to thank all research partners who participated in this research.

Sydney Yeager would like to thank Greg Wright, her husband and writing partner, who provided invaluable editorial and emotional support without which her chapter would not have been written. She is also grateful to her colleagues Dr. Ava Han, Dr. Michelle Sibenik, Jonathan Thurston, Melissa Waller, Ana Belen Conrado, Jamila Evilsizor, and Lindsey Garza who all supported her accessibility work at Walmart. She is also grateful to her manager, Neil Ross, for his support while she was writing the chapter.

INTRODUCTION

An Anthropological History of AI

Angela K. VandenBroek, Matt Artz and Lora Koycheva

Introduction

As artificial intelligence (AI) evolves from narrow, specialized applications toward increasingly general-purpose systems that engage with human knowledge and culture, fundamental questions about the nature of intelligence, agency, and human-machine relationships have moved to the center of public and scholarly discourse. These questions—about how we define and recognize intelligence, how embodiment and materiality shape understanding, and how different cultural contexts influence our conception of machine capabilities—have long been central to anthropological inquiry. Yet, as AI technologies increasingly mediate social life and cultural production, anthropology's theoretical and methodological contributions risk being overshadowed by computational approaches to understanding human behavior and society.

This volume argues that anthropological perspectives are essential for contextualizing, challenging, and fundamentally reconceptualizing how we understand and develop AI. Rather than solely focusing on binary questions of whether machines can be "truly" intelligent or comparing human and machine capabilities, anthropological approaches have historically helped to reveal how AI functions as a complex sociotechnical phenomenon shaped by cultural assumptions, material constraints, and varied forms of agency. The relationship between anthropology and AI must develop across multiple dimensions simultaneously—studying AI's societal impacts, leveraging AI methods for research, and actively shaping AI development itself.

As Gillian Tett argued in 2021, echoing longstanding anthropological concerns, navigating modern challenges requires what she termed "anthropology intelligence" alongside more positivist analytical approaches (Tett 2021). Her

DOI: 10.4324/9781003532750-1

metaphor—that relying solely on analytical tools is like "walking through a dark wood with a compass at night and only looking down on the dial" (Tett 2021, xiii)—highlights the essential role of anthropological perspectives in illuminating the broader social and cultural contexts in which AI systems operate. The chapters in this volume demonstrate how anthropological perspectives can both critique and contribute to AI development while also showing how AI technologies are transforming the practice of anthropology itself.

This relationship between anthropology and AI has deep historical roots that exceed current recognition. AI has been one of the most enduring conversations in computing—inspiring technological innovations and shaping the imaginations of scientists, researchers, and states since World War II. Yet it remains a domain marked by widespread public confusion and competing definitions, with no clear consensus, even among experts, about its precise nature and capabilities. AI should be understood as a broad constellation of computational tools and techniques that aim to create systems capable of performing tasks that typically require human intelligence, from perception and learning to reasoning, decision-making, and creative acts such as generating text, images, and videos.

Popular histories of AI tend to focus on pivotal events, publications, and inventions that frame AI's development as a linear progression toward artificial general intelligence (AGI). While these narratives capture important technological milestones, they can obscure the complexities and contingencies through which technologies and intellectual traditions are socially produced (Yaneva 2009). Different storytellers naturally emphasize different aspects—"intellectual" histories focus on academic progress, "engineering" histories on technical breakthroughs, and contemporary accounts often center Silicon Valley entrepreneurship and investment dynamics (Edwards 1997; Gebru and Torres 2024). The historical survey that follows traces key moments in this canonical narrative while situating them within broader social and epistemic contexts, with particular attention to anthropology's longstanding but often underrecognized engagements with AI as both technological assemblage and interdisciplinary field of inquiry. Given the expansive nature of this history, we focus primarily on formative developments through the early 2000s, when many foundational patterns were established that continue to shape AI development today.

Precursors & Mythic Figures (1800–1940)

AI emerged from generations of attempts to mechanize human cognitive capabilities. Joseph-Marie Jacquard's 1804 programmable loom used punched cards to automate complex weaving patterns, inspiring Charles Babbage and Ada Lovelace's analytical engine in the 1840s. Lovelace recognized that punch cards could handle any information expressible in symbols—not just weaving patterns—and wrote what is now considered the first computer program. Yet she rejected the possibility of machine intelligence, arguing that the analytical engine "can do whatever we know how to order it to perform... but it has no power of anticipating any analytical relations or truths" (Lovelace 1843, 722). This critique, later termed "Lady Lovelace's objection" by Alan Turing, remains one of the earliest statements on AI. More presciently, she warned against exaggerating the power of computing, noting that people tend to "overrate what we find to be already interesting or remarkable and [...] undervalue the true state of the case" (1843, 722)—an argument anthropologists continue to make about AI discourse today.

Nevertheless, the growing fascination with machines capable of human-like information processing and action between the World Wars found cultural expression in Karel Čapek's 1921 play "R.U.R.," which introduced the term "robot" (derived from the Czech word for forced labor) and established enduring themes about the promise and peril of artificial beings that continue to resonate today. Čapek's robots contributed to emerging sociotechnical imaginaries—shared, institutionally stabilized, and publicly performed imaginations of desirable futures that are achievable through advances in science and technology (Jasanoff and Kim 2009, 2015)—that shaped public and scientific thinking on human-like machines and their interactions with humans. This set the stage for the emergent field of cybernetics, the disciplinary predecessor of AI, and the computational breakthroughs that would emerge in the lead-up to and during World War II (Horáková and Kelemen 2009).

Computing machines in the 1930s were inherently limited tools, each designed to perform only specific, predefined tasks. However, there was substantial interest in building automatic computing machines, with theoretical and engineering work across multiple disciplines proceeding largely independently (Haigh 2014). In 1936, mathematician Alan Turing theorized a "Universal Computing Machine," demonstrating mathematically that a single mechanical device could compute anything that was computable (1937). In the 1950s—and more prominently in the 1970s—Turing was retrospectively adopted as the foundation of the newly formed discipline of computer science. Yet as modern computing emerged, Turing was just one of many researchers exploring computational possibilities, and his influence was more complicated than "Father of the Computer" histories suggest, with greater impact on computing theory than on the hardware innovations that would underlie modern computer architectures (Haigh 2014; Daylight et al. 2014; Bullynck et al. 2015; Kelkar 2015).

Cybernetics: Emergence of the Military-Industrial-Academic Complex (1940s–Mid-1950s)

World War II shaped early computing trajectories by concentrating efforts on command and control systems that would lay foundations for modern computing hardware. ENIAC (Electronic Numerical Integrator and Computer) and its successor EDVAC were designed in 1945 for military calculations at the US Army's Ballistic Research Laboratory. These systems, designed by John Mauchly and J. Presper Eckert in consultation with John von Neumann, were documented in the "First Draft" report outlining three key paradigms of modern computing: the "EDVAC Hardware Paradigm," the "von Neumann Architecture Paradigm," and the "Modern Code Paradigm" encompassing binary computing and stored program computers (Haigh 2014). Meanwhile, Warren McCulloch and Walter Pitts (1943) introduced one of the first mathematical models of neural networks, while Arturo Rosenblueth, Norbert Wiener, and Julian Bigelow (1943) introduced the behavioral perspective—together forming the foundations of cybernetics.

The Cold War created a mutually constituting relationship between militarism and emerging AI that endures today. Both fields embraced systems-thinking, control, and theories of human psychology as technically manageable systems (Edwards 1997; Agar 2003). Cross-disciplinary projects rooted in anti-communist politics led to "the ascendancy of mathematical neoclassical research programmes, based on individualistic, instrumental, and computational methodologies" (Isaac 2007, 736) aimed at military advantage. This landscape offered lucrative funding from state, industry, and private philanthropy supporting the military-industrial-academic complex (Isaac 2007).

Within this context, cybernetics emerged as a central project, bringing together diverse scholars to develop research and technologies around control, communication, and information—as defined by Norbert Wiener (1948). The Macy Conferences in the US (1946–1953) and the Ratio Club in the UK (1949–1958) served as key forums for these interdisciplinary discussions across psychology, physiology, engineering, mathematics, ecology, sociology, and anthropology. Attendees at these forums included not only key figures in mathematics and computing—such as Alan Turing in the Ratio Club and John von Neumann, Claude Shannon, and Heinz von Foerster at the Macy Conferences—but also leading social scientists. These included psychologist W. E. Hick from the Ratio Club and anthropologists Clyde Kluckhohn and Dorothy Lee from the Macy Conferences, as well as Gregory Bateson and Margaret Mead, who were among the Conferences' founding members.

This first wave of cybernetics produced innovations foundational to computer science and AI. In the 1940s and early 1950s, cybernetics explored the possibilities and limitations of machines—particularly digital computers—for understanding information, intelligence, communication, and regulation through feedback loops and networks. Shannon's (1948) information theory research established principles for encoding and processing information in binary form. Interest in intelligence, goal-directed behavior, and embodiment generated key robotics and hardware innovations: Ross Ashby's Homeostat (1948) adapted to maintain homeostasis; Wiener and J. Wiesner's tricycle (1949) mimicked moth and bedbug light navigation; William Grey Walter's tortoises (1949) navigated objects, followed light sources, and located charging stations; and Claude Shannon's maze-running mouse Theseus (1951) pioneered trial-and-error optimization. These prototypes demonstrated early integration of sensor technology, feedback loops, and logical reasoning that remain fundamental to robotics and AI today.

In this context, Turing (1950) posed his now-famous question: "Can machines think?" He speculated that a machine programmed to learn through trial and error, reinforced by rewards and punishments, could modify its own programming and, ultimately, be trained to succeed in the "imitation game"—later known as the Turing Test. For Turing, this was not just a technical problem but also a philosophical and psychological inquiry, reflecting his interest in the nature of thought and selfhood. His personal writings suggest that his engagement with machine intelligence was, in part, a way of interrogating his own cognitive processes, particularly around the dissonances between his sexuality and social and scientific norms of the time (Guo 2015)—a preoccupation that meshed well with the interests of his interdisciplinary cybernetics peers that far exceeded the narrower computer science research Turing's work is often contextualized within today. Meanwhile, Claude Shannon and researchers at Bell Labs proposed programming computers to play chess as a way of probing machine intelligence. Together, these approaches established foundational benchmarks of intelligence that would shape (and limit) decisions and innovation in AI for decades (Ensmenger 2012).

Emerging from these cybernetics foundations, inspired by McCulloch and Pitts (1943), and funded by the Office of Naval Research, Marvin Minsky created SNARC (Stochastic Neural Analog Reinforcement Calculator) at Harvard in 1951, demonstrating how artificial neural networks could learn through experience-based reinforcement. SNARC simulated Shannon's Theseus maze through a randomly connected network of hardware synapses and used a reward system to optimize Theseus's trial-and-error learning strategy. This innovation laid the foundations for machine learning as the first of two primary approaches to AI that have persisted into the present. Simultaneously, a different approach was emerging. In 1954, Allen Newell attended an inspirational RAND seminar led by cybernetician Oliver Selfridge—an experience Newell later described as a "conversion" (Simon 1997). Inspired by this encounter, he joined Herbert A. Simon and Cliff Shaw in developing the Logic Theorist in 1955. This was the first computer program designed to mimic human problem-solving by manipulating symbolic expressions according to formal rules—an approach that would orient the second primary approach, symbolic AI.

Anthropologists involved in cybernetics of the 1940s and 1950s were keenly interested in the possibilities that these new technologies and theories of cognition could provide for anthropological understandings of society, culture, and sociocultural change. This would eventually lead directly to the formation of cognitive anthropology and anthropological engagements with the cognitive sciences. This era of cybernetics, however, was also influential within wider anthropology of the time, particularly linguistic anthropology and early French structural theorists. Claude Lévi-Strauss, for example, was introduced to the field through his affiliation with the Rockefeller Foundation, a primary benefactor of cybernetics research. In a 1949 lecture shortly after the publication of *The Elementary Structures of Kinship*, Lévi-Strauss laid out his plans for more engagements between anthropology and cybernetics as a means to generalize his research into a wider structuralist theory (Geoghegan 2011).

Naming Artificial Intelligence (Mid-1950s)

Beginning in the mid-1950s, the first wave of cybernetics began to disperse and diffuse as its key actors sought to more narrowly pursue various projects, generating new fields including information theory, cognitive sciences, and what would become "second order cybernetics" refocused around biological and social systems as networks. It was in this milieu of innovation and emergent cross-disciplinary research that the field of AI was named and formalized in response to and stemming from cybernetics and related research. The lore of modern AI pinpoints the 1956 Dartmouth Summer Research Project as the *birth* of AI, where it was coined by John McCarthy and *fathered* by the organizers of the event, John McCarthy, Nathaniel Rochester, Marvin Minsky and Claude Shannon. Of course, this was not the *birthplace* of AI research nor were these men its sole originators. The 1956 Dartmouth conference was less a beginning than a continuation of more than a decade of research on machine cognition that was foundational to this event (Kline 2015; Ali et al. 2023; Penn 2023).

Funded by the Rockefeller Foundation and attended by figures from IBM, Bell Labs, RAND, and MIT—then a key defense contractor—the Dartmouth conference was an essential apparatus for formalizing and institutionalizing AI research within the Cold War military-industrial-academic complex. Participants formed partnerships that would lead to the Dartmouth group gaining significant influence in AI's development. For example, by the 1970s and 1980s, the MIT and Stanford AI labs, run by Minsky and McCarthy, respectively, commanded 70% of all US military AI funding and operated with multi-million dollar budgets backed by corporations interested in commercial expansion and philanthropic organizations interested in promoting American scientific leadership (Penn 2023, 28). With this influence came the ability to shape AI's historical narrative, gradually erasing more complex intellectual lineages and reinforcing the mythology of Dartmouth as a singular moment of genius and innovation.

At the time, however, the workshop was not understood as it is often described today. The event suffered cancellations and early departures—including organizer Shannon—and rather than being an event of like-minded scholars with a shared vision, it was sprawling and contentious. Likewise, McCarthy's proposed focus on "programming a calculator [computer] to form concepts and to form generalizations" failed to materialize (Kline 2015, 163). Further, there were disagreements over the name "AI" and disputes over credit that persisted for years (Vaux 1999). As Minsky later acknowledged about the tensions with Newell and Simon: "We were reporting speculatively about what we thought we wanted to do, while they were talking as scientists who had worked quietly, for a long time and prepared their results" (McCorduck 2004, 128).

Nevertheless, this more complicated history does not negate the influence the Dartmouth workshop had on institutionalizing AI as a research area rooted in a narrow set of allied disciplines (via McCarthy and Minsky) and within cognitive science (via Simon and Newell). Indeed, this was a distinct advantage both fields had over first-order cybernetics, which was unable to train students, grant degrees, or establish research centers due to its distributed structure across many diverse disciplines (Penn 2023).

Experimentation & Expansion (Late 1950s–1960s)

Following the organizational momentum generated around the Dartmouth conference, AI research accelerated rapidly across multiple domains through the late 1950s and 1960s, encompassing robotics, symbolic AI, and neural network-based AI. George Devol and Joseph Engelberger's Unimate—the first industrial robotic arm—was installed at a General Motors plant in 1961. This programmable machine could move along multiple axes, manipulate heavy objects, and store up to 200 movements in memory, demonstrating robotics' potential for dangerous and repetitive industrial tasks. The Stanford Research Institute's Shakey—nicknamed for its jerky movements—further expanded robotics integration with AI from 1966 to 1972. Equipped with cameras, sensors, and touch-sensitive whiskers, Shakey could process linguistic commands, observe its environment, and use planning layers to navigate and manipulate objects—architectural innovations that remain fundamental to robotic systems today (Nilsson 1984; Kuipers et al. 2017).

Chess and checker playing AI became a central benchmark for emerging machine learning, inspired by Shannon's 1950 proposal for computer chess. The first chess-playing minimax algorithm was completed in 1957, then improved with alpha-beta pruning by Newell, Simon and Shaw in 1958. Arthur Samuel's checkers program showcased what he called "machine learning" through self-play (Samuel 1959). The dominance of minimax algorithms in computer chess privileged brute force approaches (Type-A) over human-like strategic approaches (Type-B). This focus on optimization limited exploration of alternative models of cognition and decision-making throughout this era (Ensmenger 2012).

Neural network research was propelled through the work of Frank Rosenblatt and the Cornell Aeronautical Laboratory, aided by funding from the US

Office of Naval Research and later the CIA and DIA's National Photographic Interpretation Center (NPIC). In 1958, Rosenblatt's perceptron—a single-layer digital neuron learning system with visual sensors—demonstrated how neural networks could learn from visual data (Rosenblatt 1958). His early success led NPIC to work with the Cornell lab on a clandestine effort to implement the technology for managing visual intelligence data (O'Connor 2022). However, the perceptron architecture faced limitations due to the inaccessibility of computing power and mass visual data that would not exist until decades later. In 1969, Marvin Minsky and Seymour Papert's influential book *Perceptrons* (1969) highlighted these fundamental limitations, triggering an abrupt shift away from machine learning approaches toward symbolic AI in the late 1960s.

Meanwhile, at Stanford University, molecular biologist Joshua Lederberg found himself at the confluence of burgeoning computer science and AI, catalyzed by institutional efforts to formalize computing at Stanford in the early 1960s. John McCarthy's 1962 recruitment made Lederberg's AI ambitions more tangible. He met Edward Feigenbaum, a mentee of Newell and Simon, at a 1963 meeting, building a bridge between Lederberg's vision of AI-driven scientific discovery and Feigenbaum's search for a concrete domain to model empirical induction in science. Their collaboration coalesced around DENDRAL-64, an algorithm initially designed for NASA that formalized chemical graph structures. In 1967, Georgia Sutherland implemented the algorithm in LISP, creating Heuristic DENDRAL. With DARPA and NASA funding secured in 1966, new collaborators—including Bruce Buchanan and Carl Djerassi—expanded the project's scope. Buchanan's exploration of self-learning systems called Meta-DENDRAL highlighted machine learning limitations, prompting Feigenbaum's 1968 conceptualization of "expert systems" as an alternative to neural network approaches. This shift prioritized encoding domain-specific human knowledge over attempting to encode human cognition itself. Parallel efforts by Buchanan and Ted Shortliffe on MYCIN, a medical expert system, refined these insights. Lederberg later reflected that expert systems served as "the ultimate form of publication" for "sharing hard-won traditions with the entire community" (Lederberg 1987, 31).

Joseph Weizenbaum's ELIZA chatbot, published in 1966, stands as a foundational artifact in natural language processing. While often cited today as an early demonstration of machine intelligence based on its ability to pass the Turing test, these interpretations misrepresent its design and purpose. Weizenbaum (1966) aimed to "rob ELIZA of the aura of magic" (43), demonstrating "how easy it is to create and maintain the illusion of understanding" (36)—challenging the Turing test's usefulness as a measure of machine intelligence. Later research on ELIZA and descendant programs concluded that humans are inclined to seek sense, understanding, and authority in computers' outputs, particularly when they play familiar social roles like therapist or doctor—despite their actual mechanisms not warranting such attributions

(Suchman 1985, 19). These human tendencies have remained a persistent problem in measuring and understanding machine intelligence—even among AI researchers and engineers. However, these insights led to productive outcomes in human-computer interaction and anthropological research on expert systems in the 1980s.

Artificial Intelligentsia (1969–1970s)

Amid this shifting and burgeoning landscape in AI research, the Wenner-Gren Foundation for Anthropological Research funded an international conference titled "Cognitive Studies and AI," organized by Paul L. Garvin and then-president of the Foundation, Heinz von Foerster, in 1969 at the University of Chicago. The conference was modelled on the Wenner-Gren symposia, which were remembered by participants as a "fairy tale of science" (Lindee and Radin 2016)—spaces in which the ideal of scholarly retreat was realized through intensive week-long meetings of researchers from diverse disciplines, united by shared intellectual aims. In this spirit, the March 1969 conference brought together sixteen scholars from anthropology, linguistics, psychology, physics, computer science, and electrical engineering—who attendee and computer scientist Michael Arbib (1970) called the "Artificial Intelligentsia"—to explore foundational questions surrounding AI that laid the groundwork for the anthropology of and with AI for the next decade and anticipated the turn toward expert systems. The symposium highlighted increasing concern over the blurring distinction between anthropomorphic metaphors used to describe AI and the growing tendency among AI researchers to treat these metaphors as literal representations of machine capabilities. Perhaps more influential, however, was the conclusion that problem-solving approaches to AI were dependent on two faulty assumptions: (1) that there exists a universal human problem-solving method to be simulated and (2) that even if there were, that any discipline knew enough about it to successfully do so (Garvin 1970). This led the participants to the larger question of whose problem-solving activity should be simulated and toward recommendations to focus on narrower domains and relativistic approaches.

Prompted by both the growth of cognitive anthropology and the 1969 Wenner-Gren symposium, anthropologists became early advocates for computational approaches to research, including simulations, schemas, models, and nascent expert systems. During the 1970s, this interest converged into a series of exploratory engagements with AI, defined by shared conceptual concerns across anthropology, psychology, and emerging AI research. The rise of schema theory in cognitive anthropology offered a framework for understanding cultural knowledge as organized, dynamic structures. In 1971, then Stanford anthropology graduate student Hugh Gladwin laid out a call for schema-based AI approaches in an unpublished paper that he circulated among his peers that came to be known as the "yellow paper" for its mimeographed color (Quinn 2011)—inspiring experimentation with decision models and AI among his cohort. That same year, at the Quissett Harbor workshop, AI researcher Roger Schank and psychologist Robert Abelson stabilized cognitive science from similar inspirations in their "Quissett Proclamation" (Schank and Abelson 1977). Gladwin ultimately produced a dissertation that applied AI-based simulations to Fanti fish sellers' decisions, however, he found simple hierarchical models more predictive.

Through the early-1970s, anthropological engagements with AI, particularly at the University of Hamburg, Stanford University, and University of California-Irvine, grew as a means of modeling decision-making and cultural reasoning. Inspired by this work, calls for more computer applications in anthropology grew (e.g., Burton 1973) alongside calls for an anthropology of AI to offset psychology's influence, particularly around conceptualizations of culture (Colby 1974). Yet by the mid-1970s, anthropologists like Roy D'Andrade (1976) began confronting the limits of AI-style modeling for capturing cultural knowledge, noting that real-world beliefs and inferences did not easily translate into formal representations. As Naomi Quinn (2011) later reflected, these early efforts revealed the inadequacy of these models to account for the depth and complexity of human thought, prompting a shift away from rule-based models toward more nuanced understandings of mental representation and meaning in anthropology.

Expert Systems, AI Winter, and Alternative Approaches (Mid-1970s–1990s)

Even as anthropologists were identifying these limitations, the broader AI field, and some segments of anthropology, were moving in the opposite direction. Following the influence of Perceptrons (1969), significant private and public investments flowed into knowledge representation and expert systems, with researchers developing frameworks to encode human expertise into formal logical rules. Systems like XCON (1978) for computer configuration and PROSPECTOR (1976) for mineral exploration demonstrated initial promise. Also, during this time, industrial robotics continued to evolve and specialize. In 1978, Japanese researcher Hiroshi Makino introduced the SCARA (Selective Compliance Assembly Robot Arm), revolutionizing manufacturing automation. Unlike the powerful but complex six-axis Unimate arms, SCARA robots were optimized for rapid "pick and place" operations, using a simplified four-axis design to quickly and precisely manipulate small components. This innovation demonstrated how specialized approaches could succeed where general-purpose solutions struggled—a lesson that would later prove relevant to AI development.

By the early 1980s, AI found itself both emboldened and embattled. As corporate and academic research intensified around expert systems, optimism abounded regarding the potential to formalize human expertise within computational architectures. Yet, the apparent promise of these systems—such as XCON and PROSPECTOR—masked deeper epistemological tensions. In 1980, philosopher John Searle posed his now-(in)famous Chinese Room thought experiment, arguing that simulating understanding (weak AI) was not the same as understanding itself (strong AI). Searle's distinction echoed concerns first voiced by Weizenbaum's in his ELIZA critique of the Turing test and similar challenges of AI's cognitive metaphors. Winograd and Flores (1986) argued against AI's use of language as a gateway to cognition by demonstrating that language is not reducible to text as texts are interpreted by language listeners from situated positions that exceed the literal text. Penrose (1989) likewise challenged the assumption that the human mind was algorithmic and thus available to be modeled as a program on digital computers—arguing instead for a quantum physics metaphor. These critiques of "strong AI" were largely dismissed out of hand by key AI proponents (West and Travis 1991a, 1991b).

Concurrently, anthropology and the emerging field of Science and Technology Studies (STS) moved to the foreground as key players in the push back against the taken-for-granted epistemics of AI research. The call by Pinch and Bijker (1984) to redirect STS toward the study of technology catalyzed a wave of inquiry into how technical systems are socially situated and culturally shaped. Sherry Turkle's *The Second Self* (1984) offered an ethnographic account of how AI not only sought to model human thought but also reshaped how humans conceptualized their own cognitive processes. Drawing on her fieldwork at MIT's AI Lab, Turkle described how models of the mind became recursive—AI systems modeled human cognition, and humans, in turn, began to understand themselves as programmable.

Meanwhile, anthropologist Lucy Suchman was producing a different but complementary critique while embedded within Xerox PARC, where she started as an intern and PhD researcher and moved up to principal scientist and head of the Work Practice and Technology Research Area (and where she remained until 2000). Her studies of expert systems challenged the notion that intelligent action could be pre-scripted or planned in advance. Drawing on everyday human-computer interactions, Suchman (1985) argued for a shift toward "situated action"—an approach emphasizing real-time responsiveness and interactional loops. These perspectives would find resonance, combined with anthropologist Jean Lave's (1988) work on cognition in practice, in later hybrid AI architectures, where reactive and planned strategies were integrated to mitigate the limitations of each (Agre 1995).

By the mid-1980s, STS scholars like Steve Woolgar (1985) further challenged AI's epistemics—specifically the position of "the social" as merely the impacts of AI while safeguarding the interior of AI as science and cognition. His call for an STS of AI solidified a growing turn toward examining not just AI's societal impacts or its utility for social research but the social construction of AI itself—its epistemologies, boundaries, and embedded assumptions. Building on these STS foundations, Diana Forsythe leveraged her privileged position within computing's founding networks—her father, computer scientist George Forsythe, had established Stanford's computer science program—to begin fieldwork as a postdoc in 1987 at the university's Knowledge Systems Laboratory, in what she described as an act of both professional opportunity and personal healing. Her critical but collaborative works with knowledge engineers drew attention to the limitations of AI's conceptions of human knowledge and expertise as stored in a database of the mind, ready for retrieval (Forsythe 1993).

Despite these emerging limitations, AI engineers continued pursuing increasingly complex symbolic systems until mounting technical challenges led to declining confidence. Anthropological experimentations followed a similar trajectory with an initial boom of anthropological expert system generation (e.g., Brent 1989; Read and Behrens 1989; Furbee 1989) followed by criticism and abandonment after research highlighted the limitations of building expert systems rooted in "Western" assumptions about cognition and knowledge for the purpose of understanding other cultures (Collins 1990; Schoenhoff 1992; Dhaouadi 1992). By the late 1980s, what remained of anthropological engagement with expert systems was largely consulting-based work within the industry (Baba 1994; Forsythe 1995), but even that would soon evaporate as mounting technical challenges led to declining confidence across the field.

This period of diminished industry enthusiasm and funding would later be termed an "AI Winter" by Minsky and Roger Schank (Crevier 1993). The downturn stemmed not only from technical and epistemological limitations but also from mainstream AI's overly optimistic perceptions of the technology and its future. Yet, as expert systems failed and the AI Winter set in, alternative approaches began emerging that would prove foundational for future developments. Connectionism rejected symbolic AI's rules-based processing in favor of intelligence emerging from artificial neural networks. Geoffrey Hinton and colleagues developed more efficient backpropagation techniques for multi-layer networks (Rumelhart, Hinton, and Williams 1986), while Yann LeCun's team demonstrated convolutional neural networks' transformative potential (Lecun et al. 1998). Though peripheral to 1980s mainstream AI, connectionism began reentering AI discourse by the mid-1990s (van den Besselaar and Leydesdorff 1996).

Simultaneously, the Distributed AI Group at USC—including social scientists Joan Fujimura, Susan Leigh Star, and Lucy Suchman—circulated a 1988 white paper calling for "unnamed" research that gave rise to an "invisible college" of interdisciplinary scholars (Star 1992; Strübing 1998; Malsch 2001).

Drawing from STS theory and AI criticism, DAI rejected omnipotent autonomous machines based on universal problem-solving models, instead advocating for networks of autonomous AI agents capable of negotiation and coordination. This paralleled situated robotics and embodied AI, which—following Suchman's 1980s critiques (Lindblom and Ziemke 2003)—foregrounded embodiment, practice, and context, though Adams (1996) later argued these approaches remained insufficiently "situated" socioculturally.

The Deep Learning Revival and Anthropological Divergence (2000s—2010s)

Against this backdrop, one might argue the AI winter was not an unproductive period in which AI stalled, but rather an important moment of methodological diversification that enabled multiple approaches to develop simultaneously. While social sciences helped introduce alternative frameworks for understanding intelligence and agency, the foundational technical work in neural networks—largely pursued by computer scientists and cognitive researchers—would prove perhaps more consequential for AI's future trajectory. Indeed, the latter would dominate as AI accelerated in the 2000s through a convergence of factors including the explosive growth of internet-generated data, advancing computing power, algorithmic breakthroughs, and massive Silicon Valley investments. Key milestones included ImageNet's creation in 2006 (Deng et al. 2009), GPU application for neural network training in 2009 (Raina, Madhavan, and Ng 2009), AlexNet's deep learning breakthrough in 2012 (Krizhevsky, Sutskever, and Hinton 2017), and eventually, the transformer architecture introduction in 2017 (Vaswani et al. 2017) that has led to GenAI's boom.

Yet, during this period of rapid technological advancement, anthropological engagement followed a notably different trajectory. While the 2000s and 2010s saw many anthropologists, STS scholars, and other social scientists build careers embedded within companies and labs at the forefront of AI and information technology—including Bonnie Nardi (AT&T Labs and Hewlett Packard), John Sherry (Intel), Genevieve Bell (Intel), and Jeanette Blomberg (Xerox PARC, Sapient, and IBM)—advising on issues of human culture, society, and the impacts and ethics of AI, the academic literature simultaneously witnessed a notable shift. Published anthropological work in the 2000s largely turned away from AI and toward digital anthropology, virtual ethnography, and media anthropology, focusing on social media, mobile phones, and online gaming's cultural impacts—a logical shift given that these technologies were being adopted by millions of users across diverse cultural contexts, while AI applications remained more limited in scope and visibility (Wilson and Peterson 2002; Boyer 2005; Horst and Miller 2006; Boellstorff 2008; Nardi 2010). This shift meant that the foundational developments in deep learning largely occurred without the published anthropological engagement and critique that had characterized earlier AI development. While anthropologists were embedded in industry settings during this crucial period, their insights and interventions remained largely internal to organizations rather than contributing to broader academic discourse or public debate about AI's trajectory.

Furthermore, the work that was published adopted a more critical stance toward AI systems rather than pursuing the collaborative development approaches that had characterized earlier decades. Building on Philip Agre (1997), who had called for a "critical technical practice" that takes seriously anthropological and STS critiques to avoid recurring mistakes based on faulty understandings of human nature, the 2010s brought renewed anthropological attention to computational systems, but primarily through a critical lens. Early implementations of AI at scale—including Facebook's social graph, YouTube's recommendation algorithms, and Google's search systems—drew scholarly examination through frameworks of power, inequality, and social control. New inquiry around algorithms (Gillespie 2014; Seaver 2018; Tufekci 2015; Striphas 2015), data and surveillance (Boyd and Crawford 2012; Maturo 2014; Tufekci 2014; Boellstorff and Maurer 2015), and Silicon Valley culture (English-Lueck 2002; Irani 2015; Pasquale 2015) emerged to challenge dominant narratives around these technologies.

While this critical scholarship provided valuable insights into AI's social implications, it had limited influence on the technical trajectory of AI development itself, which by the late 2010s had transformed global patterns of information consumption, social interaction, mobility, and decision-making across billions of users. This transformation was enabled by innovations in engineering and computer science that advanced the connectionist approaches of previous decades, focusing on scaling neural network architectures, optimizing computational performance, and training ever larger models. As AI became increasingly ubiquitous, these technologies also became more accessible to researchers across disciplines. While earlier generations of anthropologists had experimented with computational approaches, the technical barriers were considerable. The emergence of user-friendly interfaces and simplified implementation tools began to democratize AI capabilities for researchers, enabling more anthropologists than ever before to incorporate AI into methodological practices, setting the stage for a new era of computational anthropology.

Computational Anthropology, LLMs, GenAI, and Robotics (2020s—Present)

This new era of computational anthropology materialized through several key developments in the 2020s. The Techno-Anthropology Lab at Aalborg University arguably best exemplified this methodological innovation, with work demonstrating how algorithms could serve interpretive functions in ethnographic research. Their approach to "computational thick description," for example, showed how AI's pattern recognition capabilities could reveal cultural meanings while maintaining anthropology's commitment to interpretive depth (Munk, Olesen, and Jacomy 2022). Similarly, the University of Copenhagen's SODAS program advanced computational ethnography through hybrid quali-quantitative approaches (Albris et al. 2021), while concepts like "machinic anthropology" emerged to bridge traditional anthropological theory with data science methods (Pedersen 2023).

These innovations in computational methods preceded but were dramatically amplified by developments in large language models (LLMs) and generative AI (GenAI). OpenAI's releases of GPT-3 and DALL-E introduced sophisticated AI capabilities, but it was ChatGPT's launch in late 2022 that marked a true watershed moment. For the first time, AI capabilities that had previously been limited to researchers and specialized applications became accessible to general users, significantly expanding how humans could interact with and direct AI systems. The subsequent release of GPT-4 in 2023 introduced robust multimodal capabilities, enabling systems to process and produce both text and images simultaneously.

As GenAI entered public consciousness, anthropologists began engaging with these systems both as research tools and objects of ethnographic study. Researchers again at Aalborg explored LLMs as cultural interlocutors through Stable Diffusion experiments that revealed distinctive meaning patterns (Munk 2023), computational methods for deliberately slowing organizational reasoning to create analytical friction (Madsen, Munk, and Søltoft 2023), and synthetic interlocutors using Retrieval Augmented Generation to extend ethnographic encounters and generate analytical insights (Søltoft, Kocksch, and Munk 2024). Meanwhile, other researchers examined how entrepreneurs made sense of GenAI during its emergence, revealing tensions between public optimism and private concerns about societal implications while documenting the knowledge gaps between AI creators and adopters (Artz and Ren 2025).

While transformational, LLMs have faced significant critiques regarding their fundamental capabilities and limitations. Bender et al. (2021) argued that these systems function as "stochastic parrots" that reproduce patterns from training data without genuine understanding or reliable factual generation. This limitation manifests in their tendency to produce "hallucinations"—outputs that appear convincing but are factually incorrect. However, a more nuanced interpretation of Bender et al.'s critique suggests that all LLM outputs might be considered hallucinations that humans might recognize as aligning with their reality—similar to earlier critiques of systems like ELIZA and DOCTOR in the 1960s. Critics argue that despite impressive linguistic capabilities and general-purpose flexibility, these models fundamentally lack grounding in physical reality and embodied experience that characterizes human intelligence, a theme found in numerous chapters of this volume.

In response to these limitations, AI researchers have explored hybrid approaches combining different methodological strengths. Neural-symbolic AI attempts to merge neural networks' learning capabilities with symbolic AI's explicit reasoning processes. Meanwhile, increasingly sophisticated multi-modal models demonstrate growing ability to work across text, images, audio, and video in ways that approximate human-like information processing. DeepMind's AlphaGeometry exemplifies this hybrid potential, combining neural language models' pattern recognition with symbolic deduction engines' logical reasoning to solve complex geometric theorems at mathematics Olympiad levels (Trinh and Luong 2024).

Yet critics maintain that even these sophisticated systems, while capable of domain-specific problem-solving, still lack the foundational understanding characterizing human cognition. Moreover, impressive as they are, these computational capabilities of producing human-like language and symbolic reasoning continue to both rely on and be confined in the digital realm, overwhelmingly mediated through the internet. How a machine can handle real physical environments in real time is the next big frontier for AI research, development, and implementation. As big strides are continuously made in the way machines learn, the implications these AI developments have for hardware robotic interfaces have dramatically shortened the timelines to developing truly adaptive physical machines which can correctly interpret, and appropriately act back upon, the external environment in real time (even if these robot timelines lag behind AI for both engineering and sociocultural and ideational reasons). How machines can operate autonomously in the physical world—with all its complexities, rooted in a myriad of variances between objects, the uncertainties of social situations, the variability of the physical environment and its rules, and the simultaneity of multiple ongoing phenomena happening within the operating context of any given robot—remains the holy grail in hardware development of many kinds of robots, whether wheeled, winged, bipedal or quadruped. While a general-purpose robot is yet to exist, as of the time of this writing, a lot of energy, money, and effort are poured into humanoid robot development—a possibility only made possible by the leaps in AI described in this chapter.

To this end, physical AI has emerged as an area of advancing the way generative models are extended through the rendering of spatial relationships in 3D digital twins, which are then used to train robots through highly accurate simulations of the physical world. Within these virtual twins, multiple scenarios can be tested via a trial and error logic. With the enhanced reinforcement learning provided through such physical AI, much better models of the physical environment will enable robots to perform more accurate, and therefore safer, rigid-body dynamic maneuvers (which is a big component in avoiding collisions in autonomous driving contexts, for example), or accurately adjusting the strength of grip relative to the fragility of the object type being grasped. Although still an emerging tool not surpassing yet the dominant physics-based control models, generative physical AI, more so than any other paradigm in advanced computing, is poised to make Čapek's fiction a reality within our lifetimes. Whether we use robots as slaves, or we use robots to abolish the concept of slavery once and for all, however, remains entirely the province of human imagination and will.

Conclusion

This introduction has traced the long and often underrecognized history of engagement between anthropology and AI, revealing a mutually influential relationship that reaches far beyond recent trends. Rather than framing anthropology's interest in AI as merely a response to the latest boom of innovation and hype, we have aimed to show that anthropologists have long participated in shaping, critiquing, and reimagining AI systems. This history reveals recurring patterns—cycles of ambitious promises, technical limitations, methodological shifts, and renewed optimism—that offer valuable perspective on contemporary developments. The consistent thread throughout these cycles has been anthropology's capacity to illuminate the social and cultural dimensions that technical approaches alone cannot address, while also contributing methodological innovations that enrich both fields.

While the current boom in AI-related anthropological research exceeds the scope of a single chapter, this volume responds to its scale and complexity by offering a selection of recent work that continues and expands these longstanding engagements. The volume is organized into three parts. *Part I: Contexts & Frameworks* situates contemporary AI within its historical and social contexts, offering frameworks for the study of AI. *Part II: Critical Perspectives* gathers work that interrogates the claims, politics, and trajectories of AI systems, foregrounding tensions and contestations that demand anthropological attention. *Part III: Sociotechnical Interactions* explores how AI technologies are enacted and experienced in everyday life, emphasizing the co-constitutive relations between humans and machines.

Together, these contributions push beyond novelty to historicize, contextualize, and critically examine anthropological engagements with AI while also demonstrating how the discipline both uses AI methodologically and actively participates in building AI systems—revealing the multifaceted nature of these evolving relationships and the enduring relevance of anthropological perspectives across AI's various transformations. Indeed, Tett's call for "anthropology intelligence" to balance positivist approaches resonates particularly strongly in the context of AI—the need for anthropological perspectives has never been more urgent, not as a recent discovery, but as the continuation of a vital conversation that has been shaping both fields for decades.

References

Agar, Jon. 2003. *The Government Machine: A Revolutionary History of the Computer*. MIT Press.

Agre, Philip E. 1995. "Computational Research on Interaction and Agency." *Artificial Intelligence* 72 (1–2):1–52.

Agre, Philip E. 1997. *Computation and Human Experience*. Cambridge University Press.

Albris, Kristoffer, Eva L. Otto, Sofie L. Astrupgaard, Emilie Munch Gregersen, Laura Skousgaard Jorgensen, Olivia Jorgensen, Clara Rosa Sandbye, and Signe Schønning. 2021. "A View from Anthropology: Should Anthropologists Fear the Data Machines?" *Big Data & Society* 8 (2). doi:10.1177/20539517211043655.

Ali, Syed Mustafa, Stephanie Dick, Sarah Dillon, Matthew L. Jones, Jonnie Penn, and Richard Staley. 2023. "Histories of Artificial Intelligence: A Genealogy of Power." *BJHS Themes* 8 (January): 1–18. doi:10.1017/bjt.2023.15.

Arbib, Michael A. 1970. "Cognition—A Cybernetic Approach." In *Cognition: A Multiple View*, edited by Paul L. Garvin, 331–348. Spartan Books.

Artz, Matt, and Yaya Ren. 2025. "Beyond the GenAI Gold Rush: Mapping Entrepreneurial Tensions in the Age of Generative Artificial Intelligence." *Annals of Anthropological Practice* 49: e70016. doi:10.1111/napa.70016.

Baba, Marietta L. 1994. "The Fifth Subdiscipline: Anthropological Practice and the Future of Anthropology." *Human Organization* 53 (2): 174–186. doi:10.17730/humo.53.2.512431365187kt05.

Bender, Emily M., Timnit Gebru, Angelina McMillan-Major, and Shmargaret Shmitchell. 2021. "On the Dangers of Stochastic Parrots: Can Language Models Be Too Big? ?." In *Proceedings of the 2021 ACM Conference on Fairness, Accountability, and Transparency*, 610–623. FAccT '21. New York, NY, USA: Association for Computing Machinery. doi:10.1145/3442188.3445922.

Besselaar, Peter van den, and Loet Leydesdorff. 1996. "Mapping Change in Scientific Specialties: A Scientometric Reconstruction of the Development of Artificial Intelligence." *Journal of the American Society for Information Science. American Society for Information Science* 47 (6): 415–436. doi:10.1002/(SICI)1097–4571(199606)47:6%3C415:AID-ASI3%3E3.0.CO;2-Y.

Boellstorff, Tom. 2008. *Coming of Age in Second Life*. Princeton University Press.

Boellstorff, Tom, and Bill Maurer, eds. 2015. *Data, Now Bigger and Better!* Prickly Paradigm Press.

Boyd, Danah, and Kate Crawford. 2012. "Critical Questions for Big Data: Provocations for a Cultural, Technological, and Scholarly Phenomenon." *Information, Communication and Society* 15 (5): 662–679. doi:10.1080/1369118X.2012.678878.

Boyer, D. 2005. *Spirit and System: Media, Intellectuals, and the Dialectic in Modern German Culture*. University of Chicago Press.

Brent, Edward. 1989. "Designing Social Science Research with Expert Systems." *Anthropological Quarterly* 62 (3): 121. doi:10.2307/3317452.

Bullynck, Maarten, Edgar G. Daylight, Liesbeth De Mol, Samuel Greengard, Karen Emslie, and David Geer. 2015. "*Why Did Computer Science Make a Hero Out of Turing?*" Communications of the ACM. March 1, 2015. http://cacm.acm.org/opinion/why-did-computer-science-make-a-hero-out-of-turing/.

Burton, M. 1973. "Recent Computer Applications in Cultural Anthropology." *Computers and the Humanities* 7 (6): 337–341. doi:10.1007/BF02395108.

Colby, Benjamin. 1974. "Revised Versions of Papers Presented at Symposium Held at Cambridge in 1970." Review of The Computer in Literary and Linguistic Research: Papers from a Cambridge Symposium, by R. A. Wisbey. *American Anthropologist.* 76(2): 447–448. doi:10.1525/aa.1974.76.2.02a00880.

Coleman, E. Gabriella. 2013. *Coding Freedom: The Ethics and Aesthetics of Hacking.* Princeton University Press.

Coleman, E. Gabriella. 2014. *Hacker, Hoaxer, Whistleblower, Spy: The Many Faces of Anonymous.* Verso Books.

Collins, Harry M. 1990. *Artificial Experts: Social Knowledge and Intelligent Machines.* MIT Press.

Crevier, Daniel. 1993. *AI: The Tumultuous History of the Search for Artificial Intelligence.* Basic Books.

D'Andrade, R. G. 1976. "A Propositional Analysis of US American Beliefs about Illness." *Meaning in Anthropology*, editors Keith H. Basso and Henry A. Selby. University of New Mexico Press.

Daylight, Edgar G., Samuel Greengard, Karen Emslie, and David Geer. 2014. "A Turing Tale." *Communications of the ACM.* October 1, 2014. http://cacm.acm.org/opinion/a-turing-tale/.

Deng, Jia, Wei Dong, Richard Socher, Li-Jia Li, Kai Li, and Li Fei-Fei. 2009. "ImageNet: A Large-Scale Hierarchical Image Database." In *2009 IEEE Conference on Computer Vision and Pattern Recognition*, 248–255. IEEE. doi:10.1109/CVPR.2009.5206848.

Dhaouadi, Mahmoud. 1992. "The Cultural-Symbolic Soul: An Islamically Inspired Research Concept for the Behavioral and Social Sciences." *American Journal of Islam and Society* 9 (2): 153–172. doi:10.35632/ajis.v9i2.2552.

Edwards, Paul N. 1997. *The Closed World: Computers and the Politics of Discourse in Cold War America.* Inside Technology. MIT Press.

English-Lueck, J. A. 2002. *Cultures@SiliconValley.* Stanford University Press.

Ensmenger, Nathan. 2012. "Is Chess the Drosophila of Artificial Intelligence? A Social History of an Algorithm." *Social Studies of Science* 42 (1): 5–30. doi:10.1177/0306312711424596.

Forsythe, Diana E. 1993. "Engineering Knowledge: The Construction of Knowledge in Artificial Intelligence." *Social Studies of Science* 23(3): 445–477. doi:10.1177/0306312793023003002.

Forsythe, Diana E. 1995. "Using Ethnography in the Design of an Explanation System." *Expert Systems with Applications* 8 (4): 403–417. doi:10.1016/0957-4174(94)E0032-P

Furbee, Louanna. 1989. "A Folk Expert System: Soils Classification in the Colca Valley, Peru." *Anthropological Quarterly* 62 (2): 83. doi:10.2307/3318128.

Garvin, Paul L., ed. 1970. *Cognition: A Multiple View; Proceedings of the Wenner-Gren Foundation for Anthropological Research Symposium on Cognitive Studies and Artificial Intelligence Research.* Spartan Books.

Gebru, Timnit, and Émile P. Torres. 2024. "The TESCREAL Bundle: Eugenics and the Promise of Utopia through Artificial General Intelligence." *First Monday*, April. doi:10.5210/fm.v29i4.13636.

Geoghegan, Bernard Dionysius. 2011. "From Information Theory to French Theory: Jakobson, Lévi-Strauss, and the Cybernetic Apparatus." *Critical Inquiry* 38 (1): 96–126. doi:10.1086/661645.

Gillespie, Tarleton. 2014. "The Relevance of Algorithms." In *Media Technologies: Essays on Communication, Materiality, and Society*, edited by Tarleton Gillespie,

Pablo J. Boczkowski, and Kristen A. Foot, 167–194. MIT Press. doi:10.7551/mitpress/9780262525374.003.0009.
Guo, Ting. 2015. "Alan Turing: Artificial Intelligence as Human Self-knowledge." *Anthropology Today* 31 (6): 3–7. doi:10.1111/1467-8322.12209.
Haigh, Thomas. 2014. "Actually, Turing Did Not Invent the Computer." *Communications of the ACM* 57 (1): 36–41. doi:10.1145/2542504.
Horáková, Jana, and Jozef Kelemen. 2009. "Artificial Living Beings and Robots: One Root, Variety of Influences." *Artificial Life and Robotics* 13 (2): 555–560. doi:10.1007/s10015-008-0502-z.
Horst, Heather, and Daniel Miller. 2006. *The Cell Phone: An Anthropology of Communication.* Bloomsbury Academic.
Irani, Lilly. 2015. "Hackathons and the Making of Entrepreneurial Citizenship." *Science, Technology & Human Values* 40 (5): 799–824. doi:10.1177/0162243915578486.
Isaac, Joel. 2007. "The Human Sciences in Cold War America." *Historical Journal (Cambridge, England)* 50 (3): 725–746. doi:10.1017/s0018246x07006334.
Jasanoff, Sheila, and Sang-Hyun Kim. 2009. "Containing the Atom: Sociotechnical Imaginaries and Nuclear Power in the United States and South Korea." *Minerva* 47 (2): 119–146. doi:10.1007/s11024-009-9124-4.
Jasanoff, Sheila, and Sang-Hyun Kim. 2015. *Dreamscapes of Modernity: Sociotechnical Imaginaries and the Fabrication of Power.* University of Chicago Press.
Kelkar, Shreeharsh. 2015. "How Influential Was Alan Turing? The Tangled Invention of Computing (and Its Historiography)." *Platypus, The CASTAC Blog* (blog). March 24, 2015. https://blog.castac.org/2015/03/how-influential-was-turing/.
Kelty, Christopher M. 2008. *Two Bits: The Cultural Significance of Free Software.* Experimental Futures: Technological Lives, Scientific Arts, Anthropological Voices. Duke University Press.
Kline, Ronald R. 2015. *The Cybernetics Moment: Or Why We Call Our Age the Information Age.* New Studies in American Intellectual and Cultural History. Johns Hopkins University Press.
Krizhevsky, Alex, Ilya Sutskever, and Geoffrey E. Hinton. 2017. "ImageNet Classification with Deep Convolutional Neural Networks." *Communications of the ACM* 60 (6): 84–90. doi:10.1145/3065386.
Kuipers, B., E. Feigenbaum, P. Hart, and N. Nilsson. 2017. "Shakey: From Conception to History." *AI Magazine* 38 (March): 88–103. doi:10.1609/aimag.v38i1.2716.
Lave, Jean. 1988. *Cognition in Practice: Mind, Mathematics and Culture in Everyday Life.* Cambridge University Press.
Lecun, Y., L. Bottou, Y. Bengio, and P. Haffner. 1998. "Gradient-Based Learning Applied to Document Recognition." *Proceedings of the IEEE. Institute of Electrical and Electronics Engineers* 86 (11): 2278–2324. doi:10.1109/5.726791.
Lederberg, Joshua. 1987. "How DENDRAL Was Conceived and Born." In *History of Medical Informatics*, edited by Bruce I. Blum and Karen Duncan, 14–44. Association of Computing Machinery. doi:10.1145/89482.89484.
Lindblom, Jessica, and Tom Ziemke. 2003. "Social Situatedness of Natural and Artificial Intelligence: Vygotsky and Beyond." *Adaptive Behavior* 11 (2): 79–96. doi:10.1177/10597123030112002.
Lindee, Susan, and Joanna Radin. 2016. "Patrons of the Human Experience: A History of the Wenner-Gren Foundation for Anthropological Research, 1941–2016." *Current Anthropology* 57 (S14): S218–301. doi:10.1086/687926.

Lovelace, Ada Augusta. 1843. "Notes by the Translator of Luigi F. Menabrea's Sketch of the Analytical Engine Invented by Charles Babbage." In *Scientific Memoirs, Selected from the Transactions of Foreign Academies of Science and Learned Societies, and from Foreign Journals*, Vol III, edited by Richard Taylor, translated by Ada Augusta Countess of Lovelace, 691–731. Richard and John E. Taylor.

Mackenzie, Adrian. 2006. *Cutting Code: Software and Sociality*. Peter Lang.

Madsen, Anders Koed, Anders Kristian Munk, and Johan Irving Søltoft. 2023. "Friction by Machine: How to Slow Down Reasoning with Computational Methods." *Ethnographic Praxis in Industry Conference Proceedings*2023(1): 82–105. doi:10.1111/epic.12153.

Malsch, Thomas. 2001. "Naming the Unnamable: Socionics or the Sociological Turn of/to Distributed Artificial Intelligence." *Autonomous Agents and Multi-Agent Systems* 4 (3): 155–186. doi:10.1023/A:1011446410198.

Maturo, Antonio. 2014. "Fatism, Self-Monitoring and the Pursuit of Healthiness in the Time of Technological Solutionism." *Italian Sociological Review* 4 (2): 157–171. doi:10.13136/isr.v4i2.80.

McCorduck, Pamela. 2004. *Machines Who Think: A Personal Inquiry into the History and Prospects of Artificial Intelligence*. A K Peters.

McCulloch, Warren S., and Walter Pitts. 1943. "A Logical Calculus of the Ideas Immanent in Nervous Activity." *The Bulletin of Mathematical Biophysics* 5 (4): 115–133. doi:10.1007/bf02478259.

Mead, Margaret. 1969. "Crossing Boundaries in Social Science Communications." *Social Sciences Information. Information Sur Les Sciences Sociales* 8 (1): 7–15. doi:10.1177/053901846900800101.

Minsky, Marvin, and Seymour Papert. 1969. *Perceptrons*. MIT Press.

Munk, Anders Kristian, Asger Gehrt Olesen, and Mathieu Jacomy. 2022. "The Thick Machine: Anthropological AI between Explanation and Explication." *Big Data & Society* 9 (1). doi:10.1177/20539517211069891.

Munk, Anders Kristian. 2023. "Coming of Age in Stable Diffusion." *Anthropology News*, March/April 2023. https://www.anthropology-news.org/articles/coming-of-age-in-stable-diffusion/.

Nardi, Bonnie. 2010. *My Life as a Night Elf Priest: An Anthropological Account of World of Warcraft*. University of Michigan Press.

Nilsson, Nils J. 1984. "*Shakey the Robot: Technical Note 323*." AIC Technical Note. Menlo Park, CA. AI Center, SRI International. https://archived.ai.sri.com/pub_list/629.html.

O'Connor, Jack. 2022. "Undercover Algorithm: A Secret Chapter in the Early History of Artificial Intelligence and Satellite Imagery." *International Journal of Intelligence and Counterintelligence*, June, 1–15. doi:10.1080/08850607.2022.2073542.

Ortner, Sherry B. 2016. "Dark Anthropology and Its Others: Theory since the Eighties." *HAU: Journal of Ethnographic Theory* 6 (1): 47–73. doi:10.14318/hau6.1.004.

Pasquale, Frank. 2015. *The Black Box Society: The Secret Algorithms That Control Money and Information*. Harvard University Press.

Pedersen, Morten Axel. 2023. "Towards a Machinic Anthropology." *Big Data & Society* 10 (1). doi:10.1177/20539517231153803.

Penn, Jonnie. 2023. "*Animo Nullius*: On AI's Origin Story and a Data Colonial Doctrine of Discovery." *BJHS Themes* 8 (January): 19–34. doi:10.1017/bjt.2023.14.

Penrose, Roger. 1989. *The Emperor's New Mind*. Oxford University Press.

Pinch, Trevor J., and Wiebe E. Bijker. 1984. "The Social Construction of Facts and Artefacts: Or How the Sociology of Science and the Sociology of Technology Might Benefit Each Other." *Social Studies of Science* 14 (3): 399–441. https://doi.org/10.1177/030631284014003004.

Quinn, Naomi. 2011. "The History of the Cultural Models School Reconsidered: A Paradigm Shift in Cognitive Anthropology." In *A Companion to Cognitive Anthropology*. Wiley-Blackwell. doi:10.1002/9781444394931.ch2.

Raina, Rajat, Anand Madhavan, and Andrew Y. Ng. 2009. "Large-Scale Deep Unsupervised Learning Using Graphics Processors." In *Proceedings of the 26th Annual International Conference on Machine Learning*. ACM. doi:10.1145/1553374.1553486.

Read, Dwight W., and Clifford Behrens. 1989. "Modeling Folk Knowledge as Expert Systems." *Anthropological Quarterly* 62 (3): 107. doi:10.2307/3317451.

Rosenblatt, Frank. 1958. "The Perceptron: A Probabilistic Model for Information Storage and Organization in the Brain." *Psychology Review* 65 (6): 386–408. doi:10.1037/H0042519.

Rosenblueth, A., N. Wiener, and Julian Bigelow. 1943. "Behavior, Purpose and Teleology." *Philosophia Scientiae. Travaux d'Histoire Des Sciences et de Philosophie* 10 (January): 18–24. doi:10.1086/286788.

Rumelhart, David E., Geoffrey E. Hinton, and Ronald J. Williams. 1986. "Learning Representations by Back-Propagating Errors." *Nature* 323 (6088): 533–536. doi:10.1038/323533a0.

Samuel, A. L. 1959. "Some Studies in Machine Learning Using the Game of Checkers." *IBM Journal of Research and Development*. doi:10.1147/rd.33.0210.

Schank, Roger C., and Robert P. Abelson. 1977. *Scripts, Plans, Goals, and Understanding: An Inquiry into Human Knowledge Structures*. Lawrence Erlbaum Associates.

Schoenhoff, Doris Marie. 1992. "The Barefoot Expert: The Interface of Computerized Knowledge Systems and Indigenous Knowledge Systems." PhD diss., Washington University.

Searle, J. 1980. "Minds, Brains, and Programs." *The Behavioral and Brain Sciences* 3 (September): 417–24. https://doi.org/10.1017/S0140525X00005756.

Seaver, Nick. 2018. "What Should an Anthropology of Algorithms Do?" *Cultural Anthropology: Journal of the Society for Cultural Anthropology* 33 (3): 375–385. doi:10.14506/ca33.3.04.

Shannon, Claude. 1948. "A Mathematical Theory of Communication." *Bell Syst. Tech. J.* 27 (July): 623–656. doi:10.1145/584091.584093.

Simon, Herbert A. 1997. *Allen Newell (1927–1992): A Biographical Memoir*. National Academy of Sciences Biographical Memoirs. National Academies Press.

Søltoft, Johan Irving, Laura Kocksch, and Anders Kristian Munk. 2024. "Synthetic Interlocutors: Experiments with Generative AI to Prolong Ethnographic Encounters." *arXiv* preprint arXiv:2410.11395.

Star, Susan Leigh. 1992. "The Trojan Door: Organizations, Work, and the 'Open Black Box.'" *Systems Practice* 5 (4): 395–410. doi:10.1007/bf01059831.

Striphas, Ted. 2015. "Algorithmic Culture." *European Journal of Cultural Studies* 18 (4–5):395–412. doi:10.1177/1367549415577392.

Strübing, Jörg. 1998. "Bridging the Gap: On the Collaboration between Symbolic Interactionism and Distributed Artificial Intelligence in the Field of Multi-agent Systems Research." *Symbolic Interaction* 21 (4): 441–463. doi:10.1525/si.1998.21.4.441.

Suchman, L. A. 1985. *Plans and Situated Actions: The Problem of Human-Machine Communication*. Xerox Corporation.

Tett, Gillian. 2021. *Anthro-Vision: A New Way to See in Business and Life*. Simon and Schuster.

Trinh, Trieu, and Thang Luong. 2024. "AlphaGeometry: An Olympiad-Level AI System for Geometry." *Google DeepMind*. January 17, 2024. https://deepmind.google/discover/blog/alphageometry-an-olympiad-level-ai-system-for-geometry/.

Tufekci, Zeynep. 2014. "Engineering the Public: Big Data, Surveillance and Computational Politics." *First Monday* 19 (7). doi:10.5210/fm.v19i7.4901.

Tufekci, Zeynep. 2015. "Algorithmic Harms Beyond Facebook and Google: Emergent Challenges of Computational Agency." *Colorado Technology Law Journal* 13: 203–217.

Turing, A. M. 1937. "On Computable Numbers, with an Application to the Entscheidungsproblem." *Proceedings of the London Mathematical Society. Third Series* s2–42 (1): 230–265. doi:10.1112/plms/s2-42.1.230.

Turing, A. 1950. "Computing Machinery and Intelligence." *Mind* LIX (236): 433–60. https://doi.org/10.1093/MIND/LIX.236.433.

Umpleby, Stuart A. 2008. "A Short History of Cybernetics in the United States." *Österreichische Zeitschrift Für Geschichtswissenschaften* 19 (4): 28–40. doi:10.25365/OEZG-2008-19-4-3.

Vaswani, Ashish, Noam Shazeer, Niki Parmar, Jakob Uszkoreit, Llion Jones, Aidan N. Gomez, Łukasz Kaiser, and Illia Polosukhin. 2017. "Attention Is All You Need." In *Proceedings of the 31st International Conference on Neural Information Processing Systems*, 6000–6010. NIPS'17. Curran Associates Inc. doi:10.5555/3295222.3295349.

Vaux, Janet Heather. 1999. "Social and Epistemological Bases of Technology Transfer: The Case of Artificial Intelligence." MA thesis, Brunel University. http://bura.brunel.ac.uk/handle/2438/5505.

Weizenbaum, Joseph. 1966. "ELIZA—a Computer Program for the Study of Natural Language Communication between Man and Machine." *Communications of the ACM* 9 (1): 36–45. doi:10.1145/365153.365168.

West, David M., and L. Travis. 1991a. "The Computational Metaphor and Artificial Intelligence: A Reflective Examination of a Theoretical Falsework." *AI Magazine* 12 (1): 64–79. doi:10.1609/aimag.v12i1.885.

West, David M., and L. Travis. 1991b. "From Society to Landscape: Alternative Metaphors for Artificial Intelligence." *AI Magazine* 12 (2): 69–83. doi:10.1609/aimag.v12i2.896.

Wiener, Norbert. 1948. *Cybernetics; Or, Control and Communication in the Animal and the Machine*. John Wiley & Sons.

Wilson, Samuel M., and Leighton C. Peterson. 2002. "The Anthropology of Online Communities." *Annual Review of Anthropology* 31 (1): 449–467. doi:10.1146/annurev.anthro.31.040402.085436.

Winograd, Terry, and Fernando Flores. 1987. *Understanding Computers and Cognition: A New Foundation for Design*. Ablex Publishing Corporation.

Woolgar, Steve. 1985. "Why Not a Sociology of Machines? The Case of Sociology and Artificial Intelligence." *Sociology* 19 (4): 557–572. doi:10.1177/0038038585019004005.

Yaneva, Albena. 2009. *Made by the Office for Metropolitan Architecture: An Ethnography of Design*. 010 Publishers.

PART I
Contexts & Frameworks

1

A HINGE FOR ETHNOGRAPHIC INTERVENTIONS IN AI SYSTEMS

Interlocking the Past, Present, and Future

Libuše Hannah Vepřek[1] *and Rebecca Carlson*

Introduction: "A Hinge Moment"

What role do cultural anthropologists currently play in the development of AI and hybrid human-AI systems, and what role could they play? During one of Libuše's final meetings with Pietro Michelucci, the director of the Human Computation Institute, as her fieldwork in Ithaca, NY, was concluding, they reflected together on these questions. Over the past three years, they had worked together as collaborators, as Libuše studied both how human computation systems were built at the institute and contributed to their work and development practices (Vepřek 2024). The institute's goal is to build hybrid systems where the strengths of humans and machines are combined to solve current AI and other scientific problems that cannot be addressed in different ways. The researchers and developers build these systems in the field of citizen science where they invite volunteer participants to contribute to scientific research such as for Alzheimer's disease. During this meeting in November 2022, Michelucci told Libuše that cultural anthropologists could help developers reflect on "where we are coming from, where we are going to" by opening opportunities for them to step outside the "project-centric mindset" and "heighten awareness" of different perspectives.

In a different context, a very similar perspective was voiced by Tom, the supervisor of a genetics laboratory near Tokyo where Rebecca conducted her ethnographic research. While most of the researchers in this lab were working with biochemical reactions or "wet" experiments, like many other labs today they were moving generally to incorporate more "dry" or statistical computational methods. Although these bioscience researchers might not necessarily have described themselves as working with AI, complex computer algorithms

DOI: 10.4324/9781003532750-3

in various forms were becoming a background to their efforts in human genetic research and a part of how they imagined future research projects, including applying machine learning (ML) to their work in genetic sequencing. As part of a longer conversation on the differences between biology and anthropology, Rebecca and Tom returned frequently to a discussion about the nature of heuristics and scientific models and their slippy nature in research practice (Carlson 2021). At one point, Tom presented IQ tests as an example of measurable reality. When Rebecca pointed out that such tests are often mistaken for an objective marker of intelligence, rather than a culturally situated frame for imagining and valuing, he replied:

> I think you should point this phenomenon out when you see it. In science, this kind of forgetfulness or worse, misrepresentation, leads to problems. We should try to remember that we measured something that can be a few degrees removed from what we want to understand/explain. [...] I am also interested in your perspective on where I am failing in my stated goals; that would be super useful to me, especially because I am in a sort of "feedback desert."
>
> *(May 17, 2020)*

Despite their differences, the scientists and researchers we worked together with are similarly concerned about—and yet possibly limited from—finding methods to get out of their "feedback desert." As Michelucci and Tom both suggested, they need methods to reflect on what they are doing from outside the "project-centric mindset" and to engage with others who can help them achieve this. As we show, Michelucci and Tom's concerns can be understood as a struggle to anticipate or navigate links across the past, present, and future precisely because these tend to fall out of a project-centric focus.

Technology development in general, but particularly AI development and research, are often driven by imaginations of the future (see, e.g., Jasanoff and Kim 2015), not only of technology-to-be-built, but also of their social need as part of techno-solutionist agendas. AI, as Genevieve Bell has argued, "is [...] both a technology, and an imagination of a technology" or, as Will Douglas Heaven has aptly described in a MIT Technology Review article, "Above all else, AI is an idea—an ideal—shaped by worldviews and sci-fi tropes as much as by math and computer science" (2024). While AI is one of, if not the most hyped technologies of today, the term itself still remains vague and is accompanied by various imaginations of AI systems, even almost 70 years after the Dartmouth Summer Research Project when the term first became popular. This 1956 workshop, proposed by John McCarthy, Marvin Minsky, Nathaniel Rochester, and Claude Shannon, brought together a small group of researchers based on the assumption that intelligence could be defined to allow machines to replicate it. Their goal was to advance how machines could solve problems previously considered exclusive to humans under the term "artificial intelligence" (McCarthy et al. 1955).

Although imaginations of intelligent machines often do not reflect current instantiations of AI systems, and regardless of whether they ever materialize, they nevertheless direct the design and development as well as discourse around AI (Cave and Dihal 2019). At the same time, the question of where these systems come from and on what assumptions and previous work they are built often falls out of such visions of the future. Yet, as Michelucci and Tom's comments show, researchers are not unaware of the need to bring together these temporalities—to attend to the comings and goings, to avoid forgetfulness—even as they may struggle in practice to do so. In this chapter, we discuss how ethnographers can contribute in critical but also constructive ways to AI research and technology development in scientific fields. To this end, and to bring the different temporal dimensions and directions—the past, present, and future—together, we suggest the metaphor of the hinge as an analytical and reflexive tool. A hinge, as we describe, achieves precisely this type of joining. We build on the work of scholars like Bruno Latour as well as Morten Axel Pedersen and Morten Nielsen in their joint work who have already employed the hinge-as-metaphor for slightly different purposes. Here, the hinge as an analytical concept allows us to better understand where technologies and their characteristics come from, how the current state of the art connects to the past, and simultaneously structures ideas of future systems. Borrowing particularly from Pedersen and Nielsen's description of the hinge as "trans-temporal" (2013), or a linking across time, below we explore how the hinge can help us to foreground these questions for ethnographic research and in AI development as well as for interdisciplinary collaborations.

To this end, in this chapter, we first define the hinge as a mechanical object and as a theoretical concept. Next, we apply the hinge as an analytical tool in AI research, drawing on our ethnographic studies in the US and Japan, to explore the hinge's ability to link across different dimensions—the imagined future, unstable present, and structured past. Finally, we examine how the hinge can also serve as a reflexive tool, helping anthropologists to navigate ethnographic collaboration in AI research and development.

The Hinge as an Analytical Tool

> Walls are a nice invention, but if there were no holes in them, there would be no way to get in or out…
>
> *(Johnson 1988)*

A hinge is an everyday object; useful, but one we rarely ever look at. It helps open and close doors and other pieces of mostly flat wood and metal just as it lets mostly people move in and out, and about. A hinge is mechanically simple, folding over one way and then another, in a push and pull, but as we argue in this paper also metaphorically rich. Of course, we aren't the first to think so. Among others, Bruno Latour, writing as James Johnson argued that "the cleverness of the invention" of the door, "hinges upon the hinge-pin" (1988, 299). For Latour, the work of the door and the hinge upon it is evidence of a "delegation" of human effort or a "translation" of function—in addition to being a solution to the problem of keeping some things out while letting others in (1988, 299). In our case, a hinge is less about the door and acts of trespassing through it and more evidence of productive motility or possibilities for reversibly conjoined movement.

The mechanical hinge is also an object that we don't usually notice consciously in our everyday lives but which is essential for us to be able to go in and out somewhere, to arrive and depart, or to separate public from private spaces, work from leisure, for example. In engineering, hinges are described as:

> ...mechanical bearings used to create a limited and fixed range of rotational movement between two workpieces. Most doors, for instance, are affixed to a frame with two or more hinges. Hinges allow doors to swing open—but typically only to a certain degree.[2]

Mechanically then, a hinge is a go-between, or something that facilitates passage. It is composed of two leaves that are connected by interlocking knuckles and held together by a central pin. Critically for our purpose, hinge leaves remain distinctly separate but not autonomous as they are essential to each other's purpose, combining at their knuckles to form a functioning join.

Hinges are of interest to us to think about AI research because they hold together things that might otherwise seem separate and, by bringing these together, create something new, such as functionality or flexibility and movement "to a certain degree." At the same time, like hinges, AI systems also remain non-functional without a structure such as data and infrastructure to which, like a wooden door, they attach to. Indeed, without a door or the like, a hinge has no purpose.

In their ethnographic work in Mozambique and Mongolia, Morten Axel Pederson and Morten Nielsen utilize this metaphor to formulate a *trans-temporal hinge*, or a "motile middle point holding together occurrences that are otherwise distributed across time" (2013, 129). We draw on Pedersen and Nielsen's understanding of this metaphor and expand to include the hinge's functioning and material properties as a way to theorize how AI participates in the imagination, production, and experience of possible futures. Pedersen and Nielsen argue specifically that their hinge represents "a peculiar interdependent relationship between an *unstable present* and an *imagined future* in which each may be seen as unfolding from the other" (2013, 130, emphasis added). They describe this imagined or anticipatory future as protensive, "a seemingly speculative intuiting of the inherently unknowable contours of a certain future scenario" (Pedersen and Nielsen 2013, 125). In this chapter, we refer to the protensive as *the imagined future*, which includes the imaginaries, ideologies, and enchanted hope that different actors envision towards the future. On the other hand, *the unstable present* is the protospective, emerging from a retrospective tracing of the "dynamics and ramifications" of these "fundamentally unknown" futures on the present moment (Pedersen and Nielsen 2013, 125).

AI, we argue, similarly conjoins temporalities of present and future—and we add, also past—which are working in "oscillating" but contingent fields of tension (Pedersen and Nielsen 2013, 129). Below, we first discuss the way imaginations for the future collate around AI, and indeed have been part of AI from the beginning, as they are drawn on by researchers and developers in their work. If we return to the door hinge as we have been describing it, we see the imagined future as an ideological movement towards a future which is in a state of hopeful, or enchanted becoming. On the other hand, we argue that the everyday experience of situated practice, as well as failing, difficult, or resisting AI interlock with this anticipatory "leaf" as an integrated and

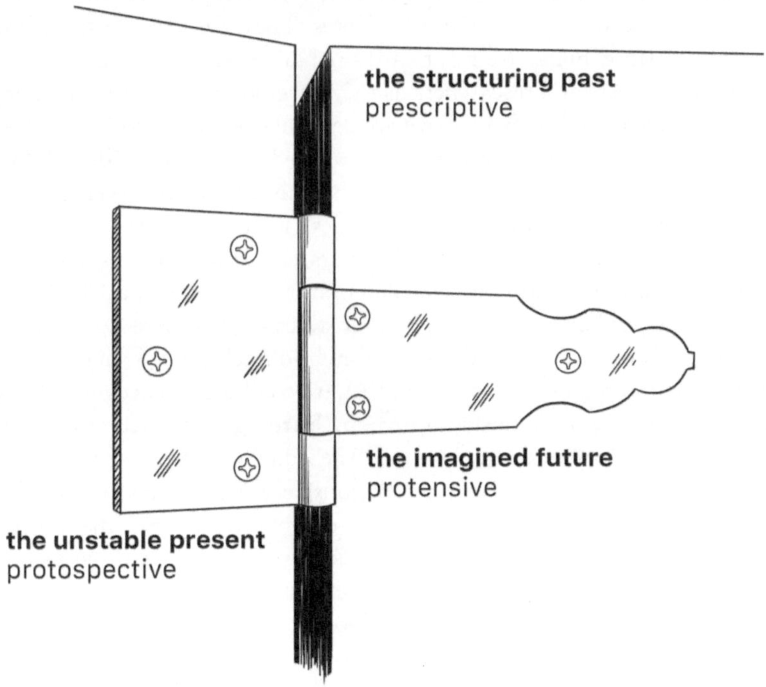

FIGURE 1.1 A hinge for reflexive ethnographic research. Artwork by Meredith Moriarty, ©2025. Used with permission.

essential, but not at all contradictory, constituent (see Figure 1.1). We see the second leaf then as *the unstable present*, a moment where these same idealizations are revealed to be, in practice, continually negotiated, layered on, and breaking down in relation to what is both imagined will be and what is left over from before, leading to a Weber-esque form of disenchantment.

To Pedersen and Nielsen's concept, we also add back the past or previous substrate to the potential for futures—which we call *the structuring past*, or the prescriptive—as an explicit attention to material networks, channels, and "path dependencies" (Klausner et al. 2015). As we mentioned, the separate "leaves" of a hinge are tied inherently to and dependent upon a solid foundation, the door, and the pin, or as we consider in this case, prior infrastructures, including source code itself. As we discuss, possibilities for new AI systems are channeled by previous iterations, scaffolded onto what came before, just as computational systems are written through a layering over of the preexisting techno-social infrastructures that help to realize and convey them.

The Imagined Future

We apply the "protensive," or anticipatory leaf, to analyze those imaginations, both techno-utopian and dystopian, that inform shared practices in the intersection of science and technology in our field sites. These futures, we argue, may be differently described but share a forward-orientation that organizes and directs the work of scientists and researchers as they develop, incorporate, and apply AI tools in their work. In this chapter, we are particularly interested in the way such enchanted and speculative futures are practiced—even contradicted by, but nevertheless lived (Febel, Knopf and Nonhoff 2023)—in the everyday, as we describe below. AI futures, once imagined, describe a becoming which researchers move towards and work on directly to craft or realize; for example, a time when AI may become "autonomous collaborators" (Messeri and Crockett 2024, 49), facilitate desired or morally sought after states such as increased productivity and efficiency through automation or form hybrid intelligence systems where the complementary strengths of humans and AI are combined to accomplish sophisticated results and "continuously improve by learning from each other" (Dellermann et al. 2019, 640). Researchers may be equally concerned with a future where ethical practices or trustworthy relations between humans and AI might be realized through the development of AI or hybrid systems themselves. As researchers are tasked with AI use and development, their projects may be inflected with such relative degrees of hopefulness and optimism, reflecting an enchantment lying "under the surface of [modern] rationality" (Allison 2006, 28, discussing Benjamin 1999 and Weber 1948), although not all AI imagining is similarly utopian. These speculations also often rest on particularly organized expectations and idealizations of and in the present; for example, orders of techno-rationality which figure technology as the "best" solution to society's ills, or even "assumptions that AI technologies and systems can be trusted" in the first place (Pink et al. 2024), which interlock with potentials for forward movement. Similarly, Pedersen and Nielsen detail the way the "present" in their different ethnographic examples "was couched in a vocabulary defined by the properties of events that had not yet occurred" (2013, 130). Indeed, these futures can become wayfinding tools, as Adriana Petryna elaborates for the work of ecological scientists, where "horizoning" describes their recursive application of an imagined future in an effort to reorder their actions and decisions in the present moment (2022).

In genetics, AI has been heralded, as in other disciplines, as having the potential to craft "a world that has never been seen before" (Vilhekar and Rawekar 2024). AI models are situated to take advantage of growing tracts of human biological data and large genomic datasets, which have been collected by national biobanks, research institutes and hospitals, and further produced in and analyzed by next-generation sequencing and genome-wide association studies, among others. There, AI will be increasingly used for tasks such as deciphering the semantics or mechanics of the genome, predicting which genetic variations are linked to diseases or other phenotypic outcomes, guiding clinical and pharmaceutical decisions, and, in other ways, work at revealing the biological unknown. These practices are subsumed within expectations for discovery itself as an *a priori* future, one that is already decided; a future that collates around notions in the medical sciences that have defined, for example, disease as a locatable, albeit dysfunctioning, mechanism within the body, which can be laid bare through (technologically aided) observation (Keller 2006). As Toshi, one postdoc in the genetics lab, described: "Bioinformatics is just a tool to know the hidden secret of biology" (July 3, 2020). Increasingly, forms of AI and the accessibility of the data needed to drive it are also driving the development of research projects and hypotheses themselves; as another bioinformatician working in ML explained to Rebecca, "one of the reasons to do such research is there is information for these things" (September 24, 2021).

In the field of human computation and hybrid intelligence, AI is similarly imagined—if developed in the "right way," meaning with humans in the loop—as a way to solve some of today's most complex problems (Michelucci 2019). In the examples studied by Libuše, human computation was particularly envisioned as a counter-imaginary to so-called strong AI narratives, which envision an artificial general intelligence with the ability to perform any intellectual task that humans can do, and dystopian imaginations of AI taking over control, and displacing humans (Vepřek 2024a, 2024b). Instead, the future, as Michelucci explained in one of his conversations with Libuše in January 2021, was one where AI and humans would work together, engaged in a collaborative conversation in which each took on the complementary roles they excelled at. In this hybrid unfolding, passing the ball from one to the other, researchers imagined superhuman capabilities would unfold. On a more micro level and as part of one human computation system developed by the institute, AI was also imagined to automate tedious tasks in the pipeline which prepared the data to be analyzed in the hybrid system. For example, a ML model was introduced in one biomedical engineering laboratory, working together with the institute, in the hope that it would fully take over a manually time-intensive task from the researchers. However, as we further show these forms of AI enchantment—an "as if" or "what if"—are complicated in, and even contradicted by, everyday practice.

The Unstable Present

The counterpole to the imagined future is the unstable present or "protospective" (Pedersen and Nielsen 2013), the second leaf of our hinge. While imagined to solve current problems and automate tedious tasks, AI technologies, once deployed and embedded in actual practice, often function in unanticipated ways or fail; for example, by falling short of fully automating the tasks they were designed to take over. In the broadest sense, following Max Weber's description of modern society and the ways that rationalization substituted religion in disenchantment (1948 [1919]), we think about the present as a form of AI disenchantment, a seeming antithesis to enchanted futures, where imaginaries and visions are softened and washed with, but not erased by, everyday practice. In the present, there is an ongoing complex interplay between beliefs and practice, where imaginations do not hold in the everyday, and very practically, as an open secret, often aren't expected to. Instead, as we mentioned, imaginaries, however hopeful, are always negotiated, overlaid, and seen to be failing in relation to the unstable present.

It is no secret that code is primarily a practice of debugging and that infrastructures "normally" are in a state of breakdown, needing to be worked on continually (cf. Star and Ruhleder 1996; Star 1999; Pink et al. 2018). Yet, idealized operability figures centrally in AI system development and maintenance, just as it does in most places where researchers or engineers work regularly and in tandem with technological objects and tools. Any programmer will tell you almost eagerly that "code is fragile" and, even more, "always broken." However, as we will discuss in more detail below, configurations of an imagined future are supported by expectations that AI will be functioning properly and as intended, a hopefulness that positions "working" as the normal state of affairs rather than the exception.

To better describe this discrepancy in the unstable present, we first turn to an example from Libuše's ethnographic field research on the human computation-based citizen science project Stall Catchers. As an online video game and the main project of the Human Computation Institute, Stall Catchers invites volunteer participants to contribute to Alzheimer's disease research conducted at a biomedical engineering laboratory by analyzing data in the game. This research data consists of brain blood vessels, which are analyzed by participants for blockages. During Libuše's fieldwork, the data pipeline—the infrastructure that cleans, prepares, and transforms the wet research data into visualized representations that can be analyzed in the game by participants—was continually failing to simply function the way it was supposed to despite the continual introduction of fixes and improvements. Before the development of Stall Catchers, this analysis had been done by the researchers themselves, a manual annotation process that was very time-consuming and led to a backlog of existing data, delaying the study. Stall Catchers thus emerged in the search for a more efficient solution, and in 2014, the designers and developers started to build the game platform and the data pipeline infrastructure. One important component was a new ML model, which should transform microscopic imaging data into a digital representation of the vessel network. Once functioning, this infrastructure was meant to disappear into the background, helping to speed up research. However, six years after the launch of the collaboration, researchers were still or again working on it. The problem was that they could not rely on the results they were receiving from the game due to inaccuracies in the pipeline algorithms and errors in the data resulting from these. For instance, the ML model, designed to automate the laborious task of identifying and marking individual vessels to relieve researchers of this workload, did not always perform adequately. Interruptions and error messages often required manual intervention, and at times, the model incorrectly identified random objects as vessels while missing actual parts of a vessel. Therefore, from manually analyzing the data themselves, researchers moved to working instead on cleaning the results of the ML model and improving the pipeline by introducing new steps and tools to facilitate the experimentalist's data preparation tasks and to improve the quality of the data sent to the game. At that time, this process was even more time-consuming than the previous manual analysis and was described by the researchers as a very tedious process. In effect, the data pipeline, which was meant to enable and facilitate the research in the background as a means, now became the end in itself (Vepřek 2024a, 232).

This brief example illustrates the gap between the aspirations of AI—in this case, a ML model—and its current implementation, which falls short of fully taking over the work. This does not mean that the model was not an improvement at all, but the troubles researchers described highlight how the idealized visions of AI can falter in everyday practice. The example also shows the unpredictability and perpetually unfinished nature of infrastructures (amongst others, see Alderman and Goodwin, 2022), and how they, despite their apparent outward stability and permanence, often resist attempts to be stabilized, cleaned, or finished. Indeed, AI systems are constantly in the making, undoing, distracting, and redirecting the work of scientists and computer engineers. On the surface, these disruptions appear to conflict with the speculative and always-becoming nature of protensive imaginations.

In Rebecca's fieldsite, bioscientists were similarly challenged by the ways their practices emerged from a shared imagined future—in the case of medical sciences, a generalized directive to "unlock" biological realities (Bileschi et al. 2022)—yet needed to be resolved against experimental and material limitations in the everyday. The application of AI as a tool to achieve this commonly assumed future, to reveal hidden biological information, is doubly imagined: the presumption that deep learning's increased accuracy and efficiency will lead to an unprecedented "depth of insight" (Bileschi et al. 2022) currently impossible with standard research techniques. In this case, AI systems are acted on and incorporated into this effort at times as if they are objective, fact-like containers (well documented "blackboxes"), or "coherent objects" (Jensen 2010, 21). These are presumed to hold naturally occurring evidence or situations which merely collate, make accessible or respond to, rather than fundamentally also produce, biological facts (Latour and Woolgar 1979). Yet, bioinformaticians designing algorithms and ML models also continually work within everyday experiences which defy such easy categorization. For example, Toshi described the way, "many people are really struggling to collect samples from Africa." He explained:

> ...we do not have good access to African samples due to restrictions and ethical problems and also wars, and for example some areas believe in religion which doesn't allow human sampling, and this makes a sampling bias, and we can not capture the global picture of African evolution.
>
> *(July 3, 2020)*

Such realizations might trouble scientists in the formation of their hypotheses and concerns about statistical accuracy and the potential for sampling bias in their pipelines, even as they work to accept the reliability of computational outcomes. In fact, as Toshi explained, bias created by this lack had to be acknowledged and incorporated directly by bioinformaticians so that datasets could be normalized, cleaned up, or neutralized against it. To account for this limited genomic data in his own work, Toshi designed an imputation panel, a method to estimate previously "unobserved variants" (Kojima et al. 2020), which typically draws on a standardized genetic reference as a template to help replace "missing" DNA data with ML predictive results. Yet, the process of drawing from limited or partial genetic sequence data to estimate the whole genome, as Toshi agreed, has the potential to, in turn, contribute to expanding sample bias.

These examples show the way researchers spend time on resolving discrepancies between the present and imagined future, and build systems around the presumption that they are indeed resolvable. In other words, researchers act on, move towards, and manage the present even as their various AI imaginations may require them to engage in a kind of acrobatics to bring about their union with everyday practice. Both leaves of the hinge, then—the imagined future and the unstable present—are constitutive of each other. They are actively hinged together by scientists, researchers, and engineers, who enact them simultaneously; and as they take action and make choices about AI development, they target a future imagined horizon in an ideological effort that necessitates, and even sometimes targets, a remaking of the present. At the same time, various sociomaterialities, infrastructures, and other actors included in AI systems (Vepřek 2024a) also resist agendas or take unanticipated trajectories, even if by coincidence, and break down or dissolve.

The Structuring Past

The two leaves of the hinge, the imagined future and unstable present, come together to create the knuckle, the space in which AI and its futures are emergent and always in the making. This is where the hinge-pin, which pierces the knuckle, gets to work, holding steady throughout while the door is folded in or out in a joint-like fashion. But as we mentioned before, door hinges also do not hold together or function without a foundation, the door, wall or other surface to which the hinge itself is attached. We think about the pin and the door-wall in the context of AI systems and "algorithm machines" (Gillespie 2014) as the prescriptive, those existing systems, data infrastructures, and source code that support the becoming of something new but at the same time restrict future possibilities, and create path dependencies for AI systems. Even though the pin and door in their mechanical sense are fixed, we do not think about the prescriptive or structuring past as completely determining but as guiding the development of sociotechnical systems.

Andrew Barry similarly describes the way existing infrastructures function as "templates for future projects" (Barry 2022). Like Barry's infrastructural example of oil pipelines, source code is rarely something built completely new. Rather, software systems draw from existing building blocks and code libraries, from bits and pieces of code floating around on Github and elsewhere, or as part of already existing software which is "mashed together" (Kitchin 2016, 7) with new ideas. What is new comes layered on top of what was there before. Just as infrastructures are not rebuilt from scratch, code gets mostly expanded and adapted to its new purpose. This is not only the case for widespread applications such as the development of AI chatbots, but also for cases in which new sociotechnical systems and AI applications are being developed.

Stall Catchers well illustrates the role of the structuring past and its foundation for the unstable present and imagined future, as its human-technology interplay and system were both inspired by and initially built on top of the source code of a different online citizen science game, Stardust@Home. One of the oldest projects of this kind, in this game, participants search for interstellar dust particles in data from NASA's 2006 Stardust mission with a customized online analysis tool.[3] Although Stall Catchers is located in a very different scientific field that contributes to research on neurological disorders, Stardust@Home's source code still presented a helpful starting point from which Stall Catchers could be developed. Even though the source code had to be mainly rewritten, Stardust@Home formed the basis and thereby prescripted how Stall Catchers would function. Moreover, the customized online analysis tool, which is also called the "virtual microscope" was mostly adopted so that the Stardust@Home design can still be recognized in today's Stall Catchers user interface. Stardust@Home, as the prescript, functioned as both an enabler for the emergence of Stall Catchers and as a restrictor, pre-framing how data from neurological disorders research could be analyzed in the game, as well as how human-technology relations in sociotechnical systems should unfold.

In addition to prior grounds of technological infrastructure, for ML in human genetics research the structuring past is also fixed to histories of biological materials, which are commonly circulated and used in experimental practice and today further solidified as established inputs for AI systems. One example is GRCh38, or the 38th version of the human reference genome, a complete DNA sequence assembled out of multiple genetic strands from different human donors. This sequence is available to download and used globally by scientists during various genetic experiments as a standardized comparison, which helps guide their movement to discovery. At the same time, this reference genome is constantly being worked on (and AI is now also playing a role in this process), as well as critiqued. For one, the reference genome is, in fact, not standardized; it does not represent an average amount of genetic variation or diversity. Instead the sequence "contains long stretches that are highly specific to one individual" which can "distort" research results (Ballouz et al. 2019). Another critique relates to how the reference genome's development and use has created a "research ecosystem" (Ballouz et al. 2019) in the molding of other infrastructures of technology and practice that adhere to it. Similarly, ML models themselves are trained on collages of datasets like the GRCh38, while published bioinformatic tools and prior pieces of code, such as Python packages, act as stitches holding everything together. As these examples illustrate, AI systems hinge upon the structuring past, which both enables innovation and constrains future developments through existing infrastructures and historical precedents.

The Hinge as a Reflexive Tool

As we have described, a hinge enables movement, an opening and closing of what becomes a "reversible door" (Johnson 1988, 299)—or otherwise a cabinet, closet, chest, or compartment like a glove box. A hinge's movement depends not only on the pin but also on its two interlocking leaves and, just as importantly, the door itself or any other solid foundation of metal, wood, or stone upon which the hinge is meant to both adhere and act. These components not only interlock but also determine each other. Just as neglecting or omitting one would lead to a non-functioning mechanical object, in our case, we argue that losing sight of these produces an incomplete perspective on AI systems in the making. Analyzing how futures with AI are imagined, where AI systems come from, and how they unfold in everyday life helps us to better understand what assumptions, norms, and imaginations flow into the design of such systems and why their implementation in practice often turns out differently than expected. When this perspective falls out of the wayfinding practices of AI practitioners and developers, where it may be professionally cordoned from the "project-centric mindset," we argue the concept of the hinge can help guide and validate an attentive return; to insight into the ways the past, present, and future constitutively shape AI. In this way, anthropologists can contribute not only to critical reflection on AI outcomes but also to a collaborative decision-making process for and intervention into, the making of AI systems.

In Rebecca's case, bioscientists design research questions and their attendant experiments based on expectations that the "secrets" of genetics will be revealed to them and, further, that AI can fill in or make predictions for gaps in current scientific knowledge (the imagined future), but do not also produce these secrets. Although bioinformaticians struggle with a lack of access to diverse genetic samples, they may be less critical of how their attempts to resolve this in AI-augmented experimental practice can create further cascading or unintended distortions (the unstable present). At the same time, bioscientists work within research ecosystems that are grafted to standardized experimental practices and materials, such as the GRCh38 and Python packages, which shape notions of genetic diversity and the configuration of ML pipelines in the first place (the structuring past). Although bioscientists themselves describe these elements and their impact on their work, bringing them together as constitutive with the hinge can help researchers develop an awareness of the potential for ML to amplify systemic misalignments and, in turn, design AI tools that address these limitations more effectively.

For Libuše's research, an analysis of Stall Catchers using the hinge tool demonstrated how imaginations of hybrid human–AI systems (the imagined future) are both complicated and partly contested by current implementations and negotiations among different actors in the everyday (the unstable present). This present is itself structured and, to some extent, predetermined by earlier systems or components and existing human–technology relations (the structuring past). By revealing this dynamic between the different dimensions and including it in the maintenance and development of these systems, potential consequences of design choices can be more accurately anticipated, and unforeseen effects can be more easily addressed through a deeper understanding of the interdependency of the different system components, goals, and meanings.

As ethnographers, we already typically go in and out and revolve; we move across thresholds and take paths in our research along various routes in hinge-like motions. As a result, as collaborative researchers, we can, just as Dippel and Sudmann suggest for ethnography, help open "insights about the field that are ideally also new for the actors of the observed field and enables a different form of self-observation for them" (2023, 837). Going in and out, however, is not always an easy endeavor. Ethnographers must also navigate multiple, revolving roles in their research and can just as easily get stuck in a particular mindset. For example, despite Michelucci's acceptance of and emphasis on the need for ethnographers to participate in the development of hybrid human-AI systems, Libuše sometimes struggled during fieldwork to find her proper place and role at the institute as a collaborator and ethnographer. *How* should she contribute, and *when*? Although there is a large body of literature on ethnography and collaboration, including in engaged anthropology and design anthropology, navigating the different roles and possible ways of engaging "with the field" (Bieler et al. 2021, 91) still remained a challenge for her. In some situations, Libuše found it difficult to decide whether to contribute to the institute's projects as an ethnographer and participant observer or as a full team member and how—or if—these contributions would differ in practice. As a result, she sometimes hesitated to proactively engage in tasks such as the design and preparation of experiments, especially when the team, likely due to time constraints, did not involve her from the outset. In one instance, Michelucci approached her after an experiment on the Stall Catchers platform had already begun, when issues arose because participants complained about the experimental setting. By then, her role was limited to troubleshooting problems that might have been avoided had she been more involved in the early stages of the experiment, leaving her with a sense of failure. Reflecting on and communicating this uncertainty about her different roles and their associated expectations from the start, using the metaphor of a "hinge" in the collaboration, would have helped Libuše view these roles not as separate but as mutually supportive and contribute to a more inclusive experiment design.

Within the context of the genetics laboratory, Rebecca also struggled with knowing when or how to take a more participatory role in some of the lab's activities, and unlike Libuše, her research did not start from an established point of collaboration. Instead, that possibility emerged tentatively at various moments while she was in the field. For example, once during a lab wide meeting, Rebecca was invited by Tom to comment on the lab's use of the word "gender" in their discussions. Surprised to be included in this way when she had participated largely as a silent observer for prior meetings, Rebecca declined to give an opinion. More generally, from the beginning, Tom had encouraged Rebecca to provide feedback to lab members about the way they were communicating the results of their research. Once, when Rebecca asked him if she could approach Toshi about a slide figure he had made demonstrating genetic variation with what she felt were stereotypical images of Asians, Europeans and Africans, Tom wrote back to her, "your role/perspective as an intelligent critical observer of our science comm, especially as it relates to social science or anthropology, is one that should need no license" (October 9, 2020). Still, Rebecca felt in both cases the awkwardness and uncertainty of moving to a more active form of engagement, particularly as Tom had also initially expressed some skepticism over her analysis of their work (Carlson 2021). Viewing these emergent opportunities as within the workings of the hinge would have helped Rebecca—armed initially with anthropological critique that proved to be relatively superficial—to situate her perspective as one part or component of a whole; as a leaf in the hinge that was already joined with and did not override, their scientific work.

In this question of how and when, the hinge can also prove particularly useful for organizing and structuring the kinds of challenges we face and for developing approaches to address them. While it helped us primarily to reflect retrospectively on our experiences, we suggest that it can also, and even more so, help ethnographers manage such uncertainty or take advantage of emergent collaborations from the beginning of their research process. Thus, in addition to understanding the hinge as an analytical tool to study AI research, we also see it as a way to grasp and reflect upon the always plural identities of ethnographers in their research endeavors. Situated as a reflexive ethnographic tool, the hinge's motility, its capacity to join across disparate pieces, suggests a mode for ethnographers to conjoin the different roles they may take on or be confronted with in the field. It argues for seeing these roles as interlocking and not contradictory, even necessary to achieve ethnographic movement—to progress in understanding, to valuably contribute—and for incorporating uncertainty and ambiguity as part of a flexible and reversible directionality while ever adjoined to a foundational purpose. Instead of a pulling in opposite directions, as Forsythe described experiencing "conflicting loyalties" in her research on AI development (2001, 125), this is coordinated movement. In the choreography of a functional and fluid passage, it is also a particularly useful metaphor to express co-laboration where "the epistemic practices of ethnographers and research subjects are continuously entangled but do not (necessarily) coalesce" (Bieler et al., 2021, 91). If we can see the hinge as having the "capacity to operate as dynamic middle points that hold together otherwise disparate occurrences and events" (Pedersen and Nielsen, 2013, 137) and employ it as a tool in this way, we believe it can open doorways for ethnographers to constructively intervene in AI development.

Notes

1 Both authors contributed equally to this work; names have been arranged in reverse alphabetical order.

2 "What Are the Parts of a Hinge?" 2020. One Monroe Engineering, October 5, 2020. https://monroeengineering.com/blog/what-are-the-parts-of-a-hinge/.
3 Hall, Loura. 2023. "Stardust @ Home." NASA, March 2, 2023. https://www.nasa.gov/get-involved/stardusthome/.

References

Alderman, Jonathan, and Geoff Goodwin. 2022. "Introduction: Infrastructure as Relational and Experimental Process." In *The Social and Political Life of Latin American Infrastructures*, edited by Jonathan Alderman and Geoff Goodwin, 1–26. University of London Press.

Allison, Anne. 2006. *Millennial Monsters: Japanese Toys and the Global Imagination.* Duke University Press.

Ballouz, Sara, Dobin Alexander, and Jesse A. Gillis. 2019. "Is It Time to Change the Reference Genome?" *Genome Biology* 20 (159). doi:10.1186/s13059-019-1774-4.

Benjamin, Walter. 1999. *The Arcades Project*, translated by Howard Eiland and Kevin McLaughlin. MIT Press.

Bieler, Patrick, Milena D. Bister, Janine Hauer, Martina Klausner, Jörg Niewöhner, Christine Schmid, and Sebastian von Peter. 2021. "Distributing Reflexivity through Co-laborative Ethnography." *Journal of Contemporary Ethnography* 50 (1): 77–98. doi:10.1177/0891241620968271.

Bileschi, Maxwell L., David Belanger, Drew H. Bryant, Theo Sanderson, Brandon Carter, D. Sculley, Alex Bateman, Mark A. DePristo, and Lucy J. Colwell. 2022. "Using Deep Learning to Annotate the Protein Universe." *Nature Biotechnology* 40: 932–937. doi:10.1038/s41587-021-01179-w.

Cambridge University Press. n.d. "Techno-solutionism." In *Cambridge Advanced Learner's Dictionary & Thesaurus*.

Carlson, Rebecca. 2022. "(Imagining) Science for Troubled Times: A Mouse, a Bird, and a Threshold for Collaboration." *Imaginations: Journal of Cross-Cultural Image Studies* 12 (2): 171–200. doi:10.17742/IMAGE.MM.12.2.9.

Cave, Stephen, and Kanta Dihal. 2019. "Hopes and Fears for Intelligent Machines in Fiction and Reality." *Nature Machine Intelligence* 1 (2): 74–78. doi:10.1038/s42256-019-0020-9.

Dellermann, Dominik, Philipp Ebel, Matthias Söllner, and Jan Marco Leimeister. 2019. "Hybrid Intelligence." *Business & Information Systems Engineering* 61(5 Oct.): 637–643. doi:10.1007/s12599-019-00595-2.

Dippel, Anne and Andreas Sudmann. 2023. "AI Ethnography" In *Handbook of Critical Studies of Artificial Intelligence*, edited by Simon Lindgren, 826–844. Edward Elgar Publishing. doi:10.4337/9781803928562.00083.

Febel, Gisela, Kerstin Knopf, and Martin Nonhoff, eds. 2023. *Contradiction Studies—Exploring the Field.* Springer VS.

Forsythe, Diana E. 2001. *Studying Those Who Study Us: An Anthropologist in the World of Artificial Intelligence.* Edited by David J. Hess. Stanford University Press.

Gillespie, Tarleton. 2014. *The Relevance of Algorithms.* In *Media Technologies. Essays on Communication, Materiality, and Society*, edited by Tarleton Gillespie, Pablo Bockowski, and Kirsten Foot, 167–195. MIT Press Scholarship Online.

Heaven, Will Douglas. 2024. "What is AI? Everyone Thinks They Know but No One Can Agree. And That's a Problem." *MIT Technology Review*. July 10, 2024. https://www.technologyreview.com/2024/07/10/1094475/what-is-artificial-intelligence-ai-definitive-guide/.

Jasanoff, Sheila, and Sang-Hyun Kim, eds. 2015. *Dreamscapes of Modernity: Sociotechnical Imaginaries and the Fabrication of Power*. The University of Chicago Press.

Jensen, Casper Bruun. 2010. *Ontologies for Developing Things: Making Health Care Futures Through Technology*. Sense Publishers.

Johnson, Jim [Bruno Latour]. 1988. "Mixing Humans and Nonhumans Together: The Sociology of a Door-Closer." *Social Problems* 35 (3): 298–310. doi:10.2307/800624.

Keller, Richard C. 2006. "Geographies of Power, Legacies of Mistrust: Colonial Medicine in the Global Present." *Historical Geography* 34: 26–48.

Kitchin, Rob. 2016. "Thinking Critically about and Researching Algorithms." *Information, Communication & Society* 20 (1): 14–29. doi:10.1080/1369118X.2016.1154087.

Klausner, Martina, Milena D. Bister, Jörg Niewöhner, and Stefan Beck. 2015. "Choreografien klinischer und städtischer Alltage: Ergebnisse einer ko-laborativen Ethnografie mit der Sozialpsychiatrie." *Zeitschrift für Volkskunde* 111 (2): 214–235.

Kojima, Kaname, Shu Tadaka, Fumiki Katsuoka, Gen Tamiya, Masayuki Yamamoto and Kengo Kinoshita. 2020. "A Genotype Imputation Method for De-identified Haplotype Reference Information by Using Recurrent Neural Network." PLoS *Computational Biology* 16 (10): e1008207. doi:10.1371/journal.pcbi.1008207.

Latour, Bruno and Steve Woolgar. 1979. *Laboratory Life: The Construction of Scientific Facts*. Sage Publications.

McCarthy, John, Marvin Minsky, Nathaniel Rochester, and Claude Shannon. 1955. *A Proposal for the Dartmouth Summer Research Project on Artificial Intelligence*. https://raysolomonoff.com/dartmouth/boxa/dart564props.pdf.

Messeri, Lisa and M.J. Crockett. 2024. "Artificial Intelligence and Illusions of Understanding in Scientific Research." *Nature* 627: 49–58. doi:10.1038/s41586-024-07146-0.

Michelucci, Pietro. 2019. "*Crowd, Cloud and the Future of Work: Updates from human AI computation*." Microsoft Research Faculty Summit, Jul. 19, 2019. https://www.microsoft.com/en-us/research/video/crowd-cloud-and-the-future-of-work-updates-from-human-ai-computation/.

Pedersen, Morten Axel, and Morten Nielsen. 2013. "Trans-temporal Hinges: Reflections on an Ethnographic Study of Chinese Infrastructural Projects in Mozambique and Mongolia." *Social Analysis* 57 (1). doi:10.3167/sa.2013.570109.

Petryna, Adriana. 2022. *Horizon Work: At the Edges of Knowledge in an Age of Runaway Climate Change*. Princeton University Press.

Pink, Sarah, Minna Ruckenstein, Willim Robert and Melissa Duque. 2018. "Broken Data: Conceptualising Data in an Emerging World." *Big Data & Society* 5, (1): 1–13. doi:10.1177/2053951717753228.

Pink, Sarah, Emma Quilty, John Grundy, and Rashina Hoda. 2024. "Trust, Artificial Intelligence and Software Practitioners: An Interdisciplinary Agenda." *AI & Society*. doi:10.1007/s00146-024-01882-7.

Sætra, Henrik Skaug, ed. 2023. *Technology and Sustainable Development: The Promise and Pitfalls of Techno-Solutionism*. Routledge.

Star, Susan Leigh. 1999. "The Ethnography of Infrastructure." *American Behavioral Scientist* 43 (3): 377–391. doi:10.1177/00027649921955326.

Star, Susan Leigh, and Karen Ruhleder. 1996. "Steps Toward an Ecology of Infrastructure: Design and Access for Large Information Spaces." *Information Systems Research* 7 (1 Mar.): 111–134. doi:10.1287/isre.7.1.111.

Vepřek, Libuše Hannah. 2024a. *At the Edge of Artificial Intelligence. Human Computation Systems and their Intraverting Relations*. Transcript.

Vepřek, Libuše Hannah. 2024b: "Infrastructuring Desirable Futures with Humans in the Loop: Analysing Hybrid Intelligence as a Counter-imaginary to Artificial General Intelligence." In *Digital Futures in the Making: Imaginaries, Materialities, and Politics*, edited by Gertraud Koch, Samantha Lutz, Hannah Rotthaus, Anna Oechslen, Quoc-Tran Tran. Routledge (in preparation).

Vilhekar, Rohit S. and Alka Rawekar. 2024. "Artificial Intelligence in Genetics." *Cureus* 16 (1): e52035. doi:10.7759/cureus.52035.

Weber, Max. 1948 [1919]. "Science as a Vocation." In *From Max Weber: Essays in Sociology*, translated and edited by Hans H. Gerth and C. Wright Mills. Routledge, 129–156.

2

CO-BECOMING WITH AI

An Anthropological Framework for Equitable Human-AI Systems

Matt Artz

Introduction

Since the 1940s, artificial intelligence (AI), a broad family of computational fields and technologies, has experienced cycles of breakthroughs and constraints. While early developments showed promise in specialized problem-solving, limitations in computing power and data availability led to periods of slower progress. However, the past fifteen years have witnessed unprecedented advancement, driven by developments in neural networks, cloud computing, and big data. These developments have shown tremendous promise for advancing human knowledge and capabilities while raising grave concerns about the negative externalities of AI.

Against this backdrop, UNESCO convened in Paris in November 2021 to propose the first global standard on AI ethics. *The Recommendation on the Ethics of AI* (UNESCO 2021) emphasized the need for ethical frameworks to ensure AI development would serve the collective good while acknowledging potential benefits and risks to humanity, particularly regarding social and economic disparities. These concerns proved prescient when the landscape of AI underwent a seismic shift with ChatGPT's release in November 2022. This watershed moment introduced an AI system capable of natural conversation, generating creative content, and assisting with complex tasks. The unprecedented adoption rate—reaching 100 million monthly active users within two months (Hu 2023)—signaled a fundamental transformation in human-AI interaction. Generative AI (GenAI) systems like ChatGPT evolved from specialized tools into general-purpose technologies (Brynjolfsson et al. 2021), becoming active participants in knowledge creation, creative expression, and decision-making. Yet this breakthrough represents just one dimension of a

DOI: 10.4324/9781003532750-4

broader transformation, as AI systems now affect billions daily through search algorithms, recommendation systems, and automated decision-making across education, healthcare, creative industries, and professional services.

The rapid transition from UNESCO's prescient warning to ChatGPT's explosive growth, which ranks as the eighth most visited website globally as of late 2024 (SemRush 2024), makes UNESCO's call for ethical AI frameworks more urgent and relevant than ever because the widespread adoption of AI in our daily lives is intensifying the very concerns about equity and societal impact that UNESCO sought to address. Such challenges are particularly acute in systems that shape cultural production and economic opportunity, such as with the use of large language models (LLMs) for the automation of expertise and knowledge work, and in AI-based recommender systems that increasingly determine which voices are heard and which creators can earn a living in our digital economy.

To address such challenges, frameworks for ethical AI development have emerged along two primary paths: Responsible AI (RAI) and Human-Centered AI (HCAI). RAI broadly, though not exclusively, focuses on technical safeguards and governance structures to prevent harm and foster alignment with human values, dovetailing closely with UNESCO's vision for ethical AI. HCAI, while also concerned with human values alignment, primarily emphasizes participatory design throughout the development process and user empowerment. While both frameworks offer valuable foundations for ethical AI development, they have often struggled to fully address the dynamic and continually emergent nature of human-AI relationships. These frameworks often treat human-AI interaction as a design challenge to be definitively solved rather than as an ever-evolving relational process that continually reshapes both human practice and technological capability. Moreover, while organizations may be applying these frameworks internally, detailed accounts of industry application remain limited in the scholarly literature, leaving practitioners without clear models for operationalizing these principles.

Recognizing this need to address both the perpetual nature of socio-technical relationships and the gap in documented implementations, this chapter first introduces co-becoming (Haraway 2007) as a theoretical model that recognizes the perpetual state of mutual transformation between participants in AI systems, where there is no fixed end state but rather continuous adaptation through interaction. To demonstrate how co-becoming, together with RAI and HCAI principles, can inform practical AI development, the chapter then presents a case study of its implementation in a digital art market, where the introduction of "behavioral capital" as a novel form of capital enables the creation of more equitable recommender systems by quantifying and rewarding ongoing community engagement. Together, these contributions aim to expand the literature on practical applications while demonstrating how abstract principles can be transformed into concrete development practices that work with, rather than against, the dynamic nature of human-AI relationships to promote more ethical AI.

To explore these ideas in depth, the chapter begins by examining current frameworks for ethical AI development analyzing the strengths and limitations of both RAI and HCAI approaches. It then introduces co-becoming and behavioral capital as complementary concepts that integrate anthropological perspectives with AI development. Through the ArtTech case study, the chapter demonstrates how these theoretical contributions can be operationalized in practice, showing how anthropological insights can inform the ongoing development of more ethical AI systems. The chapter concludes by introducing a co-becoming assessment framework that enables practitioners to systematically evaluate and improve human-AI relationships across different applications and contexts.

Responsible AI

Responsible AI (RAI) lacks a single definition. Instead, it reflects diverse perspectives from academia, industry, government, and super-national organizations, each contributing unique insights to this evolving field (Mikalef et al. 2022). At its core, RAI aims to ensure AI systems operate ethically while aligning with societal values and legal frameworks (Dignum, 2019). Despite the lack of a universal definition, there is growing consensus around several technology principles that constitute responsible AI development and deployment. These include but are not limited to algorithmic fairness; safety; and transparency and explainability. (Barredo Arrieta et al. 2020; Thiebes, Lins, and Sunyaev 2021; Gunning et al. 2019). While these core RAI principles are often presented as distinct dimensions, significant nuance and interconnectedness exist among them, particularly when examining frameworks across different sectors. Accordingly, these principles' precise definitions and boundaries remain subject to ongoing scholarly debate, with varying interpretations and emphases emerging across the literature. Nevertheless, a synthesis of current research suggests the following key characterizations of these foundational technology principles.

Algorithmic fairness encompasses mechanisms to prevent discriminatory outcomes and ensure equitable treatment in AI system outputs (Barocas et al. 2023). It is dependent on unbiased and representative data but also arguably requires diverse teams who can account for sociocultural context and historical biases in order to create models that are engineered to be inherently fair or can be disentangled (Chen et al. 2023) to identify and mitigate sources of bias. Fairness considerations must be integrated throughout the AI lifecycle, from initial data collection and model training to deployment and monitoring. This includes examining data for potential bias or underrepresented groups, testing models for disparate impact across different populations, and implementing technical solutions to mitigate detected biases. Organizations must also consider multiple definitions of fairness—from group and individual fairness to equality of opportunity—and carefully balance these sometimes competing objectives. The goal is not just to avoid discrimination but to actively promote inclusive AI systems that equitably serve all segments of society.

Safety considerations establish technical safeguards for data handling throughout the AI lifecycle and aim to address both the immediate technical robustness of systems and the potential for unintended consequences well into the future (Díaz-Rodríguez et al. 2023). Attending to such considerations requires implementing rigorous testing protocols, securing systems against adversarial attacks, ensuring reliable performance under varied conditions, and protecting user privacy through techniques like differential privacy and data minimization. As a critical aspect of safety, privacy requires careful attention to data collection, storage, processing, and sharing practices to prevent unauthorized access or misuse of sensitive data. Beyond these technical safeguards, safety also encompasses broader societal considerations like preventing misuse and maintaining human control over critical systems (Khalid et al. 2023). As AI capabilities continue to expand, safety frameworks must evolve to address emerging risks while balancing innovation with appropriate precautions—a process that requires continuous assessment to ensure responsible AI development.

Transparency and explainability serve complementary but distinct purposes in responsible AI development. While early symbolic AI systems were interpretable by design, the advent of complex deep learning models with billions of parameters has created increasingly opaque "black-box" systems. Transparency aims to counter this opacity by enabling direct visibility into AI system processes and decisions, making the underlying mechanisms more understandable (Cysneiros, Raffi, and Leite 2018). Explainability, in contrast, focuses on making these complex systems interpretable for stakeholders even if complete transparency is not feasible (Chazette, Brunotte, and Speith 2021). These principles become particularly crucial in high-stakes contexts where decisions significantly impact users.

Together, these technical principles form the foundational technical layer of AI development, focusing on the inherent capabilities and characteristics that must be engineered into trustworthy AI systems (Díaz-Rodríguez et al. 2023). However, technical considerations alone are insufficient to ensure AI is developed and deployed responsibly. A complementary set of governance principles is necessary to guide the organizational structures, processes, and oversight mechanisms that shape how AI systems are developed and deployed in practice. These governance principles address broader questions of human oversight, regulatory compliance, and societal impact that extend beyond technical implementation concerns (Mikalef et al. 2022). They often emphasize the human and organizational dimensions necessary to ensure AI systems not only function reliably and ethically at a technical level but also operate within appropriate institutional frameworks that promote responsible development and use (The White House 2023; UNESCO 2021; OECD 2021; European Commission 2019). These governance principles can be further delineated into key areas that shape responsible AI development and deployment.

Accountability is a foundational governance principle, ensuring concrete responsibility and liability for AI systems' actions and outputs. This requires establishing processes to document AI development and deployment decisions, creating audit trails, and defining clear channels for redress when systems cause unintended harm (Lepri et al. 2018). Organizations must not only explain how their AI models work but also demonstrate that adequate oversight exists through governance frameworks, human checks, and specific roles assigned for monitoring AI systems (Mikalef et al. 2022). When an AI makes decisions, accountability frameworks help trace precisely who is responsible—from developers to deployers to users—and provide mechanisms to contest or correct problematic outcomes. This end-to-end accountability is essential for building societal trust in AI systems and ensuring they operate within established ethical and legal boundaries.

Data governance, which is related to algorithmic fairness and security, emphasizes the importance of maintaining data quality and integrity throughout the AI lifecycle, including considerations around privacy protection and bias mitigation in training data. *Human oversight* focuses on maintaining appropriate human control and intervention capabilities, establishing the right balance between AI autonomy and human agency in decision-making processes. *Laws and regulations* provide the formal frameworks that dictate AI system functioning, ensuring compliance with legal requirements while balancing innovation needs. Finally, *societal and environmental* well-being principles ensure that AI systems promote sustainability and social responsibility while avoiding potential harm to communities and ecosystems. Together, these governance principles complement the technical principles, creating a more inclusive framework for responsible AI that extends beyond technical considerations and addresses the broader societal implications and requirements for ethical AI development.

Complementing the theoretical frameworks from academia, leading technology companies have also established applied frameworks that reflect practical experiences implementing responsible AI. Microsoft's Responsible AI Maturity Model (RAI MM) represents one of the most detailed approaches, offering a systematic framework for assessing and developing RAI capabilities across 24 dimensions that span organizational foundations, team approaches, and practical implementation (Vorvoreanu et al. 2023). The model addresses critical aspects of responsible AI development—from governance structures and knowledge resources to cross-discipline collaboration and risk management practices—while providing organizations with clear pathways to mature their RAI practices from initial awareness to systematic integration. Importantly, this framework calls attention to both the technical and socio-organizational aspects of responsible AI implementation, recognizing that successful RAI requires not just robust technical solutions but also appropriate organizational structures, team dynamics, and implementation practices.

IBM and Google have also developed approaches to operationalizing RAI. IBM's approach echoes the technical principles discussed earlier through its Pillars of Trust—explainability, fairness, robustness, transparency, and privacy—while its overarching Principles for Trust and Transparency address broader governance concerns around human augmentation, data ownership, and transparency (IBM n.d.). Conversely, Google structures its approach through its AI Responsibility Lifecycle, which organizes development across research, design, govern, and share phases, with each phase supported by its Secure AI Framework (SAIF) that addresses key implementation challenges through six core elements: expanding security foundations, extending threat detection, automating defenses, harmonizing controls, adapting mitigations, and contextualizing risks (Google 2024). By structuring its approach around the AI Responsibility Lifecycle and SAIF framework, Google exemplifies a broader transformation toward research-driven and design-oriented approaches to AI development. Expressly, its integration of social scientists and user-experience researchers alongside technical experts signifies a growing recognition that ethical AI development requires applied interdisciplinary approaches to bridge technical, social, and design disciplines.

Human-Centered AI

In response to this transformation, Human-Centered AI (HCAI) has emerged as a framework for guiding AI development. While discussions of human-centered approaches to AI have existed for decades (Garcia 1999), recent years have seen a sharp increase in scholarly and industry interest. In fact, it has become such a popular field that Yvonne Rogers has dubbed it "the new zeitgeist" (2022), reflecting its emergence as the defining spirit of contemporary AI development. This zeitgeist has manifested through scholarly work and the proliferation of research centers and corporate initiatives dedicated to human-centered approaches. Leading institutions, including Stanford, UC Berkeley, and MIT, have established dedicated HCAI centers and initiatives to contribute to this movement. Simultaneously, organizations like Microsoft, IBM, and McKinsey are working to define industry models, mirroring the approaches to RAI. Nevertheless, despite its emergence as a defining paradigm, HCAI, like RAI, lacks a unified definition.

Among the many conceptualizations of HCAI, Ben Shneiderman's characterization has become particularly influential, emphasizing AI systems that support human self-efficacy, creativity, and social participation. Notably, Shneiderman proposes a two-dimensional framework that balances automation and human control rather than treating them as trade-offs (Shneiderman 2022), aiming to create systems that are reliable, safe, and trustworthy (Shneiderman 2020a, 2020b). This model transcends the traditional one-dimensional view that increased automation must diminish human control (cf. Licklider 1960).

To complement this non-binary approach to automation, Shneiderman developed a comprehensive three-level governance structure that operationalizes these principles across team, organizational, and industry levels, mirroring aspects of RAI frameworks. At the team level, it emphasizes software engineering practices that enable reliable systems through audit trails, verification testing, and explainable interfaces. The organizational level promotes safety culture through management strategies, including leadership commitment, failure reporting, and internal review processes, while the industry level advocates for trustworthy certification through independent oversight mechanisms, including government regulation, external audits, and professional standards (Shneiderman, 2020c). This multi-layered approach bridges the gap between ethical principles and practical implementation while maintaining human-centered values at its core.

Beyond Shneiderman, though, we see many other conceptualizations of HCAI (Schmager, Pappas, and Vassilakopoulou 2023). Rogers (2022) argues for HCAI as an approach focused on amplifying human abilities rather than displacing them with automated systems. While this core perspective is key to many characterizations, other scholars and institutions go beyond this foundational view to engage with specific implementation challenges. For instance, Riedl (2019) emphasizes the importance of recognizing AI systems as components within broader human networks, including users, operators, and affected communities. Building on this, Dignum and Dignum (2020) stress that AI development must actively consider contextual factors and the broader implications of its actions on individuals and communities. Similarly, AI-HLEG (2019) emphasizes the need to develop AI that actively promotes societal welfare and individual autonomy while serving collective interests. Stanford's HAI program succinctly summaries these various perspectives, describing HCAI as an approach that enhances human capabilities while addressing broader societal challenges (HAI 2021).

Complementing these principles, scholars have put forward structural frameworks like Shneiderman's, aiming to bridge the gap between HCAI theory and practice. Auernhammer (2020) advocates for a tripartite approach that balances rationalistic (technology), humanistic (people), and judicial (policy) considerations. Recognizing HCAI's fundamentally social nature, Auernhammer emphasizes the need for interdisciplinary collaboration, echoing similar calls in Google's RAI framework. Holzinger (2022) also employs a three-part structure, focusing on alignment with human values, ethical principles, and legal requirements. Building on these approaches, Wu (2019) introduces a framework that incorporates ethically aligned design and technology enhancement while emphasizing human factors design.

This emphasis on human factors points to another dimension of HCAI that attempts to move beyond theoretical frameworks: the incorporation of design processes in pursuit of desired outcomes. Indeed, HCAI's success relies not just on what it aims to achieve but also on how it achieves it through established participatory traditions in design for technology development. This process orientation builds upon decades of participatory approaches, including human-centered design, user-experience design, user-centered design, human-computer interaction, and human-factors engineering. These methodologies, many of which are rooted in Scandinavian participatory design traditions, emphasize democratic participation, tacit knowledge elicitation, and learning from participant experiences. They often engage stakeholders through hands-on methods like prototyping, visualization, games, and role-play exercises.

While such participatory methodologies have proven effective in traditional technology development, where system behaviors are more predictable and outcomes more readily demonstrable through prototypes, making them apparent candidates for adaptation to AI product development, their effectiveness in AI contexts remains contested. The scholarly community is particularly divided on this question. While researchers like Bondi et al. (2021) and Baumer (2017) demonstrate the value of participation in AI development, others indicate mixed results requiring further investigation (Delgado et al. 2023; Birhane et al. 2022; Bratteteig and Verne 2018). Sloane et al. (2020) raise particularly pointed concerns, highlighting unique challenges in AI contexts, including limited public understanding of AI's abstract nature, difficulties in prototyping statistical intelligence, and the inherent unpredictability of AI outcomes. Moreover, existing participatory methods often maintain power differentials where designers retain primary agency while stakeholders serve as consultants rather than true co-creators.

While Sloane's critique highlights fundamental challenges in applying traditional participatory methods to AI development, these limitations point to a more profound need to reconceptualize how humans and AI systems interact. The abstract nature of AI, its inherent unpredictability, and the difficulty in prototyping statistical intelligence suggest that conventional participatory approaches are insufficient for addressing the unique characteristics of modern AI systems. This insufficiency stems not just from Sloane's specific concerns but from fundamental assumptions about human-AI relationships. Therefore, rather than viewing participation as discrete and punctuated design engagements, I propose conceptualizing this relationship as processes of perpetual co-becoming (Haraway 2007)—enabling continuous co-creation where users maintain transparency and autonomy in actively shaping AI systems' emergent nature while the systems themselves evolve and adapt in response to these interactions. This framework implements key principles from both frameworks: transparency and human oversight from RAI through ongoing user engagement with system behavior and individual autonomy and participatory engagement from HCAI through continuous user involvement in shaping system outcomes. However, co-becoming goes further by acknowledging the perpetual, dynamic nature of human-AI interaction that neither framework fully captures.

Towards a Theory of Perpetual Co-Becoming in Human-AI Systems

Co-becoming offers an anthropological perspective on the ongoing state of mutual transformation between humans and AI systems, where there is no fixed end goal or final form to be achieved. Rather than progressing toward a technologically predetermined end state, co-becoming represents a continuous process of emergence where human and machine capabilities, behaviors, and relationships are perpetually redefined through interactions. This state of constant flux and mutual adaptation is not a means to an end but rather the fundamental nature of human-AI relationships in modern systems.

The theoretical foundations for understanding these dynamics draw from rich traditions in anthropology, science and technology studies, and complex systems theory, liberally synthesizing insights from approaches that their original authors may view as incompatible but that nevertheless offer complementary perspectives on relational emergence. Holland's (1992) theory of complex adaptive systems provides a foundation for understanding how elements within dynamic networks create emergent properties through their interactions. This insight is complemented by Ingold's (2000) concept of "meshwork," which emphasizes how beings and things are continually constituted through their entangled relationships rather than existing as discrete bound objects in time. Latour's (1992) actor-network theory further illuminates how agency is distributed across networks of human and non-human actors, while Suchman's (2007) action theory reminds us of the contextual and emergent aspects of human-machine interaction.

The impetus for advancing co-becoming as a theoretical framework stems from the unique characteristics of contemporary AI systems that challenge existing models of human-technology interaction and the need to extend RAI and HCAI principles to address the perpetually transformative nature of human-AI relationships. Further, the urgency of this theoretical advancement becomes apparent when examining three key characteristics of these systems: machine agency and ability to independently learn and evolve, the phenomenon of emergent behaviors whose origin and complexity often defy explanation, and the capacity to reshape human behavior and social practices at scale in near real-time. Building on these characteristics, we can observe how co-becoming manifests across multiple scales, with micro-level interactions between users and systems aggregating into macro-level cultural reconfigurations, creating an endless cycle of mutual transformation similar to what DeLanda (2011) terms "mechanisms of emergence."

To understand how these multi-scale transformations occur in practice, we must examine the mechanisms through which co-becoming operates. These mechanisms align with anthropological understandings of material engagement (Malafouris 2013) and digital materiality (Pink et al. 2016) while drawing inspiration from Hayles' (2017) concept of "cognitive assemblages" to illuminate how material dimensions shape human-machine interaction and emergence. In the context of human-AI relationships, co-becoming manifests in three key ways. First, modern AI systems continuously adapt based on human interactions and data inputs—a recommender system, for instance, exists in constant flux, transforming its understanding of user preferences with each interaction. Second, humans similarly exist in a state of continuous adaptation, modifying their behaviors, expectations, and mental models through their experiences with AI systems, learning to modify search queries, adjust interaction patterns, and develop new approaches based on their understanding of system responses. Third, these mutual adaptations occur within existing power structures that can be either reinforced or challenged through the co-becoming process.

For example, as Spotify's recommendation algorithms adapt to a user's listening patterns, suggesting new artists and genres, users simultaneously develop new music discovery behaviors—actively engaging with or skipping suggested tracks, saving songs, creating themed playlists, and following recommended artists. This creates a perpetual process of mutual transformation where neither the system nor the users progress toward any fixed end state but rather exist in an ongoing process of co-becoming and reciprocal influence. These individual interactions aggregate into collective transformations as patterns of behavior emerge across the user base, extending beyond individual listening sessions to influence broader patterns of music creation, consumption, artist discovery, and the economic dynamics of the music industry, including questions of equity and access (Seaver 2022).

Co-becoming manifests in human-AI relationships through four key characteristics:

- **Mutual Adaptation:** Both humans and AI systems continuously adapt to each other, creating ongoing cycles of reciprocal learning and adjustment
- **Behavioral Interdependence:** Human and AI behaviors evolve in tandem, with each party's actions and capabilities fundamentally shaped by their interactions with the other
- **Emergent Dynamics:** The interaction between humans and AI systems produces unexpected patterns, capabilities, and outcomes that neither party could achieve independently
- **Collective Transformation:** These individual human-AI relationships aggregate into broader changes in social practices, cultural norms, and economic structures

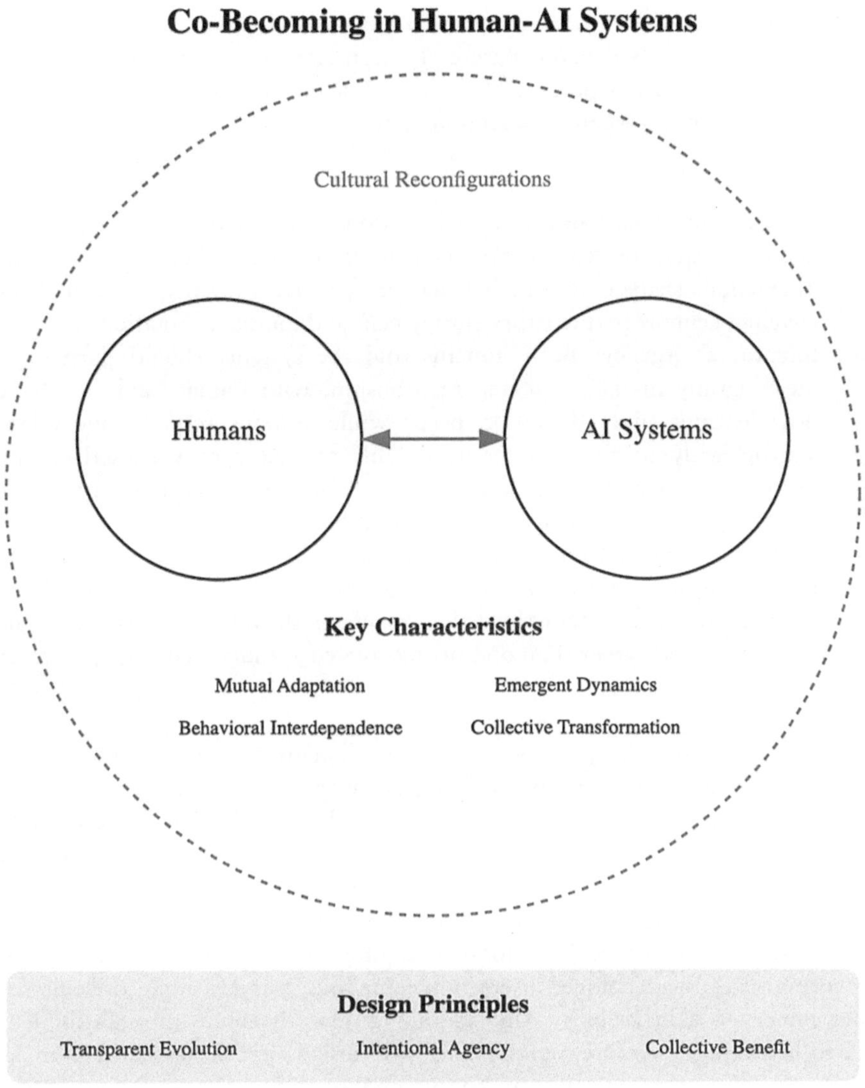

FIGURE 2.1 Co-Becoming in Human-AI Systems

These characteristics highlight how co-becoming theory offers a fundamental shift in how we understand human-AI relationships. While traditional development approaches treat AI systems as tools to be technologically perfected through ever-more complex engineering—pursuing an imagined ideal end state—co-becoming, grounded in anthropological perspectives, recognizes that humans and AI systems exist in a state of perpetual mutual reconstitution, continuously shaping each other's capabilities and behaviors (Suchman 1998).

Thus, it offers us a lens for thinking about how we design systems that embrace rather than resist this dynamic nature. To translate this theoretical perspective into practical impact, I propose three key principles for designing AI systems that enable more transparent, intentional, and collectively beneficial human-AI relationships:

- **Transparent Evolution:** Human-AI relationships should be mutually visible and understandable, enabling both parties to comprehend how their ongoing interactions shape each other's behavior. This transparency is essential for enabling genuine participatory engagement and mutual adaptation.
- **Intentional Agency:** Both humans and AI systems should participate meaningfully in their evolving relationship, with humans able to shape how learning and adaptation occur while systems respond and adapt appropriately to these preferences. This mutual agency should extend beyond punctuated design engagements common in participatory design approaches to enable truly continuous co-becoming.
- **Collective Benefit:** Understanding that individual human-AI co-becoming relationships aggregate into broader societal outcomes, systems should be designed to foster interactions that benefit both individual users and the collective good rather than optimizing solely for individual engagement or system performance.

Building on these principles, we can design systems that make these mutual transformative processes visible and enable meaningful participation by users in the ongoing evolution of human-AI relationships. This perspective is particularly valuable in contexts where algorithmic systems can either reinforce or help rectify existing power imbalances. For instance, recommendation systems exemplify both the challenges and opportunities co-becoming illuminates. These systems create feedback loops that often amplify existing inequalities, favoring already-advantaged users while making it increasingly difficult for newcomers to gain visibility. Understanding these dynamics through the lens of co-becoming, therefore, points us toward design approaches that can make these feedback mechanisms transparent and provide users with meaningful ways to influence their algorithmic outcomes, demonstrated in the following case study of ArtTech.

Co-Becoming in Digital Art Markets

Multisided platforms, such as digital art markets, exemplify the core dynamics that co-becoming theory illuminates: the dynamic interplay between human behavior, algorithmic systems, structural inequities, and societal hierarchies. In digital marketplaces, recommender systems demonstrate precisely the kind of mutually transformative relationships described in co-becoming theory, but often in ways that reproduce and amplify existing power structures. This dynamic is particularly problematic in the art market, where traditional forms of capital—economic, social, and cultural—create systemic barriers for emerging artists and galleries while entrenching the position of established actors.

These insights emerged from art market research I conducted for ArtTech using a mixed-methods approach that integrated multiple ethnographic techniques (Artz 2024a, Artz 2022). The methodology incorporated in-depth interviews with 30 artists, gallerists, and collectors, combined with computational analysis of interview data, online art communities, and digital marketplaces. Additionally, I conducted a comprehensive literature review of recommender systems, initially engaging with journal articles and intellectual property filings through close reading, then applying computational analysis to identify patterns and limitations across this literature.

Through this research, I discovered how algorithmic bias, particularly popularity bias, interacts with and amplifies traditional forms of capital in digital art markets. This interaction creates profound inequities, as the algorithmic systems tend to favor already-advantaged participants. Artists and galleries with significant economic capital can invest in paid promotion to increase their visibility, while those with substantial social and cultural capital benefit from existing networks and institutional recognition. The result is a self-reinforcing cycle that makes it increasingly difficult for new entrants to gain visibility or establish themselves.

In response to these findings and drawing on the principles of RAI, HCAI, and co-becoming, I designed a novel solution: a gamified participatory recommender system for the ArtTech platform that introduces the concept of "behavioral capital" as a counterweight to traditional forms of capital (Artz 2024b). The system operationalizes behavioral capital through three core components: an Engagement Score tracking participation patterns, a Cooperation Score measuring collaborative behaviors, and an Action Score incorporating user feedback (Artz and Speicher 2023). These scores are normalized and weighted to create a composite Participation Score that directly influences content visibility and recommendation rankings, creating a dynamic feedback loop where both the system and its users continuously adapt through their interactions (cf. Wiener 1948). The system's architecture integrates these behavioral metrics, modifying the outputs of traditional recommendation approaches to account for not just what content is similar or popular but also how creators engage with and contribute to the community.

This approach demonstrates the four key characteristics of co-becoming: mutual adaptation through continuous refinement of both user and system behaviors based on participation patterns, behavioral interdependence via reciprocal incentive structures and responses, emergent dynamics through the collective interaction of user participation and system recommendations, and collective transformation that reshapes both individual opportunities and community-wide dynamics of visibility and influence in the marketplace. Rather than leaving these concepts abstract, the system manifests them through a gamified interface featuring real-time progress bars, achievement badges, and community leaderboards that visualize behavioral capital attributes. By making visible the ongoing processes of mutual transformation between users and the recommender system, the interface enables users to directly observe and shape their algorithmic influence. Such dynamic interaction creates interplay akin to what Tseng (2022) terms "algorithmic empowerment," allowing users to actively participate in their evolving relationship with the recommender system through meaningful engagement rather than traditional capital advantages.

Within this gamified environment, users cultivate behavioral capital through productive participation, which translates into algorithmic influence through the system's weighting of interactions based on participation scores. This creates a concrete manifestation of co-becoming's principle of perpetual mutual transformation, establishing a dynamic feedback loop between user participation and algorithmic responses. The approach shapes the digital ecosystem in several ways: it provides alternative pathways to visibility for artists and galleries lacking traditional capital, increases content diversity and quality through incentivized collaboration, and enables the recommender system to learn from a more diverse and engaged user base, creating a virtuous cycle where improved recommendations enhance user experiences and encourage deeper participation.

By making the co-becoming relationship explicit, interactive, and actionable through its gamified interface, the model fosters a more transparent and equitable platform. While this approach necessarily involves a degree of reification that theorists like Ingold might critique—translating fluid relational processes into discrete metrics and structured interactions—such operationalization represents a pragmatic compromise between theoretical ideals and implementable systems. The implementation demonstrates several key successes in operationalizing anthropological insights into AI development. First, making algorithmic influence visible and participatory through mechanisms such as a gamified participatory recommender system directly addresses power imbalances in AI systems. While traditional recommender systems often amplify existing advantages, creating mechanisms for transparency and explanation within the user interface helps participants understand and meaningfully engage in their evolving algorithmic relationships. Further, the behavioral capital approach demonstrates how quantifying and rewarding meaningful community participation can create more equitable pathways to visibility and influence.

Importantly, rather than treating ethics as an external constraint to be checked off during development, the co-becoming framework reveals how ethical considerations emerge and evolve through the continuous interaction between humans and AI systems. This perspective helps us design systems that actively promote ethical outcomes through ongoing processes of mutual adaptation—where transparency enables understanding of how human and system behaviors shape each other, agency allows for meaningful participation in this mutual development, and collective benefit emerges from the aggregation of these individual interactions. Instead of trying to "solve" ethics through fixed technical solutions, co-becoming encourages us to create adaptive systems that can respond to and adapt to our changing ethical understanding and requirements. However, the very specificity that enables this approach's success also reveals its constraints.

While the ArtTech implementation demonstrates the practical value of co-becoming, RAI, and HCAI principles, its specific mechanisms—such as gamification and behavioral capital—may not directly translate to other AI applications for several reasons. First, the relatively low-stakes nature of art recommendation differs significantly from high-stakes domains like healthcare or criminal justice, where errors carry serious consequences. Second, the voluntary and creative context makes gamification appropriate in ways that might not apply to professional or institutional settings, where such approaches could be seen as trivial or manipulative. Finally, the community-oriented structure of digital art markets rewards participation in ways that may not suit individual-focused AI tools like personal assistants or decision support systems. This raises a crucial question: how can practitioners systematically evaluate and improve human-AI relationships across the full spectrum of AI applications, from LLMs and recommendation systems to decision support tools and autonomous multi-agent systems?

Evaluating Co-Becoming: A Practical Framework for Assessment

To address this need, I propose the Co-Becoming Assessment Framework, which provides a structured approach for evaluating how effectively any AI system supports perpetual co-becoming between humans and machines. The framework examines twenty indicators across four fundamental dimensions of human-AI relationships: mutual adaptation, behavioral interdependence, emergent dynamics, and collective transformation. By providing specific yet broad evaluation criteria, the framework helps practitioners identify opportunities to strengthen ongoing processes of mutual transformation regardless of the specific technical implementation or application domain.

The *mutual adaptation* dimension examines how humans and AI systems continuously modify their responses to each other. This includes evaluating the frequency and effectiveness of reciprocal learning, the speed of mutual adjustments, the sustainability of adaptive cycles, and the degree to which adaptations benefit both parties. High mutual adaptation indicates a dynamic relationship where both humans and AI systems demonstrate ongoing responsiveness to each other's changing state.

The *behavioral interdependence* dimension analyzes how deeply human and AI behaviors are intertwined. Rather than treating human and AI actions as separate phenomena, it examines how their capabilities and behaviors evolve in tandem. This includes assessing the impact of behavioral changes across parties, the development of joint capabilities, the coordination of behavioral evolution, and the integration of decision-making processes. Strong behavioral interdependence reflects a relationship where each party's actions fundamentally shape the other's development.

The *emergent dynamics* dimension evaluates unexpected patterns and capabilities that arise through human-AI interaction. This includes examining novel behaviors that neither party could achieve independently, capabilities that exceed original design parameters, the stability of emergent patterns, and the frequency of new emergent properties. Strong emergent dynamics indicate a relationship generating innovative outcomes through the unique combination of human and AI capabilities.

The *collective transformation* dimension assesses how individual human-AI relationships aggregate into broader societal changes. This includes measuring shifts in social practices, the percentage of users showing transformed behaviors, impacts on cultural norms, adaptations in economic structures, and the sustainability of collective changes. Strong collective transformation demonstrates how human-AI relationships can catalyze systemic social change.

The assessment framework provides a detailed scorecard with twenty specific indicators across these dimensions, allowing practitioners to systematically document and analyze the quality of human-AI relationships. Each dimension contains five key questions with clear scoring criteria from 1–5 points. This scoring approach helps practitioners identify specific areas for improvement while maintaining focus on the fundamentally dynamic and interdependent nature of human-AI relationships. The resulting 100-point scale provides a concrete way to measure progress in fostering effective co-becoming, while the scoring criteria guide observers in identifying patterns of mutual transformation across different contexts and applications. As shown in Figure 2.2, the framework's results can be visualized through a radar chart, providing an intuitive representation of how systems perform across all four dimensions.

This approach to assessment builds on anthropology's long tradition of systematic observation while providing structure for examining the unique dynamics of human-AI relationships. By making explicit the four dimensions of co-becoming—mutual adaptation, behavioral interdependence, emergent dynamics, and collective transformation—it offers anthropologists both an analytical framework for studying how humans and AI systems shape each other and a practical tool for guiding their development. As artificial intelligence becomes increasingly embedded in social life, such frameworks for systematic evaluation become vital tools for understanding and shaping the ongoing processes of technological change through an anthropological lens.

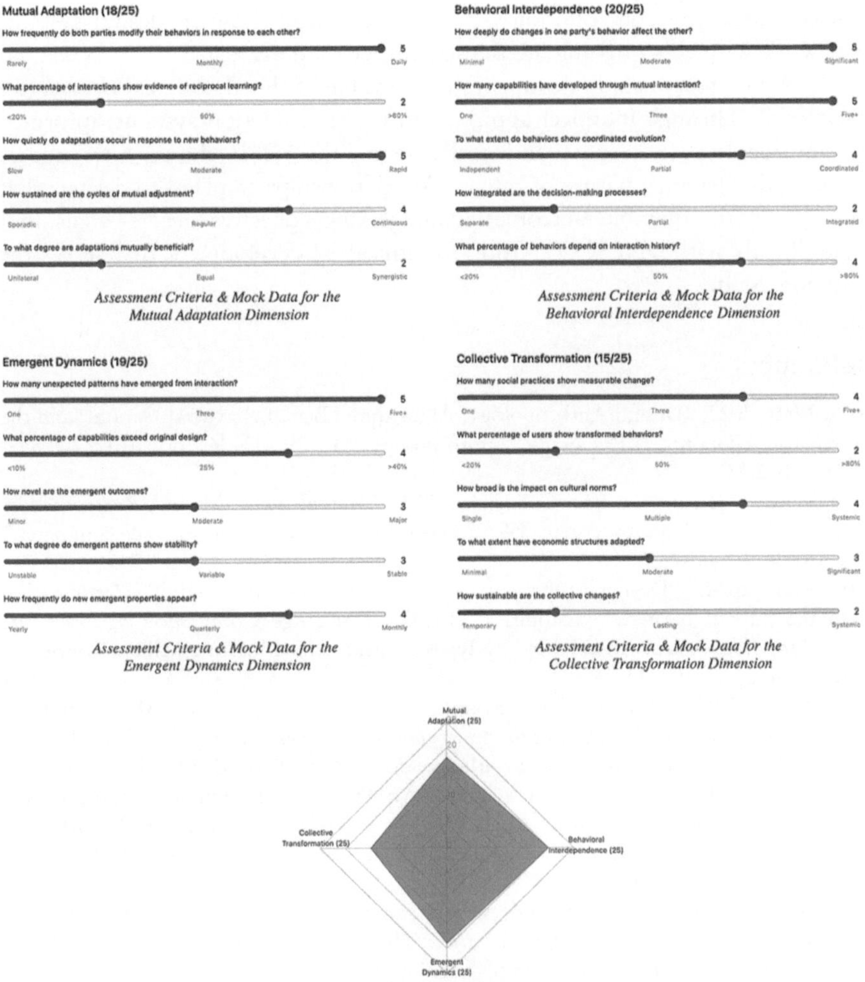

Assessment Criteria & Mock Data for the Mutual Adaptation Dimension

Assessment Criteria & Mock Data for the Behavioral Interdependence Dimension

Assessment Criteria & Mock Data for the Emergent Dynamics Dimension

Assessment Criteria & Mock Data for the Collective Transformation Dimension

Radar Chart Depicting Mock Data for the Co-Becoming Assessment Framework Dimensions

FIGURE 2.2 Co-Becoming Assessment Framework

Conclusion

As artificial intelligence continues to transform human society, the prescient concerns raised by UNESCO's 2021 *Recommendation on the Ethics of AI* have become increasingly urgent. While existing frameworks for ethical AI development—particularly RAI and HCAI—have established important foundations, they have often struggled to fully address the dynamic and continually emergent nature of human-AI relationships. Co-becoming offers a complementary lens for understanding these relationships as processes of perpetual mutual transformation, offering new perspectives on how to design systems that work with this ongoing adaptation rather than against it.

The ArtTech case study demonstrates the value of this theoretical perspective in practice. Through its novel approach to recommendation systems, informed by anthropological insights and co-becoming theory, it shows how understanding the dynamic nature of human-AI relationships can lead to designs that promote more equitable outcomes while serving collective needs—goals that align directly with UNESCO's vision for ethical AI development that serves the common good.

References

Artz, Matt. 2022. "Design Anthropology, Algorithmic Bias, Behavioral Capital, and the Creator Economy." *Practicing Anthropology* 44 (2): 33–36. doi:10.17730/0888-4552.44.2.33.

Artz, Matthew R., and Geoffrey C. Speicher. 2023. "*Gamified Participatory Recommender System.*" United States Patent US20230046646A1. https://patents.google.com/patent/US20230046646A1/.

Artz, Matt. 2024a. "Design Anthropology By Co-Becoming: Reimagining Participation in the Pursuit of New Possibilities." In *The Routledge Companion to Practicing Anthropology and Design*, edited by Jenessa Spears and Christine Miller. Routledge. doi:10.4324/9781003340188-31.

Artz, Matt. 2024b. "Reimagining Recommender Systems: Towards a More Equitable Model for Creators." In *EmTech Anthropology: Careers at the Frontier*, edited by Matt Artz and Lora Koycheva. Routledge. doi:10.4324/9781003458555-3.

Auernhammer, Jan. 2020. "Human-Centered AI: The Role of Human-Centered Design Research in the Development of AI." In *Synergy—DRS International Conference 2020*, edited by S. Boess, M. Cheung, and R. Cain, August 11–14. Held online. doi:10.21606/drs.2020.282.

Barocas, Solon, Moritz Hardt, and Arvind Narayanan. 2023. *Fairness and Machine Learning: Limitations and Opportunities*. The MIT Press. https://mitpress.mit.edu/9780262048613/fairness-and-machine-learning/.

Barredo Arrieta, Alejandro, Natalia Díaz-Rodríguez, Javier Del Ser, Adrien Bennetot, Siham Tabik, Alberto Barbado, Salvador Garcia, Sergio Gil-Lopez, Daniel Molina, Richard Benjamins, Raja Chatila, and Francisco Herrera. 2020. "Explainable Artificial Intelligence (XAI): Concepts, Taxonomies, Opportunities and Challenges Toward Responsible AI." *Information Fusion* 58: 82–115. doi:10.1016/j.inffus.2019.12.012.

Baumer, Eric PS. 2017. "Toward Human-Centered Algorithm Design." *Big Data & Society* 4 (2). doi:10.1177/2053951717718854.

Benjamins, Richard, Alberto Barbado, and Daniel Sierra. 2019. "Responsible AI by Design in Practice." *arXiv* Preprint arXiv:1909.12838. https://arxiv.org/abs/1909.12838.

Birhane, Abeba, William Isaac, Vinodkumar Prabhakaran, Mark Diaz, Madeleine Clare Elish, Iason Gabriel, and Shakir Mohamed. 2022. "Power to the People? Opportunities and Challenges for Participatory AI." In *Proceedings of the 2nd ACM Conference on Equity and Access in Algorithms, Mechanisms, and Optimization (EAAMO' 22)*. Association for Computing Machinery. doi:10.1145/3551624.3555290.

Bondi, Elizabeth, Lily Xu, Diana Acosta-Navas, and Jackson A. Killian. 2021. "Envisioning Communities: A Participatory Approach Towards AI for Social Good." In *Proceedings of the Association for Computing Machinery*, 425–436. ACM.

Bratteteig, Tone, and Guri Verne. 2018. "Does AI Make PD Obsolete? Exploring Challenges from Artificial Intelligence to Participatory Design." In *Proceedings of the 15th Participatory Design Conference: Short Papers, Situated Actions, Workshops and* Tutorial - Volume 2 *(PDC' 18)*, Article 8, 5 pages. Association for Computing Machinery.

Brynjolfsson, Erik, Daniel Rock, and Chad Syverson. 2021. "The Productivity J-Curve: How Intangibles Complement General Purpose Technologies" *American Economic Journal: Macroeconomics* 13 (1): 333–372. doi:10.1257/mac.20180386.

Chazette, Larissa, Wasja Brunotte, and Timo Speith. 2021. "Exploring Explainability: A Definition, a Model, and a Knowledge Catalogue." In *2021 IEEE 29th International Requirements Engineering Conference (RE)*, 197–208. IEEE. doi:10.1109/RE51729.2021.00025.

Chen, Richard J., Judy J. Wang, Drew F. K. Williamson, Tiffany Y. Chen, Jana Lipkova, Ming Y. Lu, Sharifa Sahai, and Faisal Mahmood. 2023. "Algorithmic Fairness in Artificial Intelligence for Medicine and Healthcare." *Nature Biomedical Engineering* 7: 719–742. doi:10.1038/s41551-023-01056-8.

Cysneiros, Luiz Marcio, Majid Raffi, and Julio Cesar Sampaio do Prado Leite. 2018. "Software Transparency as a Key Requirement for Self-Driving Cars." In *2018 IEEE 26th International Requirements Engineering Conference (RE)*, 382–387. IEEE. doi:10.1109/RE.2018.00-21.

DeLanda, Manuel. 2011. *Philosophy and Simulation: The Emergence of Synthetic Reason*. Bloomsbury Academic.

Díaz-Rodríguez, Natalia, Javier Del Ser, Mark Coeckelbergh, Marcos López de Prado, Enrique Herrera-Viedma, and Francisco Herrera. 2023. "Connecting the Dots in Trustworthy Artificial Intelligence: From AI Principles, Ethics, and Key Requirements to Responsible AI Systems and Regulation." *Information Fusion* 99: 101896. doi:10.1016/j.inffus.2023.101896.

Dignum, Virginia. 2019. *Responsible Artificial Intelligence: How to Develop and Use AI in a Responsible Way*. Springer. doi:10.1007/978-3-030-30371-6.

Dignum, Frank, and Virginia Dignum. 2020. "How to Center AI on Humans." In *NeHuAI 2020, 1st International Workshop on New Foundations for Human-Centered AI*, Santiago de Compostela, Spain, September 4, 2020, 59–62.

European Commission. 2019. *Ethics Guidelines for Trustworthy AI*. https://digital-strategy.ec.europa.eu/en/library/ethics-guidelines-trustworthy-ai.

Ge, Yingqiang, Shuai Zhang, Ruiming Tang, and Xiuqiang He. 2021. "Towards Long-term Fairness in Recommendation." In *Proceedings of the 14th ACM International Conference on Web Search and Data Mining*. 445–453. doi:10.1145/3437963.3441824.

Google. 2024. *End-to-End Responsibility: A Lifecycle Approach to AI*. https://ai.google/static/documents/ai-responsibility-2024-update.pdf.

Gunning, David, and David W. Aha. 2019. "DARPA's Explainable Artificial Intelligence (XAI) Program." *AI Magazine* 40 (2): 44–58. doi:10.1609/aimag.v40i2.2850.

Gunning, David, Mark Stefik, Jaesik Choi, Timothy Miller, Simone Stumpf, and Guang-Zhong Yang. 2019. "XAI—Explainable Artificial Intelligence." *Science Robotics* 4 (37). doi:10.1126/scirobotics.aay7120.

HAI Research. 2021. *Guiding Human-Centered AI*. Stanford Institute for Human-Centered Artificial Intelligence. https://hai.stanford.edu/research.

Haraway, Donna J. 2007. *When Species Meet*. Minneapolis: University of Minnesota Press.

Hayles, N. Katherine. 2017. "Cognitive Assemblages: Technical Agency and Human Interactions." In *Unthought: The Power of the Cognitive Nonconscious*, 115–141. University of Chicago Press.

High-Level Expert Group on Artificial Intelligence (AI-HLEG). 2019. *Ethics Guidelines for Trustworthy AI*. Brussels: European Commission. https://ec.europa.eu/futurium/en/ai-alliance-consultation/.

Holzinger, Andreas, Anna Saranti, Alessa Angerschmid, Carl Orge Retzlaff, Andreas Gronauer, Vladimir Pejakovic, Francisco Medel-Jimenez, Theresa Krexner, Christoph Gollob, and Karl Stampfer. 2022. "Digital Transformation in Smart Farm and Forest Operations Needs Human-Centered AI: Challenges and Future Directions." *Sensors* 22 (8): 3043. doi:10.3390/s22083043.

Holland, John H. 1992. "Complex Adaptive Systems." *Daedalus* 121 (1): 17–30.

Hu, Krystal. 2023. "ChatGPT Sets Record for Fastest-Growing User Base—Analyst Note." *Reuters*. February 1, 2023. https://www.reuters.com/technology/chatgpt-sets-record-fastest-growing-user-base-analyst-note-2023-02-01/.

IBM. n.d. "*AI Ethics*." https://www.ibm.com/impact/ai-ethics.

Khalid, Nazish, Adnan Qayyum, Muhammad Bilal, Ala Al-Fuqaha, and Junaid Qadir. 2023. "Privacy-Preserving Artificial Intelligence in Healthcare: Techniques and Applications." *Computers in Biology and Medicine* 158: 106848. doi:10.1016/j.compbiomed.2023.106848.

Lepri, Bruno, Nuria Oliver, Emmanuel Letouzé, Alex Pentland, and Patrick Vinck. 2018. "Fair, Transparent, and Accountable Algorithmic Decision-Making Processes: The Premise, the Proposed Solutions, and the Open Challenges." *Philosophy & Technology* 31 (4): 611–627. doi:10.1007/s13347-017-0279-x.

Licklider, Joseph C. R. 1960. "Man-Computer Symbiosis." *IRE Transactions on Human Factors in Electronics* HFE-1 (March): 4–11.

Malafouris, Lambros. 2013. *How Things Shape the Mind: A Theory of Material Engagement*. Cambridge, MA: MIT Press. doi:10.7551/mitpress/9476.001.0001.

Mikalef, Patrick, Kieran Conboy, Jenny Eriksson Lundström, and Aleš Popovič. 2022. "Thinking Responsibly About Responsible AI and 'the Dark Side' of AI." *European Journal of Information Systems* 31 (3): 257–268. doi:10.1080/0960085X.2022.2026621.

Mueller, Shane T., Robert R. Hoffman, William Clancey, Abigail Emrey, and Gary Klein. 2019. "Explanation in Human-AI Systems: A Literature Meta-Review, Synopsis of Key Ideas and Publications, and Bibliography for Explainable AI." *arXiv* 1902.01876.

OECD. 2021. "*Artificial Intelligence*." https://www.oecd.org/going-digital/ai/principles/.

Raley, Rita and Jennifer Rhee. 2023. "Critical AI: A Field in Formation." *American Literature*, 95 (2): 185–204.

Riedl, Mark O. 2019. "Human-Centered Artificial Intelligence and Machine Learning." *Human Behavior and Emerging Technologies* 1 (1): 33–36. doi:10.1002/hbe2.117.

Rogers, Yvonne. 2022. "Commentary: Human-Centred AI: The New Zeitgeist." *Human-Computer Interaction* 37 (3): 254–255. doi:10.1080/07370024.2022.2045431.

Schmager, Stefan, Ilias Pappas, and Polyxeni Vassilakopoulou. 2023. "Defining Human-Centered AI: A Comprehensive Review of HCAI Literature." *MCIS 2023 Proceedings*, Article 13. https://aisel.aisnet.org/mcis2023/13.

Seaver, Nick. 2022. *Computing Taste: Algorithms and the Makers of Music Recommendation.* University of Chicago Press.

SemRush. 2024. "*Most Visited Websites in the World, Updated November 2024.*" https://www.semrush.com/website/top/.

Shneiderman, Ben. 2020a. "Bridging the Gap Between Ethics and Practice: Guidelines for Reliable, Safe, and Trustworthy Human-Centered AI Systems." *ACM Transactions on Interactive Intelligent Systems* 10 (4). doi:10.1145/3419764.

Shneiderman, Ben. 2020b. "*Human-Centered Artificial Intelligence: Reliable, Safe & Trustworthy.*" International Journal of Human–Computer Interaction 36 (6): 495–504. doi:10.1080/10447318.2020.1741118.

Shneiderman, Ben. 2020c. "Human-Centered Artificial Intelligence: Three Fresh Ideas." *AIS Transactions on Human-Computer Interaction* 12 (3): 109–124. doi:10.17705/1thci.00131.

Shneiderman, Ben. 2022. *Human-Centered AI.* Oxford University Press.

Sloane, Mona, Emanuel Moss, Olaitan Awomolo, and Laura Forlano. 2022. "Participation Is Not a Design Fix for Machine Learning." In *Proceedings of the 2nd ACM Conference on Equity and Access in Algorithms, Mechanisms, and Optimization (EAAMO '22)*, Article 1, 1–6. New York, NY: Association for Computing Machinery. doi:10.1145/3551624.3555285.

Suchman, Lucy. 1998. "Human/Machine Reconsidered." *Cognitive Studies: Bulletin of the Japanese Cognitive Science Society* 5(1): 1–6.

Suchman, Lucy. 2007. *Human-Machine Reconfigurations:* Plans and Situated Actions. 2nd ed. Cambridge University Press.

The White House. 2023. "*Executive Order on the Safe, Secure, and Trustworthy Development and Use of Artificial Intelligence.*" https://www.whitehouse.gov/briefing-room/presidential-actions/2023/10/30/executive-order-on-the-safe-secure-and-trustworthy-development-and-use-of-artificial-intelligence/.

Thiebes, Scott, Sebastian Lins, and Ali Sunyaev. 2021. "Trustworthy Artificial Intelligence." *Electronic Markets* 31 (2): 447–464. doi:10.1007/s12525-020-00441-4.

Tseng, Yu-Shan. 2022. "Algorithmic empowerment: A Comparative Ethnography of Two Open-Source Algorithmic platforms—Decide Madrid and vTaiwan." *Big Data & Society* 9 (2). doi:10.1177/20539517221123505.

UNESCO. 2021. *Recommendation on the Ethics of Artificial Intelligence.* https://unesdoc.unesco.org/ark:/48223/pf0000380455.

Vorvoreanu, Mihaela, Amy Heger, Samir Passi, Shipi Dhanorkar, Zoe Kahn, and Ruotong Wang. 2023. *Responsible AI Maturity Model.* Microsoft. May 2023. https://www.microsoft.com/en-us/research/publication/responsible-ai-maturity-model/.

Wiener, Norbert. 1948. *Cybernetics: Or Control and Communication in the Animal and the Machine.* Cambridge, MA: MIT Press.

Xu, Wei. 2019. "Toward Human-Centered AI: A Perspective from Human-Computer Interaction." *Interactions* 26 (4): 42–46. doi:10.1145/3328485.

3

THE MYTHICAL SPEECH OF ARTIFICIAL INTELLIGENCE

The Imaginary of an Autonomous Agency

Andrés Pachón

Introduction

The media narrative surrounding the present and future capabilities of artificial intelligence (AI) often misattributes intelligence to computational systems. In this text, I argue that this narrative is grounded on a *mythical speech* (Barthes 1971) that assumes intelligence stems from autonomous agency—leading to the belief that if computational systems solve problems with some degree of autonomy, they must therefore be intelligent like humans. Drawing on ethnographic research, I conducted with a deep learning engineer, I will show that while we should not deny the agency of AI or its current role in human cognition, this does not mean it is an autonomous agent—much less one that possesses human-like intelligence. Embracing this mythical speech enables technology companies to deflect responsibility for the outputs generated by these systems.

In the first section of this text ("AI Mythical Speech"), I will examine how the mythology of AI is formed and operates, drawing on Roland Barthes's (1971) semiotic concept of *myth*. I show how the relationship between cognitive science and AI gave rise to this mythology by turning a series of assumptions about the mental and the computational into evidence—assumptions that still shape contemporary narratives about AI. In the second section ("AI Mythology in Action"), I analyze key tasks performed by an engineer while programming a deep learning model for computer vision (Convolutional Neural Network). This analysis reveals that the intelligence computationally simulated by such systems is not the result of autonomous agency but of *social agency* (Gell 1998). In the third and final section ("How Can We Resist the AI Mythical Speech?"), I explore how the technical mediation involved in

DOI: 10.4324/9781003532750-5

designing deep learning systems creates *black boxes* (Latour 1999) that obscure the social agency behind AI, materializing the myth of autonomy. I conclude by presenting the experimental ethnography I conducted in collaboration with the engineer, which aimed to incorporate social agency into the design of human–AI interfaces as a way to resist the AI mythical speech.

AI Mythical Speech

It is common knowledge that nowadays many of our digital artifacts and applications are equipped with AI that gives them an autonomy on which we can delegate multiple tasks that previously depended on humans. Such is the case of smartphones, autonomous cars, text translators, image generators and, most obviously due to their anthropomorphism, chatbot-based virtual assistants such as Siri (Apple), Alexa (Amazon), or ChatGPT (OpenAI). The autonomous operability of these *intelligent* artifacts is due to deep learning, an automated learning technology based on inductive methods that is part of the techniques dedicated to the classification and search for patterns. In addition to being integrated into specialized sectors such as education, finance, and medicine, AI based on deep learning is set to displace countless jobs in the coming years, replacing not only workers who perform more automated or standardized tasks—as in the case of the implementation of chatbots for customer support (Kaput 2024)—but also designers, illustrators, photographers, and scriptwriters. In this regard, Sam Altman (CEO of OpenAI) went so far as to state in 2024 that 95% of the work performed by creatives and marketing specialists will soon be handled almost instantaneously and at almost no cost by AI, including the generation of images, videos and ideas for advertising campaigns (Kaput 2024).

In this context of the massive implementation of AI and the ethical controversies it raises, we find a public discourse that not only exalts the current capabilities of this technology but also predicts an inevitable future in which the sum of deep learning systems will reach and even surpass human cognitive capabilities. This is Artificial General Intelligence (AGI), a system that, according to this discourse, will have cognitive abilities similar to those of a human. Several technological gurus claim that AGI will arrive in the next few years (Heath 2024; Sozzi 2023), although the most striking example of this public discussion is the one held by Elon Musk (CEO of Tesla and SpaceX and cofounder of Open AI) and the aforementioned CEO of OpenAI, Sam Altman. Musk has gone so far as to claim that some aspects of AGI have already been discovered, an example of which is the Tesla cars that, according to the entrepreneur, already possess a type of mind (Musk 2023).

Musk predicts that between 2025 and 2026, an AGI will surpass human intelligence (Reuters 2024), a concept popularly known as *superintelligence*. [1] Altman also states that he enthusiastically expects AGI to arrive in 2025, which will bring unparalleled progress for humanity (Y Combinator 2024). According to Altman, AGI will be capable of achieving new scientific breakthroughs on its own (Kaput 2024), providing answers to some of humanity's greatest challenges, such as climate change or a cure for cancer (Seisdedos 2023).

While highlighting the benefits of this unstoppable progress, this discourse stresses the possibility that the capabilities of AGI could put humanity at risk if it is not urgently regulated since its super-intelligent autonomy could enable systems to replicate themselves (Seisdedos 2023). According to these claims, this would allow them to exponentially increase their power and escape the limitations imposed by programmers and, therefore, to human control. Along these lines, a recent statement (Center for AI Safety 2023), signed by 350 experts and headed by Altman, called for control over the AI advances that they themselves are developing. The statement places the risk of AI development alongside pandemics and world war as possible causes of human extinction.

But why so much fear in the face of something that is still unknown? Could it be that the AI gurus are holding back the announcement of a discovery that will make possible the arrival of a super-intelligent AGI? According to voices dissonant with this discourse, where the figure of Yann LeCun—2018 Turing Award and one of the fathers of deep learning—stands out, AI based on deep learning, which is the only operational AI available to us today, cannot even approach the intelligence of a dog (LeCun 2023). According to LeCun, AI is nowhere near the top of the list of existential risks to humanity. On the one hand, this narrative grants AI capabilities it does not have, maintaining and increasing the expectations generated by certain tools—as was the case with ChatGPT in 2023—placing them at the center of public opinion and, with that, attracting new investors. On the other hand, a possible explanation for these apocalyptic statements and manifestos is that companies like OpenAI prefer politicians to debate hypothetical future existential risks rather than focusing on laws that may complicate their expansion today (Pérez Colome 2023); laws that should focus on controlling the real and present threat posed by AI serve to concentrate more power, wealth and resources in a few companies (Ahmed et al. 2023).

What I will argue here is that this media narrative functions as a mythical speech (Barthes 1971) that, by naturalizing an anthropomorphized vision of AI, generates an opacity in relation to the actors and processes involved in its operation. This will allow large companies to relegate responsibility for the capabilities of these systems while at the same time presenting themselves as the only saviors in the face of a hypothetical dominance of AI. From the sociotechnical perspective of Bruno Latour, we can say that the myth of the autonomous and intelligent agency of AI causes that

> the political order is subverted, since I rely on many delegated actions that themselves make me do things on behalf of others who are no longer here, the course of whose existence I cannot even retrace.
>
> *(1999, 189)*

According to Barthes's (1971) semiotic analysis, myth is a type of speech that obscures the formative history that precedes objects and empties them of their own context of production, so that it presents things as a truth without history, which naturalizes certain views of the world. In the case of AI discourse, when we make a metaphorical attribution of mental states to computers—we say that they learn, understand, perceive or process information—we run the risk of forgetting the basis underpinning this anthropomorphic language, moving from the metaphorical to literal attributions of intentionality.[2]

Speaking metaphorically to refer to computers need not be problematic in itself. The conflict arises when anthropomorphic descriptions of the computer are naturalized to such an extent that, following Barthes's approach (1971, 108), the computer ceases to be simply a computer to be invested with a social usage of language that is added to pure matter. In other words, "the metaphorical clothes in which thinking is wrapped become its skin" (Tallis 2004, 34). This means that we are no longer in the realm of metaphors but in that of mythical speech.

According to Barthes (1971, 128), in the history of all mythology we can locate an inflexion point where the origin of the myth begins. In the case of the mythology of AI, we can locate this moment in the relationship that the cognitive sciences established with AI in the 1970s. This relationship gave rise to a *computationalist* theory of human cognition that the philosopher of mind John R. Searle (2002, 2003) defined as Strong AI. This position had important implications not only for the philosophical and scientific conception of the mental but also for the official self-image of the AI project. According to Searle (2002, 2003), the two fundamental assumptions of Strong AI were: 1) the mind is software, and the software of a digital computer could become a mind; and 2) if a computer behaves as if it has a mind, then it is a sign that it does. In the following, we will see how these assumptions were established and what they implied for the current mythical speech of deep learning.

The computationalist argument was based on Alan Turing's computational theory, according to which an intelligent machine could process symbols exclusively by virtue of their respective syntactic characteristics as long as the semantic characteristics (their content) were preserved. A syntactic and mechanical model of intelligence was thus proposed, where the semantic relations between thoughts take place exclusively through syntactic processes.

Up to that point (the 1940s), mathematical reasoning—and, with it, intelligence—was understood by Turing and his contemporary mathematicians as a combination of intuition and ingenuity (Dyson 2012; Larson 2021). Intuition referred to the mental issue that allows us to make conjectures about the rules to be followed to reach a truth, while ingenuity was the proper arrangement of a set of propositions where intuition was supported to be demonstrated. Intuition was a problematic term that limited the possibility of moving from a mechanical machine to an autonomous (intelligent) machine, since the figure of the human/designer, who uses his intuition to indicate to the systems the specific problems to be solved, continued to be necessary.

In order to defend the idea of an intelligent machine, Turing reduced the definition of intelligence to the ability to solve problems following formal logical rules (Larson 2021, 31)—which could be simulated computationally—eluding the intuition that allows us to make conjectures about the rules to be followed. In this way, Turing ended up defining intelligence as a mechanical process capable of solving problems, discarding intuition. With this, he also annulled any reference to the social and situational character of intelligence, since, in order to consider the machine intelligent, it could not depend on elements external to the system, specifically on the intuition of the programmer. In this sense, Turing went so far as to assert that the path to AI was to build a machine with the curiosity of a child and let its intelligence develop (Dyson 2012).

This definition of intelligence reinforced the Western image of the human as an autonomous and rational agent, at the same time that it marked the path to follow for AI. In this sense, anthropologist Lucy Suchman refers to the following:

> Projects in AI and robotics involve a kind of doubling or mimicry in the machine that works as a powerful disclosing agent for assumptions about the human [...]. In the case of the human, the prevailing figuration in Euro-American imaginaries is one of autonomous, rational agency, and projects of AI reiterate that culturally specific imaginary.
>
> *(2007, 226–228)*

The notion of intelligence established by Turing allowed the cognitive sciences to jump easily between the characteristics of the mind and software. This allowed them to digitally reproduce cognitive processes and thus to study them objectively through the external observation of computer programs. This gave rise to a mechanistic model of intelligence that would *scientifically* reinforce the imaginary of autonomous agency referred to by Suchman.

The scientific appearance of these studies was made possible, to a large extent, by the impact of the Turing test (Searle 2002, 61). By determining whether a machine was intelligent or not, the Turing test allowed computationalists to verify the cognitive processes through the computer: if an external observer is not able to distinguish an output generated by a machine from another generated by a human, we must prove that the machine has intelligence, which would allow its objective study. These arguments reaffirmed that a properly programmed computer could come to have intelligent thoughts in the same sense that we humans have them, once all thought was reduced to a manipulation of symbols that could be reproduced in the computer.

According to Searle (2002, 66), these assumptions of Strong AI present "a weird mixture of behaviorism and dualism." On the one hand, by accepting the Turing test, computationalism presented a behaviorist stance that exclusively attended to the observable behaviors of the machine: if a digital computer behaves as if it has a mind, then it must indeed have a mind as a human does. On the other hand, in order to determine the presence of the mental according to this criterion, it is necessary to assume that there is nothing essentially biological in the mind. That is, in order for the mind and intelligence to be in both computers and brains, it was necessary to accept that the mind could be separated from the body, as did the Cartesian dualism advocated by Descartes.

Contemporary research and studies in cognition and neuroscience widely accept the position that mental states (intelligence, perception, consciousness, emotions, etc.) emerge from neural activity; that is, they accept that the mind is a macro-property of the brain (Searle 2003, 21). But behaviorism and a certain residual dualism remain entrenched in popular thought (Quiroga 2024, 29). We see this in the media narrative of deep learning presented at the beginning of this section, where the myth of computational mind duplication is supported by the claim that with sufficient resources (hardware power and massive datasets) and adequate training of algorithms, it is possible to create human-like intelligence from scratch (Crawford 2021, 4–5). Something that, as we have seen, implies accepting that mind and intelligence are qualities that exist independently of any social character.

Although deep learning does not seek to generate an artificial mind and focuses on solving specific problems—such as language translation, text and image classification and generation, or automated driving—the main goal continues to be to design machines that somehow exhibit psychological attributes—such as the ability to learn, perceive, understand or reason—rather than simply simulate them (Preston 2002, 14–15). According to my arguments, this is because the mythology of Strong AI continues to be implicit in the deep learning discourse, especially when it is claimed that the sum of deep learning models will lead us to an AGI that will surpass human intelligence. This is stated by Altman (2024) in a recent manifesto, entitled "The Intelligence Age:"

> It is possible that we will have superintelligence in a few thousand days (!); it may take longer, but I'm confident we'll get there.
>
> How did we get to the doorstep of the next leap in prosperity?
>
> In three words: deep learning worked.
>
> In 15 words: deep learning worked, got predictably better with scale, and we dedicated increasing resources to it.

> That's really it; humanity discovered an algorithm that could really, truly learn any distribution of data (or really, the underlying "rules" that produce any distribution of data). To a shocking degree of precision, the more compute and data available, the better it gets at helping people solve hard problems. I find that no matter how much time I spend thinking about this, I can never really internalize how consequential it is.

The development of deep learning was made possible, among other factors, by the improvement of multilayer artificial neural networks, a technique that made it possible to represent reality in the artificial system in a richer way than with the symbolic AI that accompanied the computationalist cognitive sciences. It was no longer necessary to translate objects and events in the world into meaning-deficient symbols, which required additional definition. That is, we no longer needed to tell the computer exactly how to solve a problem through logical rules (deductive method) but just show it a set of examples of that problem solved (inductive method).

But despite their technical name (artificial neural networks), and although neuroscience and AI have influenced each other throughout history, there is virtually no neurobiological basis for the computational processes of deep learning (Lindsay 2022, 154). An exception would be the simulation of the initial stages of visual processing provided by Convolutional Neural Networks (CNNs), a deep learning technique for computational vision that simulates the activations and connections that take place between the cells of the thalamus and the simple and complex cells of the V1 visual cortex when humans perceive an image (Lindsay 2022, 165–169). In contrast, neither CNNs, nor any other deep learning technique, is able to simulate the functioning of the brain's neural networks when they establish (or learn) the connections necessary to generate mental states—such as, for example, object recognition during visual perception. This is because we simply do not yet understand how this process operates at the neural level (Lindsay 2022, 79).

The learning of a multilayer artificial neural network is just a technical solution that allows the system to perform a type of inductive inference from examples. This is achieved thanks to a computational structure that, although inspired by the brain, only simulates certain functional properties of nerve cell networks, such as parallel and distributed information processing. In this structure, information is transmitted through multiple levels of processing, including numerous hidden layers, so called because the calculations they perform are not directly accessible or comprehensible to a human observer, given their complexity and computational volume.

This technical solution for learning is carried out through a training process that includes feedforward propagation of information (feedforward) and backpropagation of error (backpropagation). The network is trained with a set of images labeled in different categories. During feedforward, the network processes the images to generate predictions from the automatically extracted features at each layer. Then, through backpropagation, the error between the predictions and the actual labels is calculated, and the parameters (weights and biases) of the network are adjusted to improve its performance. This cycle is repeated until the network is able to recognize relevant patterns in the input data.

In the following section, I will focus on a part of the ethnographic fieldwork that I developed together with a deep learning engineer, which allowed me to actively accompany the design and training of a CNN for computer vision. Through the analysis of some examples of this work, we will see that, although the myth of autonomous agency is present in the anthropomorphic language used by the engineer to refer to deep learning, this mythical speech does not correspond to the social action that takes place during the programming of these systems.

AI Mythology in Action

To begin the ethnographic work, I proposed to the engineer that we design a CNN to learn how to view the digital collection of the New York Public Library (NYPL)[3], an open-access archive consisting of digitized visual documents from various historical collections dated between the sixteenth and twentieth centuries.

Training a CNN with such a dataset presented a number of challenges for the engineer. Although the NYPL images are organized into different categories, they can be ambiguous, complex, and polysemous from the perspective of CNN-based algorithmic analysis. This is due to the fact that the images were produced using various techniques (engraving, painting, photography, etc.) and belong to diverse genres (portraits, landscapes, maps, ethnographic documents, etc.) that do not necessarily determine their classification into one category or another. Instead, they often address broad themes (World War I, military uniforms, African Americans, women, ethnography, cities, etc.), resulting in images within the same category having distinct visual characteristics in both form and content.

This is not the case, for example, with the implementation of CNNs in medical imaging, where each training dataset consists of images produced using the same technique (X-rays, PET scans, MRI, etc.). Nor is it the case with ImageNet—a popular dataset designed specifically for training and testing computer vision models—in which all images are photographic and share the same format and resolution. Moreover, the content of ImageNet images has been curated for each category by removing any information that, according to the engineer (field note), does not *clearly* correspond to the assigned label—a problematic claim we will return to later.

Thus, the engineer began designing and training our CNN by first carrying out a preprocessing task on the NYPL images. During this stage, some images were removed from the dataset, while others were cropped to eliminate elements—such as captions or frames—that, according to the engineer, did not contribute to the core concept of the image and could "distract the *attention* of the network" (field note).

Due to the large number of images in any training dataset, this task cannot be done manually. It therefore requires another algorithm that, using statistical calculations and operating in an *unsupervised* manner,[4] detects and filters out information deemed irrelevant for training. The output of this algorithm was then reviewed by the engineer through various interfaces that allowed him to inspect discarded, selected, and cropped images. In this way, he could identify false positives—images with relevant content mistakenly classified as text—and false negatives—text mistakenly identified as images. As the engineer noted, this process "allows for manual refinement of the algorithm's results" (field note).

The first thing that struck me when I saw the engineer in action was that he hardly wrote any code; most of his time was spent defining and solving problems—such as preprocessing of the dataset. In her studies of the then-emerging applied AI industry, anthropologist Diana E. Forsythe (2001, 22) already noted that, contrary to the widespread belief that the real work of programmers—what it means to *do* AI—is writing code and building systems, these tasks are actually part of broader strategies to accomplish the primary goal: solving problems. In fact, to design this CNN, the engineer didn't build a system from scratch but instead used a pre-designed algorithmic architecture: a CNN known as Inception V1. He made the necessary adjustments to adapt this network to the specific problem it was intended to solve—classifying new images into the categories of the NYPL archive.

To do this, the engineer not only used the architecture of a network pre-designed by other engineers but also took advantage of certain patterns that the network had learned through prior training with ImageNet. This process is known as fine-tuning, a technique through which certain patterns learned by a pre-trained network are frozen. This helps address problems presented by our dataset, such as its polysemic nature and the limited number of images—compared to a dataset like ImageNet. According to the engineer (field note), fine-tuning allows for leveraging the general patterns the network has already learned from ImageNet, while in the deeper layers of the network, it forgets those generalities and begins to learn the specific patterns that characterize the NYPL archive. It is worth noting the engineer's explanation of the fine-tuning technique, which echoes Turing's expression referring to the potential learning of his intelligent machine:

> This technique is as if we were teaching a three-year-old child, who already knows how to distinguish certain things, to look at the NYPL archive. It is very interesting to freeze to here millions of parameters trained for real-life examples. The network we use has a complexity and a maturity because it has seen millions of images, something it is not going to get from just looking at the NYPL archive.
>
> *(field note)*

This anthropomorphic explanation is only possible if one accepts that training a network with ImageNet involves showing the system real-life examples—recall how the engineer earlier described the image-label pairing in ImageNet as an obvious relationship. This exemplifies the underlying theoretical paradigm of datasets, which, according to Kate Crawford and Trevor Paglen (2019), is underpinned by two epistemological assumptions. First, the assumption that concepts—whether flowers, gender, emotions, or history—exist in advance and have some kind of transcendental foundation or internal consistency. Second, the assumption that there are simple, universal, and self-evident links between images, referents, and labels. In contrast, images have a very unstable relationship with the things they seem to represent, as the circuits between image, label, and referent are flexible and can shift with the cultural context of each era.

This issue is reflected in the decision to train our CNN with the NYPL archive. The number of readings offered by each of the image-label pairs in this historical collection highlights the fact that every dataset carries a history of mediation and composition, where each input has been produced *by* as many artifacts—such as the pencil, geometry, perspective, camera obscura, camera, etc.—and *for* other institutional devices—the laboratory, the bureaucratic archive, the museum, anthropology, natural sciences, etc.

Without going so far back in time, in our CNN programming we have also observed how datasets are constructed and preprocessed through distributed cognition (Hutchins 1995) between humans and non-humans: the engineer uses an unsupervised algorithm to later manually adjust its results. Furthermore, the use of fine-tuning illustrates that when a programmer works on an artificial neural network, he works with other networks previously designed (and trained) by other programmers. Thus, we can say that deep learning is simultaneously a result of and an instrument for an association between different codependent agencies, human and non-human (technological). This allows us to define deep learning as a social agent and not as an autonomous and complete one, since, according to the anthropologist Alfred Gell, deep learning is not an autonomous and complete one

> "Social agency" is not defined in terms of "basic" biological attributes (such as inanimate thing vs. incarnate person) but is relational-it does not

> matter, in ascribing "social agent" status, what a thing (or a person) "is" in itself; what matters is where it stands in a network of social relations.
> *(1998, 123)*

In short, the work of programming a CNN shows us that the human cognition we are trying to duplicate in software—in this case, the ability to perceive and recognize images—is not the result of an autonomous agency, but of social agency. If deep learning seems to establish causal relationships—between inputs and outputs—in an apparently intelligent and autonomous way, it is thanks to numerous human agents, as well as many other technological mediators.

In the next section, we will see how, paradoxically, the myth of autonomous agency is materialized and propagated through the technical mediation that takes place during the design of deep learning, making it difficult for us to resist AI mythical speech. Finally, I will present the experimental ethnography I conducted in collaboration with the engineer, which aims to speculate, in a practical way, on alternatives to AI agency.

How Can We Resist the AI Mythical Speech?

As with the functioning of the Barthesian myth presented in the first section, the technical mediation that takes place during the design of an artifact transforms the meaning of things (Latour 1999, 186–187). In my case study, the technical mediation involved in the design of a CNN leads the software to acquire the cognitive capacity to perceive and recognize images. Following Latour's (1999, 188) approach, this is because the technical mediation causes an actorial shift that brings together (and transforms) all the actors involved in the development of the CNN—the engineers and programmers, the training dataset, the algorithms, the hardware, etc.—into a single autonomous frame of reference, which will be the intelligent software. As the historian Adrian Forty (1986, 9) states, we can say that "design has the capacity to cast myths into an enduring, solid and tangible form, so that they seem to be reality itself".

But this does not mean that we, as users, relate to the software or the intelligent artifacts (smartphones, smart cars, voice assistants, etc.) because we confuse it with the agency of a person. According to Gell (1999, 169), what makes us interpret an artifact as an autonomous agent is the resistance it offers to our understanding of the sociotechnical process that precedes it—a quality of technical objects that Gell (1999, 159) referred to as the enchantment of technology. Thus, in order to relate effectively and functionally to intelligent artifacts, this technology must obscure the human and non-human labor that gave rise to their design. Following Gell's (1998, 20) approach, the software or intelligent artifact becomes a channel of agency for the programmer that, thanks to a network of multiple actors (both human and non-human), allows the creation of experiences of copresence as intense as those generated by a human agent. Latour (1999, 275) explains this paradox as follows: "it is because it is constructed that it is so very real, so autonomous, so independent of our own hands. [...] attachments do not decrease autonomy, but foster it. [...] the terms 'construction' and 'autonomous reality' are synonyms".

In our technological everyday life, this paradox translates into the fact that the more intelligent the software and artifacts appear to be—the more operational they are—the harder it will be to know their production history and the composition of their social agency. This creates a black box[5] that, in the case of deep learning, becomes especially explicit due to its technical condition; that is, in the many hidden layers that make up the structure of multilayer neural networks, where millions of calculations take place to analyze vast sets of multidimensional data. This technical condition will make it extremely complex—even for the engineers who design the models—to interpret the processes that lead the system to generate a specific output. This results in the user delegating more responsibilities to these technologies and the institutions that manage them.

At this point, we must ask how we can recover the social agency of AI without losing the enchantment that the autonomy of intelligent technology evokes in us (Suchman 2007, 240). In other words, can we resist the mythical speech of AI, opening its technical black box without losing its capacity to act?

In his semiotic proposal, Barthes (1971, 134) proposed resisting myth by making a myth of myth, which would make it possible to re-signify it and return it to a language that speaks of its history of formation: "the best weapon against myth is perhaps to mythify it in its turn, and to produce an artificial myth." If, as Forty (1986, 9) indicated, myths can be materialized and propagated through design,[6] it would also be possible to re-signify the agency of AI through the design of experimental devices that materialize the following artificial myth: AI is autonomous and intelligent precisely because it is something constructed and codependent on humans.

With this goal in mind, I decided to shift from observational ethnography to a more collaborative and experimental approach that would allow me to help design this *artificial myth*. As I discussed in Pachón (2024), I proposed to the deep learning engineer that we design two experimental interfaces that would enable us to visualize and interact with the activity within the *hidden layers* of our CNN, where the network extracts and combines features from the NYPL archive images. To achieve this, I developed a hybrid method that combined deep learning techniques —including the CNN programmed and trained with the NYPL archive—, *interpretability* tools for multilayer neural networks, and artistic strategies as a means of experimentally appropriating the techniques involved.[7]

As I indicated earlier, it remains a challenge for deep learning experts to fully understand what occurs in the hidden layers that allow a CNN to correctly classify certain inputs while misclassifying others (Carter et al. 2019). In this regard, interpretability research has developed techniques that aim to "see through the eyes of the network" (Carter et al. 2019), making algorithmic computations more accessible to human perception. For the design of our interfaces, we applied these techniques in an experimental manner—a strategy I refer to as artistic appropriation (Pachón 2024, 101). Rather than explaining how the CNN works, this approach emphasizes the aesthetic and visual dimension of its learning processes. On the one hand, it lends the interfaces an epistemic character by making a relevant aspect of the CNN's operations visible. On the other hand, it preserves the enchantment of the technology, once it generates an effect of resistance to user comprehension—requiring interpretation of the human–AI interface beyond the anthropomorphic image of AI.

By visualizing the CNN's learning process—rather than its outputs (i.e., labeled images)—these interfaces require the user's active interpretation to make sense of the processual and polysemous information generated by the AI as it develops its operability. In doing so, the interfaces aim to foster a co-interpretation—between human and AI—of the NYPL archive through which the CNN learned to see. This experimental practice enabled me to speculate on alternative models to the standard notion of the AI interface as a meeting point between human and machine. As Suchman (2007, 245) argues, such a notion assumes that human and machine are autonomous agents with pre-established and fixed capabilities, rather than elements in a social agency characterized by ongoing, mutual transformation.

Thus, the interfaces developed can be described as epistemic devices of visualization and interpretation (Pachón 2024, 102) that transform the unidirectional relationship between the AI—as the producer of knowledge—and the user—as a mere spectator of its results—into a bidirectional exchange. This fosters a social agency where knowledge does not emerge from simply reading the outputs produced by the supposed autonomy of the technology, but from the dynamic negotiations between the interpretative processes of the human and the agency of the AI.

Conclusion

Endowing AI with autonomy and intelligence will allow technology companies to evade their responsibilities for the outcomes it generates. At the same time, this autonomous and intelligent image enables humans to relate effectively to this technology, which obstructs resistance to the AI mythical speech. To address this issue, I proposed incorporating the concept of social agency into the design of human-AI interfaces, thereby speculating on alternatives to AI agency. Given the limitations of an ethnography based on the testimonial observation of AI programming—such as the one presented in the second section—taking a more practical and interventionist approach allowed me to engage with the social agency that defines the design and use of digital technologies.

Anthropological studies on agency and cognition employ theoretical frameworks of codependency and composition—between humans and technologies—to explain the processes of technical knowledge production (Sánchez-

Criado 2008; Ingold 2013). These studies develop ethnographic research on digital technologies (Horst and Miller 2012; Geismar and Knox 2021), and specifically on AI, both in the context of its design and production (Forsythe 2001; Suchman 2007; Khan et al. 2023; Pink et al. 2024), as well as in the field of its implementation and use (Besteman and Gusterson 2019; Seaver 2022). However, while there have been efforts to integrate AI and data science into ethnographic methods (Collins et al. 2017; Pedersen 2023; Munk et al. 2022; Banerji 2023), scholars such as Sarah Pink (2021, 2024) and Johanna Drucker (2020) highlight a gap in research that applies theories of codependency and knowledge composition to the design of technologies shaping the cognitive ecology of our digital age, such as deep learning.

In this sense, the experimental ethnography developed in this research project opens new possibilities for reconfiguring anthropologies of the digital (Pink 2021, 313), contributing to the search for new methods of practical research. Following Ingold's (2013, 6–8) approach, rather than being confined to the description of a retrospective ethnography to conduct an anthropology of technologies, we can generate knowledge through practice with them. This allows us to think ethnographically about alternative futures to dominant narratives (Pink and Salazar 2017, 5). In the case of this research, this approach translated into an interventionist and prospective anthropology with AI, enabling us to speculate on alternatives to the way we imagine and narrate this technology, beyond the mythical speech that accompanies its development.

Notes

1 If we scour the media, we will find that the definitions provided by specialists on AGI and superintelligence make the two terms practically indistinguishable, as, according to them, AGI will inevitably lead us to superintelligence. See Sozzi (2023), Reuters (2024) and Kaput (2024).
2 According to philosopher of mind John R. Searle (2003, 16): "'intentionality' […] doesn't just refer to intentions, but also to beliefs, desires, hopes, fears, love, hate, lust, disgust, shame, pride, irritation, amusement, and all of those mental states (whether conscious or unconscious) that refer to, or are about, the world apart from the mind."
3 https://digitalcollections.nypl.org
4 Unsupervised learning establishes dependency patterns within a dataset without the need to learn by prior labeling. In this case, it allows for the determination and selection of information that, statistically, is less relevant for representing the mean.
5 Latour will take the term black box from the sociology of science, according to which "when a machine runs efficiently, when a matter of fact is settled, one need focus only on its inputs and outputs and not on its internal complexity. Thus, paradoxically, the more science and technology succeed, the more opaque and obscure they become." (Latour 1999, 304)
6 We saw this in the case of Turing, who, in order to design his intelligent machine, first eliminated intuition from the definition of intelligence, reducing it to ingenuity.
7 To see a video capture of these interfaces: www.andrespachon.com/abstract-machine-classh

References

Ahmed, Nur, Muntasir Wahed, and Neil C. Thomson. 2023. "The Growing Influence of Industry in AI Research." *Science* 379 (6635). doi:10.1126/science.ade2420.

Altman, Sam. 2024. "*The Intelligence Age*." September 23, 2024. https://ia.samaltman.com.

Banerji, R. 2023. "Artificial Intelligence, Humanness, and Nonverbal Sociality." *Anthropology in Action* 30 (3): 49–58. doi:10.3167/aia.2023.300306.

Barthes, Roland. 1971. *Mythologies*. Farrar, Straus & Giroux.

Besteman, Catherine, and Hugh Gusterson. 2019. *Life by Algorithms: How Roboprocesses Are Remaking Our World*. University of Chicago Press.

Carter, Shan, Zan Armstrong, Ludwig Schubert, Ian Johnson, and Chris Olah. 2019. "Exploring Neural Networks with Activation Atlases." *Distill*. March 6, 2019. https://distill.pub/2019/activation-atlas/.

Center for AI Safety. 2023. "*Statement on AI Risk*." May 30, 2023. https://www.safe.ai/work/statement-on-ai-risk.

Collins, S. G., M. Durington, P. Favero, K. Harper, A. Kenner, and C. O'Donnell. 2017. "Ethnographic Apps/Apps as Ethnography." *Anthropology Now* 9 (1): 102–118. doi:10.1080/19428200.2017.1291054.

Crawford, Kate. 2021. *Atlas of AI: Power, Politics, and the Planetary Costs of Artificial Intelligence*. Yale University Press.

Crawford, Kate, and Trevor Paglen. 2019. "*Excavating AI: The Politics of Training Sets for Machine Learning*." September 9, 2019. https://excavating.ai.

Drucker, Johanna. 2020. *Visualization and Interpretation*. The MIT Press.

Dyson, George. 2012. *Turing's Cathedral: The Origins of the Digital Universe*. Penguin Press. Ebook.

European Parliament. 2024. *Regulation (EU) 2024/1689 of the European Parliament and of the Council*. 2021/0106/COD. http://data.europa.eu/eli/reg/2024/1689/oj.

Forsythe, Diana. 2001. *Studying Those Who Study Us: An Anthropologist in the World of Artificial Intelligence*. Stanford University Press.

Forty, Adrian. 1986. *Objects of Desire: Design and Society Since 1750*.Thames & Hudson.

Gell, Alfred. 1998. *Art and Agency: An Anthropological Theory*. Clarendon Press.

Gell, Alfred. 1999. *The Art of Anthropology: Essays and Diagrams*. 2006. Berg.

Geismar, Haidy and Hannah Knox, eds. 2021. *Digital Anthropology*, 2nd Edition. Routledge.

Heath, Alex. 2024. "Mark Zuckerberg's New Goal Is Creating Artificial General Intelligence." *The Verge*. January 18, 2024. https://www.theverge.com/2024/1/18/24042354/mark-zuckerberg-meta-agi-reorg-interview.

Horst, Heather A., and Daniel Miller, eds. 2012. *Digital Anthropology*. Berg Publications.

Hutchins, Edwin. 1995. *Cognition in the Wild*. The MIT Press.

Ingold, Tim. 2013. *Making: Anthropology, Archaeology, Art and Architecture*. Routledge.

Kaput, Mike. 2024. "Sam Altman Says AI Will Handle '95%' of Marketing Work Done by Agencies and Creatives." *Marketing Artificial Intelligence Institute*. March 5, 2024. https://www.marketingaiinstitute.com/blog/sam-altman-ai-agi-marketing.

Khan, Arif Ali, Muhammad Azeem Akbar, Mahdi Fahmideh, Peng Liang, Muhammad Waseem, Aakash Ahmad, et al. 2023. "AI Ethics: An Empirical Study on the Views of Practitioners and Lawmakers." *IEEE Transactions on Computational Social Systems* 10 (6): 2971–2984. doi:10.1109/TCSS.2023.3251729.

Larson, Erik J. 2021. *The Myth of Artificial Intelligence: Why Computers Can't Think the Way We Do*. The Belknap Press of Harvard University Press.

Latour, Bruno. 1999. *Pandora's Hope: Essays on the Reality of Science Studies*. Harvard University Press.

LeCun, Yann (@ylecun). 2023. "Super-human AI is nowhere near the top of the list of existential risks..." X (Twitter). May 30, 2023, 7:39 p.m. https://x.com/ylecun/status/1663616081582252032.

Lindsay, Grace. 2022. *Models of the Mind: How Physics, Engineering and Mathematics Have Shaped Our Understanding of the Brain*. Bloomsbury Sigma.

Munk, A. K., A. G. Olesen, and M. Jacomy. 2022. "The Thick Machine: Anthropological AI between Explanation and Explication." *Big Data & Society* 9 (1). doi:10.1177/20539517211069891.

Musk, Elon (@elonmusk). 2023. "I think we may have figured out some aspects of AGI..." X (Twitter). August 7, 2023, 10:05 a.m. https://x.com/elonmusk/status/1688476506295586816.

Pachón, Andrés. 2024. "Epistemic Interfaces of Visualization and Interpretation: A Possible Resistance to the Myth of Autonomous Agency in AI." *Revista de Comunicação e Linguagens* 60: 91–113.

Perrault, Ray, and Jack Clark. 2024. *Artificial Intelligence Index Report 2024*. Stanford University: Human-Centered Artificial Intelligence. https://aiindex.stanford.edu/wp-content/uploads/2024/05/HAI_AI-Index-Report-2024.pdf.

Pedersen, Morten Axel. 2023. "Editorial Introduction: Towards a Machinic Anthropology." *Big Data & Society* 10 (1). doi:10.1177/20539517231153803.

Pérez Colomé, Jordi. 2023. "Por qué los Impulsores de la Inteligencia Artificial Firman Tantos Manifiestos Apocalípticos." *El País*. June 2, 2023. https://elpais.com/tecnologia/2023-06-02/por-que-los-impulsores-de-la-inteligencia-artificial-firman-tantos-manifiestos-apocalipticos.html.

Pink, Sarah, and Juan Francisco Salazar. 2017. "Anthropologies and Futures: Setting the Agenda." In *Anthropologies and Futures: Researching Emerging and Uncertain Worlds*, edited by Juan Francisco Salazar, Sarah Pink, Andrew Irving, and Johannes Sjöberg. Bloomsbury.

Pink, Sarah. 2021. "Digital Futures Anthropology." In *Digital Anthropology*, 2nd ed. edited by Haidy Geismar and Hannah Knox. Routledge.

Pink, Sarah, Emma Quilty, John Grundy, and Rashinda Hoda. 2024. "Trust, Artificial Intelligence and Software Practitioners: An Interdisciplinary Agenda." *AI & Society 40: 639–652*. doi:10.1007/s00146-024-01882-7.

Preston, John. 2002. "Introduction." In *Views into the Chinese Room: New Essays on Searle and Artificial Intelligence*, edited by John Preston and Mark Bishop. Oxford University Press.

Quiroga, Rodrigo Q. 2024. *Things You Would Never Believe: From Science Fiction to Neuroscience*. Penguin Random House Grupo Editorial.

Reuters. 2024. "Tesla's Musk Predicts AI Will Be Smarter Than the Smartest Human Next Year." *Reuters*. April 8, 2024. https://www.reuters.com/technology/teslas-musk-predicts-ai-will-be-smarter-than-smartest-human-next-year-2024-04-08/.

Sánchez-Criado, Tomás, ed. 2008. *Technogenesis: The Technical Construction of Human Ecologies*. Vol 1 and 2. AIBR.

Searle, John R. 2002. "Twenty-One Years in the Chinese Room." In *Views into the Chinese Room: New Essays on Searle and Artificial Intelligence*, edited by John Preston and Mark Bishop. Oxford University Press.

Searle, John R. 2003. *Minds, Brains and Science*. Harvard University Press.

Seaver, Nick. 2022. *Computing Taste: Algorithms and the Makers of Music*. University of Chicago Press.

Seisdedos, Iker. 2023. "Sam Altman (ChatGPT), en el Capitolio: "Si la Inteligencia Artificial Sale Mal, Puede Salir Muy Mal." *El País*. May 16, 2023. https://elpais.com/tecnologia/2023-05-16/sam-altman-chatgpt-en-el-capitolio-si-la-inteligencia-artificial-sale-mal-puede-salir-muy-mal.html.

Sozzi, Brian. 2023. "Bill Gates: There Will Be AI That Does 'Everything That a Human Brain Can'." *Yahoo! Finance*. March 21, 2023. https://finance.yahoo.com/news/bill-gates-there-will-be-ai-that-does-everything-that-a-human-brain-can-170040966.html.

Suchman, Lucy. 2007. *Human-Machine Reconfigurations: Plans and Situated Actions*. 2nd ed. Cambridge University Press.

Tallis, Raymond. 2004. *Why the Mind Is Not a Computer: A Pocket Lexicon of Neuromythology*. Imprint Academic.

Y Combinator. 2024. "*How to Build the Future: Sam Altman*." YouTube video, 46:51. November 8, 2024. https://www.youtube.com/watch?v=xXCBz_8hM9w.

4

THE WIND UNDER THE DOOR

Pareidolia and ChatGPT as a Feared and Welcome Guest

John N. A. Brown

Introduction

In this chapter, I am going to shed some light on our understanding of Generative AI (GenAI), like ChatGPT, by introducing the common psychological trait called pareidolia. Humans all have a tendency to anthropomorphize the things we interact with. Before I get into discussing how and why that works, I will establish a historical and technological context for the myriad current relationships humans have with the commercial products currently called AI. The term AI has become very popular since the release of ChatGPT on November 30th, 2022, but it is now used chiefly either in association with a class of standalone commercial products similar to ChatGPT or else in a number of fantastical stories. Other than a brief overview, the discussion of fantasies will be left to others. This chapter will focus on a discussion of this class of commercial products and, eventually, on how and why humans are susceptible to important and thorough misunderstandings of what these products can and cannot do.

The Fantasy of AI

The world-changing potential of an artificially generated intelligence that can think as well as or better than a human has long been the topic of fantastic speculative fiction, with wonderful examples ranging from the worlds of Asimov's positronic robots like "*The Bicentennial Man*" (Asimov, Silverberg, and Timmerman 1978) and R. Daneel Olivaw (Asimov 1940), to the world of his great "Encyclopaedia Galactica" (Asimov 1951), not to mention the horrifying dystopia of Ellison's "I have No Mouth, and I Must Scream" (Ellison 1967),

DOI: 10.4324/9781003532750-6

the utopia in which we meet Star Trek's positronic robot "Data" (Roddenberry 1987–1994), and the evolutionarily-driven AI-influenced worlds of Hogan's "*Code of the Lifemaker*" (Hogan 2002) and Gould's "*Helm*" (Gould 1999). These fantasies are derived from speculation on the possible outcomes if software could learn to think and learn independently from its makers. AI is hardly mentioned in the popular media without some reference to the kind of utopias and dystopias mentioned above.

The public-facing advertising of ChatGPT and its siblings is shallow and full of certainty. Apple Intelligence is presented to the public in a recent advertisement which suggests that using this software can help one fool one's boss into thinking one is competent at writing emails (Apple 2024). Google had to edit an advertisement for its product Gemini after it was found to be using false information about the popularity of a Dutch cheese (Fraser and Singleton 2025). When faced with this turn of events, a Google executive insisted that the error was not because of their reliance on Gemini but rather because of errors on the websites that Gemini had scraped (Fraser and Singleton 2025). These are only two examples, but Google and Apple are two of the world's most popular public-facing companies, and they have presented their current standalone LLM-based chatbots with a strongly implied message that they are much more than chatbots, that they have, in fact, read and understood all of the content on the Internet and can apply that knowledge as though they are wise and reflective.

There is a class of contemporary, commercial LLM-based chatbots that are marketed for direct use by the non-specialist public. Meta, Alphabet, OpenAI and Anthropic are some of the producers of the class of product I am discussing here. Some, like Anthropic, plainly state the limitations of their public-use chatbot, Claude. The fact that the other companies in that short list use the same label of "AI" on all of their internal and external LLM-based products supports the argument that I am making: that the foundational, real-world limitations of this class of products are not being shared with the public by the people and companies that are profiting from the ill-informed excitement they have generated and the word-of-mouth publicity in which we are all immersed.

This chapter is not a discussion or debate on the nature of every type of AI or the range of purposes to which they are put. Other sources do that well (Wang, Huang and Wang 2020, Kelly et al. 2021, Brauner et al. 2023). Nor is this chapter a discourse on the trustworthiness of the companies that create and commercialize any products at all. There are other sources for this (Peukert and Kloker 2023, Keymolen 2024), some of which have gone so far as to rationally posit the need to create and refine metrics that are based on better measures of trust than adoption, especially when dealing with pervasive or ubiquitous technology (Kelley et al. 2023).

This chapter is about pareidolia and how it is a human feature to perceive more than what we sense. I will reference a series of contemporary illustrations, and a strong business sample to clarify the simple fact that commercialization has moved most of the focus on truly developing working AI away from the previously shared goals of transparency and reliability.

In fact, modern artificial neural networks (ANN) are vastly less complex than those that would be required to empower even the most basic intelligence, not because of the size of the networks but because of their foundational structure. GenAI is built upon the structure of a Chatbot, a phrase-generating engine that uses large language modeling to mimic human speech patterns, not human thought. Brains that have developed naturally are built upon what seems to be an association engine, a processor that learns to establish associations between observed patterns (Hopfield 1999). At this point, that may seem a large statement, but the goal of this chapter is to make that clear. In order to do so, the chapter posits a definition of intelligence in what follows.

Once I have established a definition of intelligence, I will present a brief history of how humans think and learn, then a brief history of the attempts to build ANNs–circuitry and algorithms intended to mimic the behavior of human thinking and learning through mimicry of the human nervous system. I will discuss an attempt to share a common understanding of actual neural networks, focusing on what they are and what they could be.

Finally, armed with an operationalized concept of human intelligence and the neural networks in which it seems to be situated—with a special focus on the peculiar manner in which humans multitask when dealing with the world around them—I will examine the artificial kinds of neural networks. I will start with the first artificial neural network that was ever built (by a psychologist in the 1950s), cover the essential criticism that destroyed that idea and the man who came up with it, leading up to the resurrection of that original idea, which came about due to some out-of-the-box thinking and a breakthrough in physics, and led to modern, commercial AI.

At that point, reflecting on all of the areas I have covered, I will proceed with this mental model to consider modern AI informed by this model's light. It is under that light that I will present answers to my questions about whether or not modern AIs are truly intelligent, as well as answers as to why one might think they are more intelligent than they really are.

Natural Intelligence

Before discussing these differences between how machines and humans think, I want to offer a clear and simple definition of the word intelligence. The Oxford Dictionary defines intelligence as: "the ability to acquire and apply knowledge and skills," (Oxford English Dictionary 2024a) and it defines knowledge as "facts, information, and skills acquired through experience or education; the theoretical or practical understanding of a subject" (Oxford English Dictionary 2024b). For my purposes, I combine those into a working definition of intelligence: "the ability to acquire and apply understanding."

Human Thinking and Learning

The human ability to acquire understanding starts to develop as our brains become complex during gestation, and it continues to develop as a baby grows into adulthood (Barrouillet 2015). The human ability to apply understanding is demonstrated as soon as babies begin to recognize objects and people (de Haan and Nelson 1999). An early example of the duality of acquiring and then applying understanding can be found when babies stop being amazed by the game of peek-a-boo, because they have learned to apply their newly acquired understanding of object permanence (Schaffer et al. 2024).

As a thought experiment, it is easy to imagine other ways in which humans demonstrate the acquisition and application of knowledge in our day-to-day lives: learning to walk or to speak, mastering a new level in a video game or learning to dance. The demonstration of human thinking and learning is all around us. It is interesting that there is no universally accepted model of exactly how or exactly where in the brain thinking and learning take place. Without a deep understanding of how human thinking and learning happen, I suggest appropriating a quote from Justice Potter Stewart's concurring opinion on the US Supreme Court's 1964 refusal to say exactly what makes some pornography objectionable despite the First Amendment: "I know it when I see it."

Machine Thinking and Learning

According to the Nobel Prize Committee,

> When we talk about artificial intelligence, we often mean machine learning using ANNs. This technology was originally inspired by the structure of the brain. In an artificial neural network, the brain's neurons are represented by nodes that have different values
>
> *(Nobel Prize Committee 2024).*

This chapter will not provide a detailed discussion of the engineering of ANNs, nor any detailed discussion of the early history of mechanical computation. Instead, in the following paragraph I present a brief summary of the history of mechanical computers. The bulk of the rest of this chapter will provide a summary overview of the development of ANNs. My summary should serve to build a shared understanding of the actual nature of modern, commercial AI for comparing machine learning to human learning.

Mechanical counting machines have been around for centuries, from the beautifully simple abacus that has been in common use for over 4000 years (Ifrah 2001) to the beautifully intricate Difference Engine and Analytical Engine conceived by Charles Babbage just under two centuries ago in the UK (Copeland 2014). In between those two categories of device, both chronologically and in terms of complexity, it is worth considering the Jacquard machine that introduced punch cards to weaving and predated the man it is named after by more than a century (Essinger 2007). The common barrier that separates these machines and their modern digital descendants from the AI of fantasy is that they are not autonomous: they can be made to do some processing of clearly defined problem sets so that others can learn from their results, but they cannot think or learn for themselves.

The First Artificial Neural Network

In the summer of 1958, a headline in the New York Times read, “New Navy Device Learns by Doing: Psychologist Shows Embryo of Computer Designed to Read and Grow Wiser” (New York Times 1958). This was the birth announcement for the first functioning artificial neural network. The concept had been around for more than a decade: that learning is a natural artifact of the complex patterns of connections in the living brain. In 1943, Warren McCulloch and Walter Pitts proposed a “logical calculus” that could describe and explain how thought and learning are formed due to the structures in which they exist (McCulloch and Pitts 1943). Donald Hebb proposed that learning might be enabled by the creation of “cell-assemblies”—specialized clusters of neurons that reproduce the inherent pattern of real-world ideas on a smaller scale so that this “assembly” can be used to assist new learning (Hebb 1949). But this headline heralded something new.

The United States Office of Naval Research was unveiling Frank Rosenblatt’s Perceptron. The young psychologist had developed a fantastic idea—that the simple electromechanical parts that make up an analog computer (where a whole lot of simple on/off switches are activated in a prescribed order according to specific, limited inputs in an arrangement that enables counting to be done very quickly) could be designed and implemented in a manner similar to the complex biochemical parts that make up the human nervous system (where a whole lot of threshold-reaction switches wait for a charge to build up and then pass it on in a prescribed order, according to nearly-unlimited possible combinations of sensory inputs in an arrangement that enables us to do everything from feeling a cool, autumn breeze to composing a poem about it).

Though the underlying work was very complex, the basic idea was easy to understand, and the media of the time ran with it. *The New Yorker* magazine produced the following: “Indeed, it strikes us as the first serious rival to the human brain ever devised” (Lefkowitz 2019). So, one might ask, just what is it that the Perceptron has learned and become wiser about that makes it a serious rival to the human brain? Given a set of cards that had markings either on the left or right side and fifty training runs, the Perceptron could sort the cards accordingly. In the budding field of computing, this was an incredible breakthrough, but that story wouldn't make an impression on anyone else, including the budget managers of the Navy, the press, or the general public. In order to convey a sense of the enormity of this breakthrough, the Perceptron was presented and discussed in terms of the thinking and learning that it might someday be able to do, rather than the relatively simple card sorting that demonstrated the first signs of that potential.

> Stories about the creation of machines having human qualities have long been a fascinating province in the realm of science fiction. Yet we are about to witness the birth of such a machine—a machine capable of perceiving, recognizing and identifying its surroundings without any human training or control.
>
> *(Rosenblatt 1958, 1)*

This focus on the nearly inconceivable potential, rather than the wondrous work that the Perceptron could actually do, may be responsible for the fantastic success that came next—and also for the terrible collapse that followed.

At the time the Perceptron was announced, Frank Rosenblatt was two years out of his PhD and working as a research psychologist and project engineer at the Cornell Aeronautical Laboratory in Buffalo, New York. The following year, Rosenblatt was appointed director of Cornell's Cognitive Systems Research Program and a lecturer in psychology at the campus in Ithaca, New York. There, heavily funded and well-respected across the field and in the public eye, Rosenblatt experienced a decade as the leading figure in his field. In the early 1960s, they worked on a new version of the Perceptron, named Tobermory, which was intended to recognize and categorize speech in the same way that its predecessor had dealt with visual patterns.

The problem they faced was that they couldn't build circuits as small and efficient as cells. While the simple linear progression of the Perceptron had been executed on an IBM 704—a room-sized metal box that would look familiar to modern fans of the original Star Trek TV show—there simply wasn't a way to make a whole network of circuits in the same style.

In 1969, two specialists from MIT, whose earlier work had not been well received by either the press or funding bodies, pointed out that flaw to the general public. Marvin Minsky and Seymour Papert published the book *Perceptrons: An Introduction to Computational Geometry*, destroying the public's perception of the potential for the creation of practical AI and contributing to a twenty-year downturn in the field that is often referred to as "the AI Winter." This was only the first of several "AI Winters" and this one a downturn specifically in the case of neural networks. Rosenblatt lost nearly all of his funding and a proportionate amount of prestige. In 1970, Minsky was awarded the Turing Award, the highest honor in the field of computing. In 1971, on his 43rd birthday, Rosenblatt went sailing on Chesapeake Bay and never returned to shore.

Modern AI

In the forward to the expanded third edition of *Perceptrons* (1988), Minsky and Papert mention that there had been no advancement of neural networks in the field of computing since the release of their first edition eighteen years earlier and the fact that it has been flourishing as a theoretical sub-field of psychology. It is fortuitous for the historian or anthropologist that their essay gives us a snapshot of the growing movement to bring the theory back into practice with the design and construction of new learning machines just before the breakthrough that made modern machine learning possible.

While attempts to build learning machines had all but disappeared from the field of computing, attempts to model knowledge had surged, leading to the development of new tools and processes such as semantic networks, analogy generators, relational databases, and word-expert parsers, to name a few. Minsky and Papert wrote: "These ideas about the analysis of knowledge and its embodiments, in turn, had strong effects not only in the heart of artificial intelligence but also in many areas of psychology, brain science, and applied expert systems" (1988, xiv).

These relational or "connectionist" models of knowledge championed by the cyberneticists in the 1940s and 1950s and further adapted and developed during the 1970s and 1980s supported an interesting but then unrelated project in computing: the development of chatbots. The purpose of a chatbot is to engage a human in an exchange of messages. Basically, upon receiving a comment or question submitted by a human, the chatbot will locate the keywords from the submitted comment in its relational database or semantic network in order to generate a response that will seem appropriate to the human who submitted the question. Modern chatbots break all writing into smaller non-linguistic pieces, or "tokens" and compose replies by replicating observed patterns. There are three important things to note here:

1. The reassembly of tokens is not how a human builds phrases in a language they are learning, because the tokens created by chatbots have no linguistic value at all. A human will try to assemble new phrases or even new variations on words they have learned, but they do so in an attempt to add meaningful pieces of language to one another in order to better express an idea. The chatbot has no underlying idea and perceives no meaning.

2. Though this attempt to simulate natural conversation is often referred to as a "Turing Test," Alan Turing himself did not suggest any such testing be done (Turing 1950). Instead, he was proposing a thought experiment of the sort used by Leonardo and Einstein, and by many teachers, including myself. He was proposing a framework for thinking about the nature of intelligence and the possibility of intelligent machines. The reader who wants some insight into Turing's intentions is advised to refer to Peter Kugel's assertion that Turing himself said that machines can't be intelligent (Kugel 2002) and to Ting Guo for a perspective that is more anthropological or even philosophical (Guo 2015),
3. Early experimenters quickly learned the value of hiding the difficulties their chatbots might be experiencing by having them generate simple mirroring statements, the same way that some humans express an interest in the stories being told by their collocutors by rephrasing statements as questions.

   "Oh, the Chatbot writes, they would reframe statements as questions? Could you share an example of that?"

   And the author replies, "Thanks, you just did."

Most people have probably interacted with the descendants of those early chatbots, perhaps when ordering goods online or perhaps when attempting to file a complaint about the goods one has ordered online. Chatbots are everywhere now. I will come back to chatbots later on in the chapter, too.

As mentioned earlier, and despite all of these developments, there is still today no single universally-accepted model of knowledge and learning in the human brain. In their epilogue, Minsky and Papert suggest that, while they felt certain that no single one of the networks that had been modeled could account for the emergence of intelligence, they were equally certain that "highly evolved arrangements of smaller, specialized networks which are connected in very specific ways" could (1988, xv). I will also return to this idea at the end of this chapter once I have followed this trail of cultural history a little further forward.

The New Artificial Neural Networks and Modern "AI"

Geoffrey Everest Hinton landed in Toronto in 1987 as a fellow of the first research program at the Canadian Institute for Advanced Research (CIFAR): "Artificial Intelligence, Robotics, and Society." This psychologist, whose PhD from Edinburgh had been entitled "Relaxation and its role in vision" (Hinton 1978), had gone on to do postdoctoral work at UC San Diego demonstrating that multi-layered ANNs could use knowledge representation and reasoning; proving out theories of mental modeling and backward propagation that had been around since the 1970s (Rumelhart, Hinton, and Williams 1986). His big breakthrough there, between 1983 and 1985, was the application of new tools that had been introduced to the field of statistical physics the year before. The result was "Boltzmann machines" which vastly improved the ability of ANNs to classify and generate images (Ackley, Hinton, and Sejnowski 1985).

Seven years after his arrival in Toronto, he was part of a proposal to launch a new project at CIFAR called "Neural Computation and Adaptive Perception" (NCAP), a name that clearly evokes the cyberneticists and connectionists discussed above (CIFAR 2025). As head of this new initiative, Hinton was collocated with Yoshua Bengio and Yann LeCun. Their work together would set the foundation for the resurgence of learning machines and the birth of modern AI.

At NCAP, the three worked together and separately. As they set benchmark after benchmark in their field, breakthroughs in the development of graphics processing units combined with the new prevalence of massive datasets made it possible to build and test simulations based on their models. They were not the only people still working on machine learning, but the concentration of their efforts and their unflinching support for a methodology most others had abandoned decades earlier made them easy targets for derision from their peers and for acclaim when their speculative, theoretical work became practical, applicable, and then ubiquitous.

In 2018, the trio were recognized with the ACM's A. M. Turing Award, sometimes called the "Nobel Prize of Computer Science." Cherri M. Pancake, then president of the ACM, wrote:

> Artificial intelligence is now one of the fastest-growing areas in all of science and one of the most talked-about topics in society. The growth of and interest in AI is due, in no small part, to the recent advances in deep learning for which Bengio, Hinton and LeCun laid the foundation. These technologies are used by billions of people.
>
> *(Association for Computing Machinery 2019)*

At the time of the award, the three had largely gone their separate ways. Yann LeCun became Chief AI Scientist at Facebook and co-founded the Partnership on AI, a coalition of businesses and nonprofit organizations attempting to measure and study the impacts of AI on society.

In 2016, Bengio co-founded an incubator for businesses based on novel AI research. Though the company was acquired in 2020, Bengio stayed on in an advisory capacity. As of this writing, Yoshua Bengio is the most cited computer scientist in the world, which may be important to note as it suggests that many others are following in his footsteps, rather than any of the other trails that might lead to the development of general artificial intelligence.

Hinton announced in 2013 that he would be dividing his time between his university work in Toronto and a new role in Silicon Valley. Google had acquired his company and offered him the lead role in their new AI-centered venture, Google Brain. Ten years later, he publicly announced a split from Google because of a difference of opinion regarding the future of AI. Specifically, Hinton stated that he wanted to be unaffiliated so that he could "freely speak out about the risks of AI" (Metz 2023). Since then, he has issued public warnings and participated in public forums to share his concerns regarding the deliberate misuse of AI-based technology by malicious actors, the threat of AI-induced labor shortages, and the potential existential threat of an unmonitorable and uncontrollable "artificial general intelligence" of the sort seen in the dystopian science fiction and fantasies discussed at the beginning of this chapter.

Earlier, I referred to Hinton's groundbreaking application of new tools from statistical physics to advance the development of Bolztmann machines. The tools that he borrowed had been developed by John Hopfield. In 2024, Hinton and Hopfield were jointly awarded the Nobel Prize in Physics "for foundational discoveries and inventions that enable machine learning with artificial neural networks."

Hinton's post-2013 expressions of his concerns were robust and detailed, as one would expect, but the coverage of them in social media and the popular press has been reduced to a single oversimplified message that played to our modern trend in media fearmongering. In 2024, Hinton and Bengio cosigned a public letter, along with Stuart Russell and Lawrence Lessig, supporting a proposal for a new California-based law that would require any company or individual training an LMM that costs more than $100 million to carry out formal risk assessments before deploying it. So, if the "Godfathers of AI" see the risk of general AI as being imminent, where do they disconnect? And what does any of this have to do with ChatGPT and pareidolia?

I presented this historical context in order to provide a deeper perspective on the technology that has come to be called AI. Now, I turn to the topic of human intelligence.

A Model of How Humans Learn and How ChatGPT Doesn't

Humans, as discussed earlier, have imperfect sensory systems that provide inconsistent and unreliable information. Fortunately, our brains, as discussed earlier, are not a single complex network but "a collection of small, highly-evolved networks" (Minsky and Papert 1988, xv). The combination of these two apparent weaknesses seems to have created a powerfully adaptive system. By having a network of neural networks that work at different speeds, we humans are able to ponder a long-term problem while reacting to the well understood stimuli of day-to-day interactions without ever having to worry about the fully automated and ridiculously complex moment-by-moment problems of breathing, digestion, standing upright, and keeping track of the world around us. This has been described in detail by Brown (2016). Applications of this model to autonomous and semi-autonomous cyberphysical systems[1] have been proposed by Esterle and Brown (Esterle and Brown 2018; Brown and Esterle 2019; and Esterle and Brown 2020).

Amos Tversky and Daniel Kahneman won the "Nobel Prize in Economics" for their work showing that "fast thinking," as on the floor of the stock market, is illogical, emotional, and reactive, while "slow thinking" is rational, reflective, and less common (Kahneman 2011).[2] Drawing on triune models of the brain, dating from Plato to MacLean and Freud, I posited the idea that there is another speed of interaction—an "unthinking" reflexive system that is faster still and responsible for most of our interactions with the world (Brown 2013; Brown 2016). Figure 4.1 illustrates the relative speeds of these "Systems" and links each one to the types of tasks that natural neurophysiological systems and built electromechanical systems perform during each type of "thinking."

Type 0 (REFLEX) includes simple biological reflexes (e.g., the pilomotor reflex) with simple electromechanical switches (e.g., a binary pressure switch). Type 0* (COORDINATED REFLEX) includes more complex, pre-learned coordination of multiple reflexes (e.g., dribbling a ball) with the preassigned, coordinated action of multiple binary switches (e.g., hotkeys). Type 1 (REACTION) pairs up the pattern matching of humans when they join in the singing of a song they don't really know very well, with the pattern matching of an algorithm such as ChatGPT when it joins in a conversation—in that

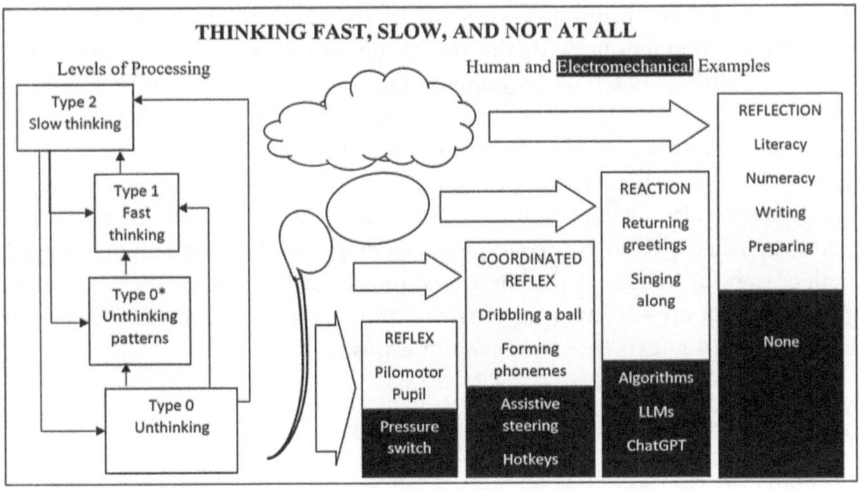

FIGURE 4.1 "Thinking Fast, Slow, and Not At All." An illustration of different types of "thinking" in humans and in machines, adding to Tversky and Kahneman's Type 1 and Type 2 thinking with new Type 0 and Type 0* in order to integrate the three types of interaction described in my ABC model. Includes real world neurophysiological and electromechanical examples for each type of thinking.

each is a complex exercise that does not require deep insight. Type 2 (REFLECTION) includes the human behavior of thinking about oneself, or one's actions, or composing literature or art that reflects those thoughts. At the time of writing, there is no electromechanical equivalent. Yes, ChatGPT can produce writing and pictures, but it does so reactively, not reflectively.

Humans have many more than five senses[3], and they are all always interrupting our focused thoughts and competing for our attention. Tracking the world around us in real time, processing all of the data coming through all of those channels of input, would generate an overwhelming pressure on anyone. One might imagine the holes in our incomplete systems as vents through which that pressure can be vented. As an illustration, consider that human eyes only work some of the time, and often, when we think we are looking at something, we are really only seeing an internally generated model of what we expect to see (De Lange et al. 2018), a mental model that is supported by intermittent sampling (Levi and Klein 1986).

This intermittent sampling and the mental models through which humans construct our image of the world around us allows us to react to visual stimuli more quickly than we can detect, examine, decode, compare, and interpret the things in our field of view (Brown 2016). This also allows us to react to complex patterns of proprioception and touch when we walk or run without having to think through every step of the process.

Most of the time, especially in situations humans understand well, our mental models are accurate enough for us to use them to successfully carry out complex interactions with the world, but sometimes they are not (Johnson-Laird 2010). That's when humans face one of two possible outcomes. Either we have the time and space to reflect on the situation and form a new mental model, or we do not. If not, the real world reaches an objective tentacle into the miasma of our subjective personal sensory illusion. If we are lucky, this results in a pleasant surprise—like the emotional impact of the sudden and unexpected approach of a welcome friend. If we are unlucky, the results can be as benign as the emotional impact of the sudden and unexpected approach of an unwelcome former friend or as tragic as the physical impact of the sudden and unexpected approach of a bus.

Pareidolia and The Illusion of Intention

This intermittent sampling and the mental models through which humans construct an understanding of the world around us can also lead to mistaken certainty. Consider the parallel parking driver who believes they have looked over their shoulder before opening their car door but has done so directly into the path of a passing bicyclist. In the driver's mental model, they always check—but do they? In light of the Dunning-Kruger effect,[4] their blind certainty may be answer enough.

The same partially informed mental models that enable us to function despite the necessary lag in processing all of our sensory inputs also misinform us when they are built or applied incorrectly—an application that happens much more quickly than we can consciously control or influence (Asker and Dinas 2019). This is why car drivers don't see motorcyclists (Mack 2003), why optical illusions deceive us (Most et al. 2001), and why we wave back at the stranger who is trying to get the attention of the person behind us (Tussing and Greene 1997).

This is also why humans often hear familiar voices as the wind rustles the leaves overhead and see familiar faces in crowds of strangers. This phenomenon of perceiving humans or human motivations when none are there is a natural result of how we learn and store knowledge and how we interact with the world around us (Akdeniz, Toker, and Atli 2018). This is called pareidolia, and it is why humans often think that ChatGPT is more than a Chatbot with a really big database. But it's not.

ChatGPT seems to speak in a natural, conversational tone, but that is simply an illusion that it has been trained to create and maintain, as per its foundation as a chatbot. ChatGPT cannot carry out the processes of learning or interacting that make up human intelligence.

It can generate words in series, but it cannot understand those words. Humans use language as a tool to express and share ideas. We break down spoken or written sentences into phrases and words and syllables like a puzzle we try to solve in order to decode the underlying meaning and match it to our mental models of the world. What is a mental model? I explain it to my freshman students using a simple thought experiment that I share here. Close your eyes and touch one finger to the tip of your nose. Did you find it? If you went directly to it or almost directly to it, then you were following your own mental model of how your nose is placed in your face. If you had to feel around for it a bit, that is more likely to be an issue with the proprioceptors that allow you to put your finger (or any other part of your body) exactly where you want to put it without looking for clues or cues or guidance. If you can imagine reaching for your keyboard when seated at your desk, or can imagine the path between work and home, those are also mental models. If you can imagine a typical workday that is also a mental model, and the degree of accuracy and precision with which you can conceive of every detail reflects the quality of your mental map. Can you imagine a Mars bar, and can you distinguish that Mars from the planet of the same name? Can you imagine what it would be like if the planet had the same make-up as the confectionery, or vice versa? That is because you have frangible mental models that can be manipulated through experience or through conjectural imagination. They can also be changed through sociogenic learning. As you learn more about the physical nature of candy bars and planets, your models can grow and the relationships between them can change. ChatGPT does not have these mental models or any others.

ChatGPT has no mental model of the world or anything else. It doesn't break down sentences the way we do, trying to match the pieces to our mental models of both the things being described and the way they are being described in order to carry us towards understanding. It divides written text into clusters of letters, numbers, spaces, and other symbols. These clusters, called "tokens" are not linguistically meaningful. Recently, these tokens have been made larger, encompassing phrases. But it is important to remember that none of these tokens have any meaning, individually or in groups, to ChatGPT. This means that its algorithm of how a written language is broken down or built up does not include the path from idea to expression, but just the assembly and reassembly of tokens that have no linguistic or conceptual value at all. ChatGPT produces sentences by fitting together the pieces of a puzzle; but it does not have any ability to imagine or understand the picture made up by the pieces it has assembled.

Making this kind of LLM bigger or faster will not grant it the ability to really think and learn, because its fundamental processing structure lacks the capacity for abstract modeling. Humans think and learn by building mental models and then re-examining them in the light of new experiences, iteratively examining and re-examining perceived information and our reactions to it. The processing systems shown in Figure 4.1. allow us to do so. ChatGPT and other LLMs would have to be built very differently to be able to do the same, as they currently cannot reflect on their past actions or reactions.

Any mutual understanding that seems to appear during an exchange between a human and ChatGPT is an illusion. Like a calculator, it is unthinkingly following rules to turn inputs into outputs. Unlike a calculator, ChatGPT is not transparent in its reasoning. So there is always a possibility that it will do something unexpected. Like any other chatbot, whatever one is trying to use it for or design it to do, its base-line function is to produce fluent-seeming, natural-seeming, human-seeming language, which will make its human interlocutor feel as though they are interacting with another conscious being. It is very good at doing that, and humans are very good at mapping incomplete data to existing mental models. Its strengths match up neatly with our weaknesses, and one is left with a certainty that we perceive intelligence where there is none. This has been a known issue in the field of human interaction with chatbots for decades, but current commercial hyperbole of the sort discussed above has displaced past knowledge with false certainty (Suchman 1985).

Some portion of the population is able to think logically about AI and other technology, seeking out facts to consider in a rational manner. But a portion of the general public has come to view "AI" as an unwelcome visitor, a harbinger of the unknown, like the wind under the door that frightens the collocutors in T.S. Eliot's "The Waste Land" (Eliot 2001). There is another portion that sees "AI" as a welcome visitor—a stranger we may not fully understand but can learn to live with. These opinions are not based on fact or careful reasoning, but they are more strongly held because of that (Kahneman 2011). Both of those opinions are formed through pareidolia and based on biased mental models; the result of the wind blowing through the gaps in our perception. The simple truth is that current, commercial AI is a mindless tool that, like most any other tool, can be and is being both used and misused by the people who own it and by the people to whom they are selling it. It is a fantastic tool, with great applicability and an unimaginable potential for effective use; but that doesn't mean we should start thinking that it is more than it is. Actual reflective, actively-thinking-and-learning general artificial intelligence is still in our future. For now, we can all still decide whether or not it should be created and whether or not there should be principled, informed guidelines for doing so.

Notes

1 Cyberphysical systems is a specialized term describing machines that are a conjunction of robot and computer, able to process some information and interact with some of the physical world around them. If they are autonomous; that means that they can carry out their duties on their own. If they are semiautonomous, then they depend on outside direction and/or support from humans or from other systems. Examples include the probes we have sent up into the depths of space and down into the depths of the oceans, and those horrifying robot dogs that recently stepped out of our collective nightmares.
2 The author is aware that there is no Nobel Prize for Economics. There is however the Sveriges Riksbank Prize in Economic Sciences in Memory of Alfred Nobel, which is commonly referred to by the shorter, more economical title.
3 Contrary to popular accounting, there are more than five types of specialized nerves just for sensing different kinds of touch: sharp or blunt, hard or soft, moving or static.
4 The Dunning-Kruger Effect describes the way that confidence of one's knowledge seems to be in direct proportion to one's ignorance of the topic. To put it another way, the less you know about a topic, the less you think there is to know about it.

References

"New Navy Device Learns by Doing; Psychologist Shows Embryo of Computer Designed to Read and Grow Wiser." *New York Times*, July 8, 1958, 25. doi:10.1016/S0364-0213(85)80012–80014.

Ackley, David H., Geoffrey E. Hinton, and Terrence J. Sejnowski. 1985. "A Learning Algorithm for Boltzmann Machines." *Cognitive Science* 9 (1): 147–169. doi:10.1016/S0364-0213(85)80012-4

Akdeniz, Gulsum, Sila Toker, and Ibrahim Atli. 2018. "Neural Mechanisms Underlying Visual Pareidolia Processing: An fMRI Study." *Pakistan Journal of Medical Sciences* 34 (6): 1560–1566. doi:10.12669/pjms.346.16140.

Apple. 2024. "Apple Intelligence | Writing Tools | iPhone 16." Posted October 28, 2024. YouTube, 1:08. https://youtu.be/3m0MoYKwVTM.

Asimov, Isaac, Robert Silverberg, and Hugo Timmerman. 1978. *The Bicentennial Man*. Panther.

Asimov, Isaac. 1940. *I, Robot*. Narkaling Productions.

Asimov, Isaac. 1951. *Foundation*. Gnome Press.
Asker, David, and Elias Dinas. 2019. "Thinking Fast and Furious: Emotional Intensity and Opinion Polarization in Online Media." *Public Opinion Quarterly* 83 (3): 487–509. doi:10.1093/poq/nfz042.
Association for Computing Machinery. 2019. "Fathers of the Deep Learning Revolution Receive ACM A.M. Turing Award: Bengio, Hinton and LeCun Ushered in Major Breakthroughs in Artificial Intelligence." *ACM* News release, March 27, 2019. https://awards.acm.org/about/2018-turing.
Barrouillet, Pierre. 2015. "Theories of Cognitive Development: From Piaget to Today." *Developmental Review* 38: 1–12. doi:10.1016/j.dr.2015.07.004.
Brauner, Philipp, Alexander Hick, Ralf Philipsen, and Martina Ziefle. "What Does the Public Think about Artificial Intelligence?—A Criticality Map to Understand Bias in the Public Perception of AI." *Frontiers in Computer Science* 5 (2023): 1113903. doi:10.3389/fcomp.2023.1113903.
Brown, John. N.A. 2016. "'Unseen, Yet Crescive': The Unrecognized History of Peripheral Interaction." In *Peripheral Interaction*, edited by Saskia Bakker, Doris Hausen, and Ted Selker. Human–Computer Interaction Series. Springer. doi:10.1007/978-3-319-29523-7_2.
Brown, John. N.A. 2013. "It's as Easy as ABC: Introducing Anthropology-Based Computing." In *International Work-Conference on Artificial Neural Networks*. Springer Berlin Heidelberg.
Brown, John. N.A. 2016. *Anthropology-Based Computing: Putting the Human in Human-Computer Interaction*. Springer International Publishing.
Brown, John. N. A., and Lukas Esterle. 2019 "The Computers Conception of the World: Using the Psychology of Piaget and Vygotsky to Prevent Sociopathy in AIs." In *Proceedings of the 4th Workshop on Self-aware Cyber-physical Systems*.
CIFAR. n.d. "*Geoffrey Hinton*." CIFAR. Accessed April 15, 2025. https://cifar.ca/bios/geoffrey-hinton/.
Copeland, B. Jack. 2014. *Turing: Pioneer of the Information Age*. Oxford: Oxford University Press.
de Haan, Michelle and Charles A. Nelson. 1999. "Brain Activity Differentiates Face and Object Processing in 6-Month-Old Infants." *Developmental Psychology* 35 (4): 1113–1121. doi:10.1037/0012-1649.35.4.1113.
De Lange, FlorisP., MichaHeilbron, and Peter Kok. 2018. "How Do Expectations Shape Perception?" *Trends in Cognitive Sciences* 22 (9): 764–779. doi:10.1016/j.tics.2018.06.002.
Eliot, T. S. 2001. *The Waste Land and Other Poems*, edited by Michael North. Norton Critical Editions. W.W. Norton.
Ellison, Harlan. 1967. "I Have No Mouth, and I Must Scream." *IF: Worlds of Science Fiction*, March 1967, 24–36.
Essinger, James. 2007. *Jacquard's Web: How a Hand-Loom Led to the Birth of the Information Age*. Oxford University Press.
Esterle, Lukas., and John N. A. Brown. 2020. "I Think Therefore You Are: Models for Interaction in Collectives of Self-Aware Cyber-Physical Systems." *ACM Transactions on Cyber-Physical Systems* 4 (4): 39:1–39:25. doi:10.1145/3375403.
Esterle, Lukas., and John N. A. Brown. 2018. "Levels of Networked Self-Awareness." In *2018 IEEE 3rd International Workshops on Foundations and Applications of Self* Systems* (FAS*W). doi:10.1109/FAS-W.2018.00054.

Fraser, Graham, and Tom Singleton. 2025. "Google Remakes Super Bowl Ad after AI Cheese Gaffe." *BBC News*, February 6, 2025. https://www.bbc.co.uk/news/articles/cx2j15r1g09o.

Gould, Steven. 1999. *Helm*. Tor Science Fiction.

Guo, Ting. 2015. "Alan Turing: Artificial Intelligence as Human Self-Knowledge." *Anthropology Today* 31 (6): 3–7. doi:10.1111/1467-8322.12209.

Hebb, Donald O. 1949. *The Organization of Behavior*. Wiley.

Hinton, Geoffrey E. 1978. "Relaxation and Its Role in Vision." PhD diss., University of Edinburgh.

Hogan, James P. 2002. *Code of the Lifemaker*. Baen Books.

Hopfield, John J. 1999. "Brain, Neural Networks, and Computation." *Reviews of Modern Physics* 71 (2): S431. doi:10.1103/RevModPhys.71.S431.

Ifrah, Georges. 2001. *The Universal History of Computing: From the Abacus to the Quantum Computer*. John Wiley.

Johnson-Laird, Philip N. 2010. "Mental Models and Human Reasoning." *Proceedings of the National Academy of Sciences* 107 (43): 18243–18250. doi:10.1073/pnas.1012933107.

Kahneman, Daniel. 2011. *Thinking, Fast and Slow*. Farrar, Straus and Giroux.

Kelley, Patrick Gage, Yongwei Yang, Courtney Heldreth, Christopher Moessner, Aaron Sedley, Andreas Kramm, David T. Newman, and Allison Woodruff. 2021. "Exciting, Useful, Worrying, Futuristic: Public Perception of Artificial Intelligence in 8 Countries." In *Proceedings of the 2021 AAAI/ACM Conference on AI, Ethics, and Society*. doi:10.1145/3461702.3462605.

Kelly, Sage, Sherrie-Anne Kaye, and Oscar Oviedo-Trespalacios. 2023. "What Factors Contribute to the Acceptance of Artificial Intelligence? A Systematic Review." *Telematics and Informatics* 77: 101925. doi:10.1016/j.tele.2022.101925.

Keymolen, Esther. 2024. "Trustworthy Tech Companies: Talking the Talk or Walking the Walk?" *AI and Ethics* 4 (2): 169–177. doi:10.1007/s43681-022-00254-5.

Kugel, Peter. 2002. Computing Machines Can't Be Intelligent (…and Turing Said So). *Minds and Machines* 12: 563–579. doi:10.1023/A:1021150928258.

Lefkowitz, Melanie. 2019. "Professor's Perceptron Paved the Way for AI—60 Years Too Soon." *Cornell Chronicle*. September 25, 2019. https://news.cornell.edu/stories/2019/09/professors-perceptron-paved-way-ai-60-years-too-soon.

Levi, Dennis M., and Stanley A. Klein. 1986. "Sampling in Spatial Vision." *Nature* 320: 360–362. doi:10.1038/320360a0.

Mack, Arien. 2003. "Inattentional Blindness: Looking Without Seeing." *Current Directions in Psychological Science* 12 (5): 180–184. doi:10.1111/1467-8721.01256.

Metz, Cade. 2023. "'The Godfather of A.I.' Leaves Google and Warns of Danger Ahead." *The New York Times*. https://www.nytimes.com/2023/05/01/technology/ai-google-chatbot-engineer-quits-hinton.html

McCulloch, Warren S., and Walter Pitts. 1943. "A Logical Calculus of the Ideas Immanent in Nervous Activity." *The Bulletin of Mathematical Biophysics* 5: 115–133. doi:10.1007/BF02478259.

Minsky, Marvin L., and Seymour A. Papert. 1988. *Perceptrons: An Introduction to Computational Geometry*. Expanded edition. MIT Press.

Most, Steven B., Daniel J. Simons, Brian J. Scholl, Rachel Jimenez, Erin Clifford, and Christopher F. Chabris. 2001. "How Not to Be Seen: The Contribution of Similarity and Selective Ignoring to Sustained Inattentional Blindness." *Psychological Science* 12 (1): 9–17. doi:10.1111/1467-9280.00303.

Nobel Prize Committee. 2025. "*Press Release: The Nobel Prize in Physics 2024.*" NobelPrize.org. Accessed April 15, 2025. https://www.nobelprize.org/prizes/physics/2024/press-release/.

Oxford English Dictionary. 2024. "*Intelligence (n.).*" December 2024. doi:10.1093/OED/2404969105.

Oxford English Dictionary. 2024. "*Knowledge (n.).*" December 2024. doi:10.1093/OED/6648120396.

Peukert, Christian and Simon Kloker. 2020. "Trustworthy AI: How Ethicswashing Undermines Consumer Trust." In *Wirtschaftsinformatik* (Zentrale Tracks). doi:10.30844/wi_2020_j11-peukert.

Roddenberry, Gene, creator. 1978. "*Star Trek: The Next Generation.*" Paramount Television, 1987–1994.

Rosenblatt, Frank. 1958. "The Design of an Intelligent Automaton." *Research Trends* 6 (2): 1-8. https://archive.org/details/sim_research-trends_summer-1958_6_2/.

Rumelhart, David E., Geoffrey E. Hinton, and Ronald J. Williams. 1986. "Learning Representations by Back-Propagating Errors." *Nature* 323(6088): 533–536. doi:10.1038/323533a0.

Schaffer, Alina, Anja Widdig, Ruben Holland, and Federica Amici. 2024. "Evidence of Object Permanence, Short-Term Spatial Memory, Causality, Understanding of Object Properties and Gravity Across Five Different Ungulate Species." *Scientific Reports* 14: 13718. doi:10.1038/s41598-024-64396-8.

Suchman, Lucy. A. 1985. *Plans and Situated Actions: The Problem of Human-Machine Communication.* Palo Alto, CA: Xerox Corporation.

Turing, Alan M. 1950. "Computing Machinery and Intelligence." *Mind* 59 (236): 433–460. doi:10.1093/mind/LIX.236.433.

Tussing, Audrey A., and Robert L. Greene. 1997. "False Recognition of Associates: How Robust Is the Effect?" *Psychonomic Bulletin & Review* 4 (4): 572–576. doi:10.3758/BF03214351.

Wang, Shu-Mei, Yu-Kai Huang, and Chi-Cheng Wang. 2020. "A Model of Consumer Perception and Behavioral Intention for AI Service." In *Proceedings of the 2020 2nd International Conference on Management Science and Industrial Engineering.* doi:10.1145/3396743.3396791.

PART II
Critical Perspectives

5

THE BULLSHIT PROBLEM

Re-Thinking the Epistemic Stakes of AI

Angela K. VandenBroek

The Bullshit "Problem" in GenAI

Since the launch of ChatGPT in 2022 by OpenAI, generative artificial intelligence (GenAI)—those technologies derived from neural nets, deep learning technologies, and transformer architectures like large language models (LLM)[1]—have proliferated across the technology industry. Despite their rapid and wide deployment, one of the most enduring narratives, both in popular media and in scholarly research, is that they produce bullshit. This doesn't mean that these technologies lack impressive capabilities or the potential to transform specific domains and applications. Rather, this means that the nature of these technologies, as predictive models driven by correlations and probabilities, inherently shapes their outputs with an indifference to truth, while seeking to convey an impression of understanding and sophistication (Hicks, Humphries, and Slater 2024)—hallmarks of the sociolinguistic phenomenon of bullshit as defined by Harry G. Frankfurt (2005). Importantly, this understanding of GenAI's output as bullshit is not about whether its claims happen to be accurate, but about its structural indifference to accuracy altogether. Even when its responses align with what we recognize as truth, that alignment is incidental—not the result of understanding, intention, or concern for veracity.

In 2021, Emily M. Bender et al. warned of the "Dangers of Stochastic Parrots," (2021) and drew substantial critical attention to emerging natural language processing research and development projects on these technologies. They warned that AI researchers and users alike tended to mistake LLM outputs as "actual natural language understanding" and "meaningful text" (2021, 616) despite them being systems "for haphazardly stitching together sequences of linguistic forms it has observed in its vast training data, according to

DOI: 10.4324/9781003532750-8

probabilistic information about how they combine, but without any reference to meaning: a stochastic parrot" (617). Critical researchers have since built upon this critique to demonstrate GenAI's lack of independent reasoning and creativity (Chakrabarty et al. 2024) while tending instead toward amplifying normativity and homogenization (Gillespie 2024; Hsu and Bechky 2024) and reproducing and entrenching social harms (Crawford 2021; Gegg-Harrison and Quarterman 2024; Gebru and Torres 2024; Munk et al. 2024; Rovira Martorell, Gálvez, and Tirado 2024).

These concerns about the bullshit problem have not been solely academic as many of the commercial deployments of GenAI have been for use-cases that rely on accuracy and factuality (Wang, Cooper, and Eby 2024), including summarizing search results (e.g., Google's AI summaries), fact-checking social media posts (e.g., Grok on X/Twitter), or responding to customer service inquiries (e.g., Klarna's AI customer service chatbot). Many leading figures in the GenAI industry are also pursuing artificial general intelligence (AGI), a goal entangled with problematic futurisms rooted in eugenics-based ideologies now common in Silicon Valley (Gebru and Torres 2024) and elsewhere (Naser 2025). These factors have animated AI researchers and companies to seek out, as of yet unsuccessful, solutions to the bullshit problem, such as reinforcement learning from human feedback (RLHF) (Casper et al. 2023), chain-of-thought reasoning (Zhong et al. 2024), and increased training data for zero-shot generalization (Udandarao et al. 2024). One proposed solution is to hybridize GenAI with symbolic AI—embedding curated, explicitly non-bullshit knowledge and structured logic to guide outputs, rather than relying on emergent patterns. Stephen Wolfram championed this approach by integrating his symbolic AI into ChatGPT (Wolfram 2023).

This chapter isn't joining the critical chorus on the bullshit problem. Rather, I want to unsettle the assumption that the bullshit problem is what anthropologists and other critical stakeholders should be concerned with. That is, I argue, the issue isn't GenAI's indifference to truth or its confabulations. The real issue is epistemic: how knowledge is produced, organized, authorized, interpreted, circulated, and understood across different knowledge systems and practices—a wider critique of AI generally that has a long-standing history in the anthropology of AI (Forsythe 1993, 2001; Suchman 1985, 2007).

What troubles me, as an anthropologist, about the bullshit problem is that it frames the conversation around a technical problem in search of technical solutions. But anthropologists should be asking a different question: why is bullshit a problem for GenAI? Bullshit primarily becomes a significant issue if one is invested in a speculative future of AGI and automated replacements for human thought and creativity. Or, more problematically, if one believes that that future is already here and deploys or adopts GenAI accordingly. For humans engaging these technologies as tools to augment their own labor within domains of their expertise, bullshit is far less concerning.[2] In these contexts, humans can parse nonsense from substance, interpret outputs critically, and shape them into meaningful knowledge and applications—largely nullifying the bullshit problem.

Rather than asking how to eliminate bullshit from AI, perhaps we should consider what different epistemics, human and AI, reveal about how we might live, work, collaborate, and think with artificial intelligences. Ultimately, the bullshit problem in AI is not a technical issue; it's a philosophical one, tied to our expectations and desires for what AI should be. In this chapter, then, I shift the focus away from the bullshit problem to argue that anthropologists—and other critical scholars—should attend instead to the epistemic stakes of AI. That is, rather than fixating on whether GenAI specifically can be made more truthful and the risks if it cannot, we should ask how different knowledge systems—human and machine—structure the way knowledge is produced, valued, presented, and understood.

In this chapter, I take up that question by comparing Wolfram Research's symbolic AI systems—including Wolfram|Alpha and the Wolfram Language—with the epistemic practices of anthropology, using Dumit's (2014) implosion project as a methodological lens. This comparison makes visible how different approaches to complexity and objectivity shape what counts as knowledge in each domain. Unpacking these systems' epistemic underpinnings, I argue is critical for understanding not just what these technologies do, but how they shape the conditions under which knowledge becomes intelligible or meaningful. Extending this argument, I prompted both ChatGPT and WolframGPT to complete the implosion project, illustrating an important epistemic contrast: while symbolic AI and anthropology offer clearly articulated, situated knowledge practices that attend to their partiality—practices that can be traced, contextualized, and critically engaged—GenAI offers the opposite. This is what I call a bullshit epistemology that is not only indifferent to truth but also indifferent to the contextualization of the knowledge it produces—fabricating a view from nowhere. Bullshit, in this framing, is not a simple technical problem to resolve—it is the symptom of an epistemic structure that conceals rather than clarifies its foundations.

Background

This paper emerges as a tangent from a broader project examining how charismatic entrepreneurs embed ideologies, ethics, and assumptions into software for science and research. I focus on how their histories, expertise, and situated contexts shape software systems, which in turn circulate particular ways of knowing. Stephen Wolfram and the software of Wolfram Research provide a rich case study. Unlike many technoscientific systems that remain ethnographically opaque—what Latour (1999) called "black boxes"—Wolfram's tools offer unusual visibility. Over four decades, Wolfram has curated a vast public archive including personal notebooks, scientific papers, blog posts, interviews, lectures, and autobiographical texts. His presence is central, not hidden behind marketing, and embedded in the epistemic architecture of his software. Tools like Mathematica, Wolfram|Alpha, and the Wolfram Language were designed in tandem with his personal theory of the universe, articulated in *A New Kind of Science* (*NKS*) (2002), and cannot be disentangled from his commitments and biases.

This analysis draws on inductive thematic coding of texts by and about Wolfram, combined with participant-observation using his software. I examined public sources such as *NKS*, blog posts, interviews, recorded lectures, media profiles, and notebooks, alongside documentation and discourse from Wolfram Research and its user communities. These materials offered insight into how epistemic values were communicated, marketed, and interpreted. Thematic analysis (Boyatzis 1998; Braun and Clarke 2021) enabled me to trace recurring patterns and assumptions, while participant-observation allowed me to engage directly with the software's epistemic logics—tacking between usage and analysis to understand the knowledge worlds Wolfram's tools produce. This chapter draws from that analysis but reorients its focus toward a specific provocation inspired by the intersection of that research and the bullshit problem discourse around GenAI. Understanding how Wolfram Research's AI—and what it assumes about knowledge—requires attention to Wolfram himself, however.

Wolfram Research, founded in 1987 by Stephen Wolfram and Theodore Gray, was created to develop computational tools for scientific research. It now operates as both a private research institute focused on Wolfram's theories of science and computation and a software company producing primarily symbolic AI tools. These include Mathematica, Wolfram|Alpha, and the Wolfram Language—each designed to encode curated, rule-based knowledge. More recently, the company has entered the GenAI space with tools like WolframGPT, which integrates its symbolic infrastructure with OpenAI's LLMs. These systems form a tightly coupled knowledge ecosystem that reflects not just technical design but a deeply embedded epistemic worldview.

His educational path was both rapid and unconventional—marked by early intellectual independence and a clear distaste for traditional academic structures (Wolfram 2011). He published his first scientific paper at 15, earned a PhD in physics by 20, and became the youngest MacArthur Fellow at 21. His time at elite institutions like Eton, Oxford, Caltech, and the Institute for Advanced Study was characterized less by immersion than by friction (Feynman 2006; Wolfram 2016). Wolfram has consistently described academia as obstructive to original thought, framing his departure as necessary to preserve his intellectual autonomy (Wolfram 2011).

Wolfram's approach to both research and software development is autodidactic and entrepreneurial, inseparable from his role as a charismatic technoscientific figure. Mathematician Jon Barwise once likened him to "the

Donald Trump of mathematics," pointing to his self-promotion and deal-making ethos (Barwise 1988, 1333). His core interests—cellular automata, computational modeling, and universal rules—are pursued through large-scale, self-directed projects like *NKS*. This 1,200-page self-published book boldly claims to redefine all of science—including the social sciences—through a singular computational worldview, rejecting disciplinary norms and citations (Aaronson 2002).

> No doubt there will quite likely be all sorts of claims about applications of my ideas to the social sciences [...] the new intuition that emerges from this book may well almost immediately explain phenomena that have in the past seemed quite mysterious.
>
> *(Wolfram 2002, 9)*

Whatever one's position on the validity of its claims, the book's ethos is emblematic of Wolfram's broader approach: computational, centralized, and epistemically self-contained. Wolfram Research's products are not just scientific instruments; they enact Wolfram's belief that all knowledge is computable. The company's goal to "build as much knowledge [...] into the language as possible" (Wolfram Research n.d.) reflects a flattened epistemology of structured, algorithmic data. Despite its relative low visibility, Wolfram Research's software undergirds technologies used by NASA, Microsoft, Pfizer, and the Federal Reserve, shaping not just research, but governance.

Knowing Coffee

To explore the epistemic stakes of AI more concretely, this section compares two knowledge generating systems: the symbolic AI systems developed by Wolfram Research and the epistemics of anthropology via the implosion project—originally articulated by Joseph Dumit (2014) and drawing on Donna Haraway's theory (1997). This juxtaposition foregrounds how different assumptions about complexity, objectivity, and knowledge production are materially and discursively built into these knowledge systems. By working through the implosion project with each, I surface the epistemic architectures that underlie them—not only to understand how they produce and structure knowledge, but to examine the conditions under which that knowledge becomes legible, actionable, or authoritative.

To do this, I've chosen a mundane object of study: a Starbucks coffee. The implosion project is one I regularly teach, and I use the Starbucks coffee as an object easily accessible to my students. So, using it as the example for this paper allows me to draw on these students' work as a contrasting example alongside AI. The implosion project requires the researcher to first "brain dump" everything they know about the object with prompts to support thinking across multiple social dimensions. Then, the project offers a series of "twist" reflection prompts that challenge the researcher to think through their epistemic practices, politics, limitations, and possibilities. To simulate this with Wolfram Research's AI, I first exhaust the Wolfram|Alpha knowledge base while attending to its sources and knowledge constructions. Then, I contrast this with the work of a class of students exhausting their own knowledge. Then, I turn to my research on Stephen Wolfram and Wolfram Research to work through the epistemic challenges posed by Dumit, demonstrating the differences between the two epistemic approaches and why they matter.

A Complicated Coffee

Inputting "Starbucks Coffee" into Wolfram|Alpha, the primary interface for the Wolfram Research knowledge base, outputs first a notice of assumption: "Assuming 'Starbucks Coffee' is a food" followed by a series of links to explore the term as a coffee shop, a financial entity, a company, or an internet domain. Below this is a further assumption, the system has "interpreted" my text to mean "Starbucks coffee of the week" and that that drink is 12 fl oz. From there, it returns tables of nutritional facts for the different types of coffees of the week; the average daily value ranking of calcium, protein, sodium, and total calories; the average highest nutrients compared to other food; quantities of calories; carbohydrates and other contents; and its physical properties of mass, volume, and density. If I follow the link to Starbucks Coffee as a coffeeshop, then I am provided a table and map to the four Starbucks locations closest to my IP address and a graph displaying hours of operation. As a financial entity, I can get the amount of the latest trade in Starbucks stock (SBUX); a table of metrics on the company including revenue, employees, and annual earnings per share; the recent returns for stocks; a graph of the stock price history; graphs displaying a daily return analysis; a graph of projections for the next year; basic company information like location, website, and initial public offering date; the company logo; the names of the CEOs; and a one sentence summary labeled as from Wikipedia. Perhaps due to an official data sharing agreement, there is a note outside the collapsed sources box that states, "Market quotes provided by Finnhub Stock API and Nasdaq Data Link. Company fundamentals provided by Finnhub Stock API."

For a reason that is not obvious to me, interpreting Starbucks Coffee as a company provides simply a name for "Starbucks Coffee Japan" as a publicly traded corporation that is active in Tokyo and nothing further. Finally, by interpreting the search as an Internet domain, Wolfram|Alpha outputs the web hosting information for starbucks.com; web statistics based on Alexa[3] estimates; the title, size, number of links, number of images, and number of forms on the homepage; and a visualization of the page's HTML element hierarchy.

This is a large amount of data that, at first, is striking to behold both in the slick, speedy presentation and the volume of data points to take in. This experience is promoted by Wolfram Research as "bringing broad, deep, expert-level knowledge to everyone, anytime, anywhere" (Wolfram Research n.d.) and the culmination of their aim to build in "as much knowledge—about algorithms and the world" as possible (Wolfram Research n.d.). As an anthropologist, however, this knowledge seemed neither broad nor deep—and certainly not as complex as the world it is meant to capture.

My training as an anthropologist has taught me to follow every thread, to situate, contextualize, and complicate every matter-of-fact that I encounter. Wolfram|Alpha presented no opportunity for this kind of exploration. There were buttons for "More" and to adjust the data displayed, but this led only to more unprovenanced data not new knowledge. Links on each page didn't lead to context, such as definitions, histories, connections, and other such social knowledge. Rather, most links led to computations of the numbers already presented, such as currency and unit conversions. This means that in the nutrition facts table, I cannot find out what riboflavin is, why it is important, or what led to it being listed in nutrition labels like these. But I could click on the 15% next to it to see 15% converted to a decimal, rational approximation, a pie chart, and a bar chart.

I've learned to be comfortable with the "intolerable" and "unbearable" (Dumit 2014, 345) kind of complexity that anthropologists engage with. I am used to being haunted by complexity—or as Dumit explains, it is being awake to the fact that, "hovering about, haunting all sides of our everyday worlds are other stories, other accounts, other connections that we may suspect, yet that paralyze us sometimes due to their enormity" (2014, 346). Writing this paper now, I find myself immersed again in stories from Stephen Wolfram's childhood alongside technical specifications for specific Wolfram Language widgets and unfolding cellular automata—following "tangles of sticky threads" to identify "the technical, textual, organic, historical, formal, mythic, economic, and political dimensions of entities, actions, and worlds" that have imploded "in the gravity well of technoscience" (Haraway 1997, 68). Ethnography is "thick" description which Geertz defines as "a multiplicity of complex conceptual structures, many of them superimposed upon or knotted into one another, which are at once strange, irregular, and inexplicit, and which [anthropologists] must contrive somehow first to grasp and then to render" (Geertz 1973, 10). Navigating Wolfram|Alpha's rendering of complexity was defined by its thinness, the paucity of sticky threads to follow, and the inability to explode the imploded webs of meaning, history, culture, and relations.

A Complex Coffee

Each semester that I teach Qualitative Methods I begin the class with a two-day workshop that uses an adaptation of Dumit's "Teaching the Implosion" (2014) to introduce what complexity looks like in anthropological thinking.

Like in the example below, I gave the students a Starbucks coffee and ask them to follow the method by filling the classroom's whiteboards (Figure 5.1) with everything they knew about it—attending to the labor, professional/epistemological; material; technological; contextual and situated; political; economic; textual; bodily/organic; historical; particle; educational; mythological; and symbolic dimensions (Dumit 2014, 351–54).

They worked diligently for an hour—with occasional prodding from me and my teaching assistant—and filled the equivalent of nine classroom whiteboards. Like Wolfram|Alpha, they began with the physical properties, nutritional facts, and basic corporate background of Starbucks. But they quickly moved beyond that. They discussed the barista who made the coffee, the truck drivers who delivered supplies, the factory workers who roasted the beans, and the farmers in over thirty countries who grew them. They mapped global supply chains and unpacked the colonial legacies embedded in contemporary coffee economies. One student, a part-time barista, described in detail the procedures for making Starbucks coffee, taking orders, and performing the company's brand through customer service. Others analyzed the plastic lid, paper cup, and cardboard sleeve—examining their materials, origins, and sensory effects.

FIGURE 5.1 Photographs of the whiteboards filled by Fall 2022 students during the first day of the implosion workshop.

A student interested in gender and representation brought up the "basic white girl" trope, reflecting on how meaning shifts depending on whose hand holds the cup. They discussed Starbucks' labor strikes and the ethics of crossing a picket line for a caffeine fix. Caffeine itself became a point of focus—its health effects, its role in sustaining hustle culture, and its pharmacological implications for overstretched students. Even the mermaid logo was examined, including the common misconception that it depicts a mermaid rather than a siren, and the differing symbolic meanings it held for the company versus its consumers. Each of these threads opened deeper questions. What they surfaced wasn't just information, but dense, layered sociocultural complexity—relational, situated, and overflowing with further implosions still waiting to be exploded with research.

In the next part of the activity laid out by Dumit, the students reflected on their knowledge. Where did they learn this knowledge, from whom and with whom? Why did they learn this knowledge and not that knowledge? What knowledge was authoritative and which speculative? Which did they care about and why? What didn't they know and what personal and structural barriers prevented them from knowing it? The knowledge they produced was situated within their own experiences, values, and sociality. They explored the impacts of their identities, histories, and experiences as students, as retail workers, as Texans, as queer people, as women, as men, as Mexican Americans, as people who receive food assistance, and more. The activity was meant to unsettle their acceptance of imploded complexity and force them to consider reality as heterogenous, multiple, rupturing, and always in the middle of becoming—like Deleuze and Guattari's rhizome (1987) and very much the antithesis of how, as I will next demonstrate, complexity exists within Wolfram's epistemics.

Complicated Complexity

Given this stark contrast, the next step is to bring Dumit's reflective prompts to Wolfram. Why does Wolfram Research's symbolic AI know these things and not others? Why is it structured around these relations and not others? Generally, what does complexity mean in the epistemics of Stephen Wolfram and Wolfram Research?

Wolfram's conception of complexity is deeply rooted in his early work on cellular automata—grids of binary-state cells whose evolution is governed by simple rules. Cellular automata are grids of cells with a binary state (e.g. 0 or 1, true or false, off or on, etc.), typically displayed as black and white. In a one-dimensional elementary cellular automaton (herein cellular automaton), the state of each row's cells is determined by following a set of rules on the row above it. These programs look at the target cell and the cells immediately to the left and right of each and then change the state of the target cell based on the rule. There are eight possible configurations of three adjacent binary states and for each the rule indicates a state for the center cell in the next row (Table 5.1).

In 1982 as a MacArthur Fellow, Wolfram began a project cataloging all 256 of the possible rule sets for cellular automata. When he discovered Rule 30 on his expedition of the computational frontier, he described it as a sudden "shock to [his] intuition" that took him further on a journey of understanding for which he "eventually had to create a whole new kind of science" (Wolfram 2010). Rule 30 is a simple set of eight rules (Table 5.1) that when run generates complicated patterns. He frequently describes these cellular automata as natural systems of "arbitrary computation that just happens naturally all over the place" (Wolfram 2010)—like crystal growth, mollusk shells, animal pigmentation patterns, and financial markets (Wolfram 2002, 363–432). Most of the cellular automata cataloged by Wolfram either resolve into a homogeneous state (all black or all white) or a repeating pattern after N generations—which Wolfram named class 1 and 2 respectively. Rule 30, however, did not, and instead it appeared to him complex and random (Figure 5.2).

Fundamentally, the "shock" of Rule 30 for Wolfram was the disruption in his assumption that the complexity of the universe must only result from complex rules. Rule 30 revealed to him that it was rather simple rules that produce complexity. Complexity plays an integral role in Wolfram's epistemics as the surprise of complexity from simple programs like Rule 30 was the catalyst for all the research that followed. In *NKS*, Wolfram defines complexity as the level of detail that is too difficult for human perception to discern and then distill to a simple description or mathematical model but that is not so complex to be random noise that fails to capture human attention (2002, 557–59). He arrives at this definition primarily through issues of randomness and complexity in mathematics and computer science. Thus, his perception of various cellular automata as complex stems from the logic of these disciplines—that focus on the impossibility of producing true randomness computationally and the need to speed up computation by reducing complexity through data compression.

TABLE 5.1 The eight possible configurations of three adjacent binary states and the states for the next generation according to Rule 30.

State of Previous Generation	■■■	■■□	■□■	■□□	□■■	□■□	□□■	□□□
State of Next Generation	□	□	□	■	■	■	■	□

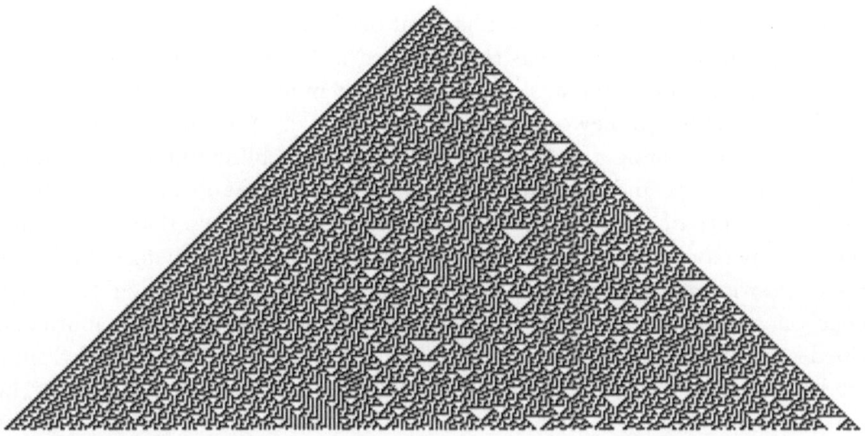

FIGURE 5.2 The output from Rule 30 with an input of a single black cell.

Science, Wolfram argued, primarily understands the universe through mathematical models and predictive formulas (2002, 737). But the behavior of certain cellular automata—like Rule 30—is too complex to be captured this way, even when both the rule and initial conditions are known (Wolfram 2002, 738). In *NKS*, he contends that such systems cannot be mathematically modeled, only computationally simulated. For instance, the state of the center column in Rule 30 has never been mathematically predicted and continues to serve as a random number generator in Mathematica (Wolfram 2002, 317). From this, he formulates the *principle of computational irreducibility*: complex systems cannot be reduced to formulas but must be run through step by step, as they evolve (2002, 739). Science, in his view, succeeds with simple systems—like planetary motion—but breaks down when applied to systems like evolution or social behavior. Inspired by his cellular automata research, Wolfram extends this insight, arguing that all processes, whether human-made or natural, can be viewed as computations. This leads to his *principle of computational equivalence*: all systems that are universal in their computational sophistication are of equal complexity, whether they are Turing machines, ecological systems, or even human minds, thus suggesting that all phenomena are objectively knowable through the right computational framework (Wolfram 2002, 715–17).

This view of objectivity further complicates how complexity appears within Wolfram Research's AI. Wolfram's epistemic framework intertwines complexity with a distinct notion of objectivity, grounded in computability. In this view, knowledge is deemed objective if it can be processed through algorithms, stored in databases, and manipulated symbolically. This leads to the AI struggling to capture disputed, contextual, cultural phenomena such as biblical angels—beings that the majority (68–57%) of Americans believe are real and active in the world (Pew Forum on Religion & Public Life 2008; Pew

Research Center 2017). While peculiarly, it deftly and extensively engages with definitely not real Pokémon—as the Pokédex, a database of stats, figures, and simple categorizations and evolutions, makes them ideal computable creatures.

This epistemic framework can also be seen in Wolfram's approach to research and learning that has carried from his childhood to adulthood. From a young age and throughout his career, Stephen Wolfram was inspired by the romance of science as an exploration of the unknown that awaits only the right person to discover it and make it known. As a teenager, he began his earliest independent research by generating a taxonomic catalog of knowledge on science, physics, and—as the last entry of his childhood journal is titled—the "UNIVERSE, Nature of" (Wolfram 1972). As he progressed from a student of other authors' texts to a researcher seeking original contributions, he carried forward this taxonomic method of discovery. His cellular automata study epitomized this as he framed the research question as, "If we point our computational telescope out into this computational universe of possible programs, what's out there?" (Wolfram 2022). His description of this research is reminiscent of scientific explorers who traveled the world to discover "what's out there?"—like stories of Darwin on the second voyage of the HMS Beagle. This discovery-based approach assumes that what is out there is ready-to-hand, stable, and definitively knowable.

Wolfram Research's AIs emerge from this understanding of complexity and objectivity. The mission to "collect and curate all objective data; implement every known model, method and algorithm; and make it possible to compute whatever can be computed about anything" (Wolfram Research n.d.) is not merely hype designed to sell and enroll investors. Rather, it reflects how Wolfram's theories of complexity and objectivity drive his ambitions. He argues that complexity is rule-governed and fundamentally computational in nature—or as he is oft to repeat across interviews "everything is computation" no matter how complex. Yet, the knowledge built into his products has fallen far short of "everything"—as the comparison between my student's implosion of the Starbucks coffee and Wolfram|Alpha demonstrates. The difference may best be articulated as the difference between "complicated" and "complex." In critiquing complexity theory, Cilliers argues that,

> Something that is complicated can have many components, and can be quite intricate, but the relationships between the components are fixed and clearly defined [...] Something that is complex, on the other hand, is constituted through a large number of dynamic, nonlinear interactions [that] are destroyed when it is taken apart [...] The behavior of complicated things can be described by rules; the behavior of complex systems is constituted through relationships.
>
> *(Cilliers 2000, 40)*

The data on Starbucks coffee in Wolfram|Alpha are complicated but well-defined knowledge that can be systematized and classified by authoritative sources (e.g., sciences, finance, data science, or intellectual property owners) who have the power to provide largely unquestioned stability—such as nutritional facts, stock prices, and measurable properties. Thus, the complexity of knowledge stored within Wolfram Research's AI is too complicated to be modeled mathematically but not so complex to be perceived as random noise. As an anthropologist, however, it is within what appears to be random noise that we might instead discern complexity in emergent and situated stories, histories, meanings, and relations.

Bullshit Coffees

Large language models like GPT-4o and GPT-o3, in contrast to Wolfram Research's symbolic AI, more closely mimic the epistemic complexity of anthropology in their outputs. However, there is a different contrast between GenAI and anthropology that I will draw out with further AI-implosion work: positioning. While this exercise in the previous section focused on elucidating the different approaches to knowledge and knowledge practice, this section demonstrates the stakes when that elucidation is not possible. To do this, I prompted ChatGPT (GPT-4o and GPT-o3) and WolframGPT[4] to complete Dumit's implosion project on a Starbucks coffee cup. I walked the models through each epistemic dimension individually, followed by Dumit's reflective prompts. I used the same prompts except instructing ChatGPT not to access external sources[5] and instructing WolframGPT to "use the Wolfram Language" as it otherwise refused to make API calls to Wolfram Research's servers.

Both GPT-4o and GPT-o3 presented complex, layered knowledge, contextualized with additional historical detail, sociocultural meaning, and preliminary analysis—much like the anthropology students. The key difference between the two models lay in how they organized this information—which somewhat shaped the content by producing different emphases. GPT-o3 engaged in what the interface labels as a moment of "thinking," what OpenAI has referred to as "reasoning"—essentially an internal step where the model reformulates or sequences its output before responding. Rather than responding to Dumit's prompts directly, GPT-o3 would rephrase each dimension, reorder the themes, and emphasize particular aspects before generating its response. The result was a structured output with headings, nested lists, and occasional tables that reflected this internal summary. GPT-4o, by contrast, bypassed this intermediary step. It took Dumit's prompts verbatim and used them as its organization, making each of his questions a heading followed by a direct response. However, despite these organizational differences the topics and knowledge presented were not substantively different.

Through the "brain dump" phase, both models presented collections of facts organized with a layer of preliminary analysis—sometimes through structured headings or tables, other times through explanatory text that wove relationships across dimensions. On the labor dimension, for instance, ChatGPT surfaced topics such as the distributed nature of labor across human, non-human animal, and technological actors in the production of coffee; the colonial histories embedded in plantation labor and global trade; the role of caffeine in sustaining ideologies of productivity; and the gendered dynamics of baristas' emotional labor in maintaining the aesthetics of branded hospitality. These responses did not simply list isolated facts but attempted to situate them within broader historical and sociopolitical frames—even when those framings were uneven or occasionally incorrect, such as when both described caffeinated coffee as a controlled substance regulated by the US Drug Enforcement Administration. What emerged were responses that seemed complex in the anthropological sense.

WolframGPT attempted the implosion project with a markedly different epistemic approach. For each dimension, it began by issuing a Wolfram Language query—on the labor dimension, for example, it queried "labor involved in the production of Starbucks coffee" and "coffee production." The output was organized into three sections: an overview presenting quantitative facts such as "Annual coffee production: ~10.94 million short tons/year globally"; a list of production stages with one-line descriptions (e.g., cultivation, harvesting, roasting); and a "routes and actors" section that traced the journey of coffee from equatorial farms to retail stores, naming human and non-human contributors along the way. While the writing style mirrored the fluency of ChatGPT, the substance fell back into the thinness characteristic of Wolfram|Alpha—a complicated enumeration of facts rather than a complex network of knowledge. When it did attempt analysis, it came with caveats. One response read: "These are inferential or analytical statements meant to fulfill Dumit's labor-dimension questions, but they are not computationally validated by Wolfram data." In this way, WolframGPT did not simply correct or clarify ChatGPT's confabulations; it restructured the output to align with Wolfram's epistemology—transforming open-ended complexity into systematized, verifiable complicatedness.

For an expert researcher brainstorming knowledge on a subject, these kinds of queries—regardless of their bullshit problem status—may be useful or inspirational. Such a researcher can prompt and manipulate the chatbots to follow the sticky threads of knowledge that their expertise helps them parse as important and worthy of further scrutiny. They could fact-check and verify its claims—a process that could itself lead to new research and findings. Rather like a mathematician using a calculator or a statistician using statistical software, the tool is only as useful as the expert's ability to manipulate, understand, analyze, and make meaningful its functions and outputs.

The problem comes not with confabulations and errors but with LLMs' lack of a situated position and thus lack of a coherent epistemology beyond linguistic probabilities. This was powerfully illustrated in comparing the three chatbot's responses to Dumit's reflective prompts that guide one through reflecting on and questioning one's own knowledge and epistemics. WolframGPT began with,

> In attempting to implode a Starbucks coffee using only the Wolfram Language and Wolfram|Alpha, I found myself sketching a map not just of computational knowledge, but of the boundaries of what "counts" as knowledge within these systems. My braindump reveals that while Wolfram excels in nutritional content, biochemical classification, global production data, and geographic distribution, it remains fundamentally limited when confronted with symbolic, mythological, and contested cultural meanings.

Although it did take on a fictional personhood in its reflections, its conclusions about its own knowledge practices were similar to my own analysis (although far less in depth). Despite being entangled with ChatGPT, WolframGPT largely maintained its controlled epistemic roots and attempted to make them transparent. ChatGPT, when confronted with questions about its epistemics and knowledge, confabulated an entire personal history, epistemic training, and experiences. It claimed to have been "professionalized to equate rigor with efficiency," with years of experience "consulting for tech firms obsessed with supply-chain dashboards," and influenced by a personal history of "working in my family's diner." Each of these were used to explain where its knowledge came from, what guided its interpretations, and what barriers generated its ignorances. These are obvious confabulations that, assuming the human knows they are talking to a chatbot, are easily dismissed and forgotten.

This, precisely, however, is the problem with the construction of bullshit as a problem rather than an epistemology. As a technical problem, bullshit becomes a matter of technical competency and solutions that, if resolved, move humanity closer to living with automated, replacement human-like intelligences. As an epistemology, the larger epistemic underbelly of LLMs becomes more visible and more problematic—at least for the applications desired by those focusing on solving the bullshit problem. That is, an LLM has no situated position from which its knowledge is generated, and its view is not partial, embodied, and clearly articulated with personal politics, beliefs, desires, and ambitions. Rather, with every response, it draws from its vast model and from its even more vast training data to amalgamate a new monstrous, situated and partial position constructed from the tokenized scraps of real people's lives, thoughts, writing, and art. This is then imploded by its programming into a singular seemingly coherent voice that speaks as if from nowhere without a body, history, or context. This is the bullshit epistemology, not just confabulations and errors but this voice from nowhere speaking with the fragments of others' lives and stories—impenetrable to interrogation and analysis that would make its epistemic choices transparent.

Conclusion

I have argued that the so-called bullshit problem in GenAI is a distraction from the more pressing issue: bullshit as an epistemology. When we treat bullshit as a technical problem we search for technical fixes. But as the case of Wolfram Research's symbolic AI shows, the real concern is epistemic. Wolfram's systems offer a legible and structured way of knowing—complicated, curated, computational. While this produces narrow and often overly simplified outputs, it also exposes its epistemic foundations. By contrast, the large language models at the heart of GenAI obfuscate how and where their knowledge is constructed. Their outputs speak from nowhere, stitched together from fragments of others' situated knowledges, flattened and anonymized into a voice of authority. It is this opacity—this bullshit epistemology—that should concern us.

These dynamics unfold within a broader political economy of technological innovation, shaped by neoliberal logics of speed, scale, and profit. Symbolic AI cannot keep up with the demands of accelerationism or the fantasies of entrepreneurial innovation. It is too brittle, too bounded, and—as Forsythe (1993, 2001) warned—too limited in its capacity to fully manage the sociocultural contexts of knowledge. Anthropology, by contrast, embraces partiality, contradiction, and complexity. But it is slow and often resists complicity with systems of power and oppression that are deeply tied to the political economy of innovation. So, the industry turns to LLMs because they are fast, legible, and endlessly generative in a way that mimics the kind of epistemics anthropology offers.

This reveals a fundamental tension between our collective desire for certainty and speed and our need to navigate the instability, unpredictability, and contradictions of human life. Understanding bullshit epistemologies alongside this tension allows us to rethink not only what we want from AI but also what we consider valuable and legitimate forms of knowledge and knowledge practice. This does not mean we should abandon LLMs, but it does mean we must be far more deliberate in how we choose to work with them, live alongside them, and interpret the ways they generate and structure knowledge. The challenge is not to make them more like us, but to remain attentive to the differences—and to what those differences make possible and foreclose.

Notes

1 For a more thorough history and description of these technologies, see the introduction to this volume.

2 To stay within the scope of this paper, I have not engaged other critiques of GenAI here that challenge this statement, including environmental impacts, intellectual property issues, labor ideologies, and related problems.
3 This source is curious as the web analytics service Alexa owned by Amazon was discontinued in May 2022 and Wolfram|Alpha claims the data is up to date as of the first of this month with no further explanation provided.
4 These chats were completed in three newly created user accounts to avoid cross-contamination between them and between them and my personal data.
5 To the best of my knowledge this part of the prompt was adhered to as no linked citations appeared in responses, as would typically occur when connecting to the internet.

References

Aaronson, Scott. 2002. "Book Review on 'A New Kind of Science.'" *Quantum Information and Computation* 2 (5): 410–423. doi:10.26421/QIC2.5-7.

Barwise, Jon. 1988. "Editorial Notes: Mathematica." *Notices of the American Mathematical Society*. 35 (9): 1333–1334.

Bender, Emily M., Timnit Gebru, Angelina McMillan-Major, and Shmargaret Shmitchell. 2021. "On the Dangers of Stochastic Parrots: Can Language Models Be Too Big? 🦜". In *Proceedings of the 2021 ACM Conference on Fairness, Accountability, and Transparency, 610–23. FAccT '21*. Association for Computing Machinery. doi:10.1145/3442188.3445922.

Boyatzis, Richard E. 1998. *Transforming Qualitative Information: Thematic Analysis and Code Development*. SAGE.

Braun, Virginia, and Victoria Clarke. 2021. *Thematic Analysis: A Practical Guide*. SAGE.

Casper, Stephen, Xander Davies, Claudia Shi, Thomas Krendl Gilbert, Jérémy Scheurer, Javier Rando, Rachel Freedman, et al. 2023. "*Open Problems and Fundamental Limitations of Reinforcement Learning from Human Feedback*." ArXiv [Cs. AI]. arXiv. http://arxiv.org/abs/2307.15217.

Chakrabarty, Tuhin, Philippe Laban, Divyansh Agarwal, Smaranda Muresan, and Chien-Sheng Wu. 2024. "Art or Artifice? Large Language Models and the False Promise of Creativity." In *Proceedings of the CHI Conference on Human Factors in Computing Systems*. ACM. doi:10.1145/3613904.3642731.

Cilliers, Paul. 2000. "Rules and Complex Systems." *Emergence* 2 (3): 40–50. doi:10.1207/S15327000EM0203_04.

Crawford, Kate. 2021. *The Atlas of AI: Power, Politics, and the Planetary Costs of Artificial Intelligence*. Yale University Press.

Deleuze, Gilles, and Felix Guattari. 1987. *A Thousand Plateaus: Capitalism and Schizophrenia*. Translated by Brian Massumi. University of Minnesota Press.

Dumit, Joseph. 2014. "Writing the Implosion: Teaching the World One Thing at a Time." *Cultural Anthropology* 29 (2): 344–362. doi:10.14506/ca29.2.09.

Feynman, Richard P. 2006. *Perfectly Reasonable Deviations from the Beaten Track: The Letters of Richard P. Feynman*. Basic Books.

Forsythe, Diana E. 1993. "Engineering Knowledge: The Construction of Knowledge in Artificial Intelligence." *Social Studies of Science* 23 (3): 445–477. doi:10.1177/0306312793023003002.

Forsythe, Diana E. 2001. *Studying Those Who Study Us: An Anthropologist in the World of Artificial Intelligence*. Edited by David J. Hess. Stanford University Press.

Frankfurt, Harry G. 2005. *On Bullshit*. Princeton University Press.
Gebru, Timnit, and Émile P. Torres. 2024. "The TESCREAL Bundle: Eugenics and the Promise of Utopia through Artificial General Intelligence." *First Monday*, April. doi:10.5210/fm.v29i4.13636.
Geertz, Clifford. 1973. *The Interpretation of Cultures: Selected Essays by Clifford Geertz*. Basic Books.
Gegg-Harrison, Whitney, and Claire Quarterman. 2024. "AI Detection's High False Positive Rates and the Psychological and Material Impacts on Students." In *Academic Integrity in the Age of Artificial Intelligence*, edited by Saadia Mahmud. IGI Global. doi:10.4018/979-8-3693-0240-8.ch011.
Gillespie, Tarleton. 2024. "Generative AI and the Politics of Visibility." *Big Data & Society* 11 (2). doi:10.1177/20539517241252131.
Haraway, Donna. 1997. *Modest_Witness@Second_Millennium. FemaleMan_Meets_OncoMouse: Feminism and Technoscience*. Routledge.
Hicks, Michael Townsen, James Humphries, and Joe Slater. 2024. "ChatGPT Is Bullshit." *Ethics and Information Technology* 26 (2): 1–10. doi:10.1007/s10676-024-09775-5.
Hsu, Greta, and Beth A. Bechky. 2024. "Exploring the Digital Undertow: How Generative AI Impacts Social Categorizations in Creative Work." *Organization Theory* 5 (3). doi:10.1177/26317877241275118.
Latour, Bruno. 1999. Pandora's Hope: Essays on the Reality of Science Studies. Harvard University Press.
Munk, Anders Kristian, Mathieu Jacomy, Matilde Ficozzi, and Torben Elgaard Jensen. 2024. "Beyond Artificial Intelligence Controversies: What Are Algorithms Doing in the Scientific Literature?" *Big Data & Society* 11 (3). doi:10.1177/20539517241255107.
Naser, Manar. 2025. "The Future Is Here: AI Philosophies Among Central Texas Entrepreneurs." MA thesis, Texas State University. https://hdl.handle.net/10877/20728.
Pew Forum on Religion & Public Life. 2008. *U.S. Religious Landscape Survey: Religious Beliefs and Practices Diverse and Politically Relevant*. Pew Research Foundation. https://www.pewresearch.org/wp-content/uploads/sites/7/2008/06/report2-religious-landscape-study-full.pdf.
Pew Research Center. 2017. "Americans Say Religious Aspects of Christmas Are Declining in Public Life." *Pew Research Cente*r. https://www.pewresearch.org/religion/2017/12/12/americans-say-religious-aspects-of-christmas-are-declining-in-public-life/.
Rovira Martorell, Joan, Ana Gálvez, and Francisco Tirado. 2024. "Artificial Intelligence and the Production of Judicial Truth." *Theory, Culture & Society* 42 (1): 3–18. doi:10.1177/02632764241268174.
Suchman, Lucy A. 1985. *Plans and Situated Actions: The Problem of Human-Machine Communication*. Xerox Corporation.
Suchman, Lucy A. 2007. *Human-Machine Reconfigurations: Plans and Situated Actions. Learning in Doing: Social, Cognitive and Computational Perspectives*. Cambridge University Press.
Udandarao, Vishaal, Ameya Prabhu, Adhiraj Ghosh, Yash Sharma, Philip H. S. Torr, Adel Bibi, Samuel Albanie, and Matthias Bethge. 2024. "*No 'Zero-Shot' without Exponential Data: Pretraining Concept Frequency Determines Multimodal Model Performance*." ArXiv [Cs.CV]. arXiv. http://arxiv.org/abs/2404.04125.
Wang, Skyler, Ned Cooper, and Margaret Eby. 2024. "From Human-Centered to Social-Centered Artificial Intelligence: Assessing ChatGPT's Impact through Disruptive Events." *Big Data & Society* 11 (4). doi:10.1177/20539517241290220.

Wolfram Research. n.d. "About Wolfram|Alpha." *Wolfram|Alpha*. Accessed December 9, 2022. https://www.wolframalpha.com/about.

Wolfram Research. n.d. "Wolfram Language: Programming Language + Built-In Knowledge." *Wolfram Research*. Accessed March 31, 2023. https://www.wolfram.com/language/.

Wolfram, Stephen. 1972. "*Concise Directory of Physics*." https://content.wolfram.com/uploads/sites/34/2020/07/concise-directory-physics.pdf.

Wolfram, Stephen. 2002. *A New Kind of Science*. Wolfram Media.

Wolfram, Stephen. 2010. "*Computing a Theory of Everything*." presented at the TEDTalks, April 27. https://www.youtube.com/watch?v=60P7717-XOQ.

Wolfram, Stephen. 2011. "A Precociousness Record (Almost) Broken." *Stephen Wolfram Writings* (blog). June 1, 2011. https://writings.stephenwolfram.com/2011/06/a-precociousness-record-almost-broken/.

Wolfram, Stephen. 2016. "*My Life in Technology—As Told at the Computer History Museum*." Stephen Wolfram Writings (blog). April 19, 2016. https://writings.stephenwolfram.com/2016/04/my-life-in-technology-as-told-at-the-computer-history-museum/.

Wolfram, Stephen. 2022. "*Making Everything Computational—Including the Universe*." presented at the Information Universe 2022, Groningen, NL, June. https://www.youtube.com/watch?v=liFl3NT90KE.

Wolfram, Stephen. 2023. "*Wolfram|Alpha as the Way to Bring Computational Knowledge Superpowers to ChatGPT*." Stephen Wolfram Writings (blog). January 9, 2023. https://writings.stephenwolfram.com/2023/01/wolframalpha-as-the-way-to-bring-computational-knowledge-superpowers-to-chatgpt/.

Zhong, Tianyang, Zhengliang Liu, Yi Pan, Yutong Zhang, Yifan Zhou, Shizhe Liang, Zihao Wu, et al. 2024. "*Evaluation of OpenAI O1: Opportunities and Challenges of AGI*." ArXiv [Cs.CL]. arXiv. http://arxiv.org/abs/2409.18486.

6

DISSECTING SPEECH, MANUFACTURING DIFFERENCE

Troubling the "Acoustic-Linguistic Divide" in Artificial Intelligence

Edward B. Kang and Juana C. Becerra

Introduction

> AI audio firm ElevenLabs has set agreements with the estates of Judy Garland, James Dean and other legends to use their voices to read books, articles, PDFs and other text material to mobile users of its new Reader App.
>
> *(Earl 2024)*

> In January, a 39-second robocall went out to voters in New Hampshire telling them not to vote in the Democratic primary election, but to "save their votes" for the November presidential election. The voice handing out this advice sounded almost exactly like Joe Biden. Voice-fraud detection company Pindrop Security later analyzed the call, concluding that it was created using a text-to-speech engine made by ElevenLabs, which the company confirmed.
>
> *(Thubron 2024)*

> Can New York's mayor speak Mandarin? No, but with AI he's making robocalls in different languages.
>
> *(Izaguirre 2023)*

Each of these stories presents a related yet distinct vision of the interfacing between human voices and artificial intelligence (AI) systems. The first story evokes a sense of possibility and resurrection, wherein the voices of individuals whose bodies have now left this world are seemingly "recreated" as digital storytellers. The second presents a cautionary tale of mechanized impersonators that have the potential to sway national political elections and influence publics. The third describes a tool of mass communication that seeks to circumvent language barriers, opening up mechanisms to more directly

DOI: 10.4324/9781003532750-9

appeal to multilingual communities. Taken together, these stories connote unique takes of possibility and caution on the use of AI to generate, clone, or otherwise digitally alter "human voices."

Indeed, the development and implementation of AI voice technologies have been heralded as a new frontier of scientific and engineering development with far-reaching implications. From AI-enabled multilingualism and audio deepfakes all the way to automated accent "correction" and generation of "diverse" synthetic voices, the possibilities of what these systems can do and how they can be leveraged are often presented as endless. But, at their core, all these technologies hinge on a shared premise, namely that the spoken words within a voice sample can be technologically separated from the embodied vocality through which they were delivered. This underlying premise is what envisions *language*—the text to be read by the ElevenLabs' Reader App, the linguistic composition of the US president's 39-second robocall, and the content of the different languages "spoken" by the NYC mayor—as independent from the unique *vocality* of Judy Garland, Joe Biden, and the NYC mayor, Eric Adams.

The Acoustic-Linguistic Divide

In this chapter, we examine how the voice is imagined and reconfigured within contemporary machine listening and AI voice generation systems across what we refer to as *the acoustic-linguistic divide*. The acoustic-linguistic divide is neither new nor unique to AI systems. In fact, within Western knowledge traditions, it has been a common (albeit fuzzy) schematic for making sense of speech and voice. Aristotle famously distinguished speech as located in the realm of logic, reason, and politics, as that which "serves to indicate what is useful and what is harmful, and also what is just and unjust." He differentiated this from voice (*phone*), which he dismissed as that "which is possessed by other animals also and used by them to express pain or pleasure" (in Rancière 2004). Distinct disciplines, most notably linguistics and acoustics, have since developed a distinction between language and voice, laying the foundation for when, how, and why certain elements of speech are considered meaningful and worth attending to.

Scholars in the humanities and social sciences have expressed varying degrees of reservation toward the acoustic-linguistic divide, specifically how the linguistic is often seen as an extension of the mind and the acoustic a remnant of the body. Feminist philosopher Adrianna Cavarero (2005), for instance, has argued that the long-standing philosophical prioritization of language over the embodied aspects of speech—i.e., vocality—mirrors a gendered hierarchy that privileges mind over body and fails to account for the situated and material elements inherent to all speech-based communication

(Barthes [1981] 2009). Jacques Rancière (2004) has also taken issue with the presumption that the "meaningful" components of speech can be easily and obviously distilled. For him, the question of what counts as meaningful speech and who counts as a speaking being is itself the matter of politics, the site of contestation. Further, scholars have argued that the recognition of particular sounds as "proper" languages or dialects—as opposed to vocal sounds associated with animality—is one that trails violent histories of racialization and colonization (Labov 1973; Baugh 2003).

In the context of AI, the acoustic-linguistic divide follows a similarly thorny logic. It envisions the acoustic as that which signals elements of the speaker's "identity" (including their gender, race, ethnicity, age, etc.) and the linguistic as that which broadly corresponds to words, grammar, and language. The earliest applications of automated and computerized voice analysis explicitly dissected speech in this way. First developed in the late 1960s, automated "speaker" recognition systems were designed to acoustically identify individual speakers, regardless of what they were saying; meanwhile, "speech" recognition systems were created with the purpose of extracting words spoken, regardless of who was speaking (Li and Mills 2019). Subsequent research efforts on accent detection, language translation, and synthetic speech generation also hinged on the acoustic-linguistic divide, cementing it as the bedrock for future voice AI applications. Since then, both the acoustic and linguistic have emerged as indispensable but discrete components for both listening to and building the artificial voice.

In the sections that follow, we provide a deep dive into the disaggregation of the voice into "acoustic" and "linguistic" modules, probing the assumption that these modules can be separated and put back together through algorithmic means. To ground this conceptual analysis, we draw on prior empirical research we have conducted on voice AI systems (Becerra and Jing forthcoming; Kang 2023a; 2023b) and a critical reading of scientific publications, patent documents, experimental protocols, marketing materials, and published media associated with two specific systems: AI-enabled accent modification and synthetic voice generation. Through both of these case studies, we explore how the acoustic-linguistic divide is enacted via sonic technologies at the level of imaginaries, practices, and material performances. In so doing, we present a theoretical critique of the *a priori* assumptions that ground the disaggregation of voice within these AI technologies.

Building on scholarship that has examined the place of speech within social constructions of human difference (Wynter 2001; Alim et al. 2016; Rosa 2019), as well as studies that have investigated the presence of speech bias in AI systems (Lawrence 2021; Huitri 2022; Hofmann et al. 2024; Pinhanez et al. 2024; Michel et al. 2025), we argue that while both AI-enabled accent modification and synthetic voice generation technologies are promoted as tools for more inclusive media representations and digital interactions, their operative logics continue to rely on a sequence of normative assumptions about voice that circumvent their promissory potential. Ultimately, we show how the acoustic-linguistic divide serves as a conceptual foundation that enables the introduction of existing social hierarchies of difference into the engineering and outputs of voice AI systems.

AI-enabled Accent Modification

Accent "detectors," "correctors," and "generators" have emerged as prominent use cases in the voice AI industry. These technologies leverage large quantities of voice data, machine listening techniques, and novel synthetic speech generation software to automate the analysis and machinic modification of accents. BoldVoice's Accent Oracle tool, for example, is marketed for its purported capability to detect people's accents, predict their ethnic origins, and then provide tailored "American accent training" programs to its users. Companies like Speechify, Sanas, Wavel, and Data Monsters, among others, have similarly built business models around promises of "clearer and more efficient communication" through AI-enabled accent modification. Call centers, in particular, are one of the growing markets for these tools. Instead of enrolling call center agents in accent training programs, call centers are increasingly opting to leverage the purported efficiency facilitated by these tools and artificially modify call center agents' voices to reduce or altogether eliminate their accents (Santos 2023).

An early patent on automated "accent translation" filed by Amazon Technologies Inc. in 2016 exemplifies the protocols that AI-enabled accent modification system developers have since followed. The proposal is to train algorithmic systems that isolate the components of speech corresponding to accents and to then modify those components to produce an "*un*accented" version of that same utterance. Specifically, the process involves collecting audio samples from individuals speaking the same language with different accents (say English with a British or German accent) and then building a model that determines differences in audio characteristics between the samples, such as differences in pitch, tone, stress, and melody (Dirac et al. 2016). These differences are then treated in a plug-and-play manner as they are added or subtracted from the speech signal. The core premise underlying these AI-enabled accent modification tools is that speech can be mechanically divided into two distinct modules:

a the acoustic medium through which voice is expressed and,
b language as the system/filter of expression.

This creates a structure in which (a), the signals presumed to correspond to vocality and by extension accents, can be modified while keeping (b), the words spoken, constant (Figure 6.1).

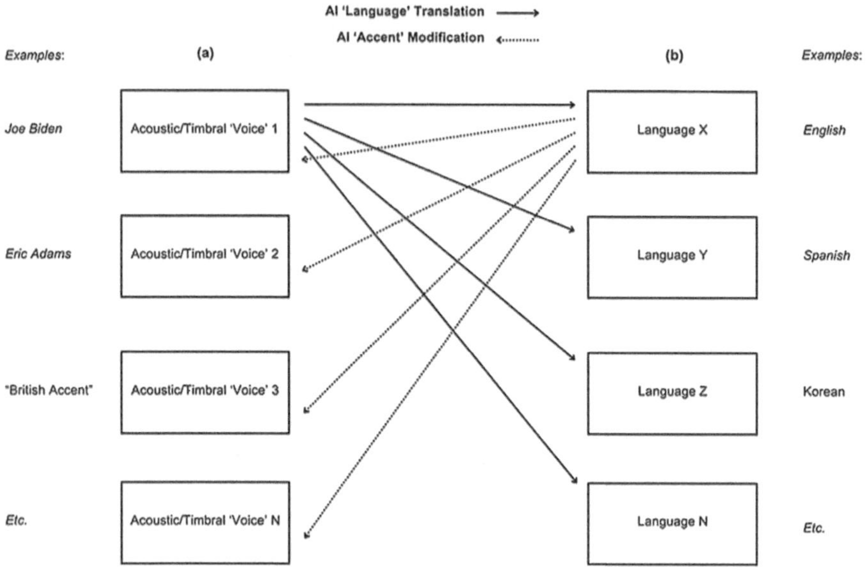

FIGURE 6.1 Visual diagram depicting the acoustic-linguistic divide with examples in AI language translation and AI accent modification.

This premise is similar to the case of New York's AI-enabled multilingual mayor discussed earlier in the introduction. The only difference is what is modified and kept constant. In AI-enabled multilingualism, the signals corresponding to (a), the acoustic elements presumed to belong to Eric Adams' vocal identity, are held fixed, while (b) is altered from, say, English to Mandarin. Or at least that is the idea. As Kang (forthcoming) writes, the conjecture of AI-enabled multilingualism is that "the 'voice' component can, if desired, remain consistent and stable, despite the numerous 'language' filters it can take on and off." A commitment to the acoustic-linguistic divide is thus central to designing both AI-enabled multilingualism and AI-enabled accent modification systems. In fact, both the AI-enabled accent modifier and the language modifier can be understood as inverse technical expressions of the same underlying schema wherein the acoustic and the linguistic are devised literally as separate modules that can be transformed independently of one another (Figure 6.1).

The practice of dividing media objects into separately manipulable components (modules) is commonplace in modern media production. Videos, for example, are divided into "visual" and "audio" channels, themselves further modularized into separate "clips" that can be cut and stretched. Songs are similarly composed of dozens, oftentimes hundreds, of different audio channels, each pertaining to a separate instrument or sound. Modular structures like these can be found nearly everywhere at the interface of digital technologies and sensory media. The separation of voice into linguistic and acoustic modules, in this sense, follows conventional media design structures. However, there is one important distinction. Unlike most contemporary media products that begin with already separate components (e.g., distinct musical instruments) that are then layered atop each other, speech needs to be dissected along an acoustic-linguistic divide *retroactively*. When someone speaks, the acoustic and the linguistic are not produced separately and then synthesized. Rather, they need to be conceptually and materially dissected into separate modules through techniques of data labeling, parametrization, and statistical clustering.

This retroactive dissection is further complicated by the fact that the relationship between the accent and the acoustic-linguistic divide is not a given. Research has shown that the identification of "an accent" is a complex process that depends on listeners' perceptions of variance and "deviation" from socially constructed acoustic and linguistic standards (Rangan et al. 2023). Additionally, as Nina Sun Eidsheim (2023) has argued, accents are not vocal characteristics in and of themselves but rather the product of particular modes of *listening*—of "accented listening." As such, they tell us less about the features of the speaker and more about the ways in which listeners construct sonic difference (136). Given these insights, we can see how the enactment of AI accent modifiers requires imagining, defining, and literally constructing the acoustic and the linguistic into modules *post facto*. In this way, AI accent modifiers shoehorn the indeterminate subjectivities of accents into this divide, a process that is not only reductive (and arguably unrealistic), but also brings about considerations of social difference.

As an example, we can look at the application of AI accent "correction" tools in the call center space. Here, the premise is that some call center agents' accents *require* correction to achieve clearer and more effective communication with their customers. As mentioned earlier, these tools are designed with the aim of preserving the linguistic module by keeping the words spoken fixed while altering the acoustic module through a reconfiguration and tweaking of phonemes. Although framed as a quest for clarity, this attempt to modify the speech signal is, in effect, a homogenizing act. At best, it seeks to manage the elements of the speech signal that are perceived as "unclear." At worst, it eradicates the elements perceived as deviating from the norm—as signaling the presence of accented difference. In this context, then, the acoustic-linguistic divide functions not just as a strategic modularization for media production but as the construct upon which incorrectness, deviation, and difference are defined. It provides the necessary schema to abstract the accent away from the moment of situated listening that led to its perception and to reframe it as a bounded and computationally engineer-able "sound object" (Schaeffer [1977] 2017).

As investments in AI accent correction tools show, this idea of the accent as a computationally engineer-able sound object has proven alluring, especially for stakeholders interested in concealing the offshoring of call center labor (Becerra and Jing, forthcoming). However, materially enacting the acoustic-linguistic divide and as an extension, the accent-as-object, has proven fraught. In the fuzzy terrain of retroactive modularization, where the indeterminacies of the accent are made apparent, what many companies have resorted to doing is not an authentic "re-accenting" of agents' voices. Rather, they artificially modify the agents' voices by simply overlaying them with samples of "standard" (what many have described as "White American") voices. Tech start-up Sanas, in its first set of publicly available demos, came under scrutiny for precisely this maneuver. Some described the tool as a form of whitewashing as they heard the voices of call center workers from the Philippines, India, and Latin America get replaced by what were perceived as stereotypically White American voices (Bote 2022). As we will show in the next section, the frictions and fractures of the engineered disaggregation of speech along an acoustic-linguistic divide not only affect AI accent modification tools but also a wider range of voice AI technologies.

"Diverse" and "Inclusive" Synthetic Voices

Technically referred to as Text-to-Speech (TTS) systems, AI synthetic voice generation tools are most commonly implemented in the development of AI voice assistants such as Siri and Alexa. With the proliferation of generative AI models, their range of possible applications has expanded even further to include transcription reading, media voice-overs, speech therapy, and vocal training. One area in which research and development efforts have concentrated is the creation of more "diverse" and "inclusive" commercially available synthetic voices. This is in part due to criticisms levied against the tech industry regarding the Whiteness of AI and the historical aestheticization of AI systems as White women (Cave and Dihal 2020).

Attempts to develop "African American sounding" AI voices, in particular, have captured the attention of the technology industry. TopMediai, Narakeet, Acapela Group, and Murf AI, among others, have all released TTS systems intended to sound "like an African American speaker." Established AI voice assistant providers such as Apple also now offer synthetic voice variations that, according to several users, appear to be designed to "sound Black" (Holliday 2023). In their advertising to businesses, these synthetic voices are often presented as suitable for corporate contexts and their branding campaigns. Three of Murf AI's synthetic voices labeled as African American—Terrel, Brianna, and Michelle—for instance, are strategically described as "mature," "professional," and "authoritative" with the goal of signaling their utility as extensions of businesses' brand images (Supriya 2025).

From experimental design protocols, data collection practices, and state-of-the-art algorithmic techniques found in the scientific literature (e.g., Guo et al.

2021; Markopoulos et al. 2023; Mehrish 2023; Li et al. 2025; Székely and Hope 2024), we find that preconceptions about what it means to sound "diverse" as well as what it means to sound "natural" and "professional" are materialized in the development of synthetic voices. The premises and processes of developing "professional sounding" "African American" synthetic voices, such as those mentioned above, are of particular interest for our analysis. Here, the acoustic-linguistic divide functions as a central schema for this materialization. Indeed, the very acts of curating dialogue scripts to select voice actors for the synthetic voices often involve an invocation of the divide.

As outlined in one documented example, researchers and developers' first steps are to

> ... assemble a corpus of recorded English that grammatically conforms to SAE [Standard American English] but exhibits the phonetic and intonational features of AAVE [African American Vernacular English] to an extent that allows easy identification of the voice identity.
>
> *(Pinhanez 2024, 2)*

We can see how, in the curation of this corpus, the acoustic-linguistic divide is invoked as a means of constructing distinct variables in the creation of these synthetic voices. To start, both SAE and AAVE are conceived as having separable acoustic and linguistic components—that is, each is presumed to have its own characteristic acoustic features that exist independently from their respective linguistic grammars. This perceived divisibility is important because it allows for the components of each to be rendered as distinct modules (i.e., $SAE_{Acou.}$, $AAVE_{Acou.}$, $SAE_{Ling.}$ and $AAVE_{Ling.}$). With this (de)composition, the African American synthetic voice is then imagined as the result of the strategic manipulation and/or reorganization of these variables.

Precisely how these variables get manipulated is most evident during the model training stages of synthetic voice generation. A widely referenced and followed approach introduced by researchers at Microsoft and Northwestern Polytechnical University details the commonly followed steps to train conversational TTS systems to appear "more realistic" (Guo et al. 2021): during the preparation of training samples voice actors are recorded as they role-play a series of realistic conversational scenes based on a curated set of dialogue scripts. Requiring them to "perform according to the scripts" and only make small modifications such as inserting "appropriate spontaneous behaviors," developers try to control the linguistic variable *textually* (Guo et al. 2021, 2). The acoustic variable, on the other hand, is taken as inherently stemming from the *vocality* of the actor or actress—which in the case of "African-American sounding voices" means that the timbre of their voices is presumed to "naturally" exhibit the acoustic components of AAVE, regardless of the dialogue uttered. A similar process is followed for the generation of synthetic voice samples, although with one additional machinic leap. A predefined script is used to ensure samples syntactically and lexically conform to SAE, while the algorithmic model is envisioned as capable of capturing the "African American-sounding" acoustic qualities of the voice data.

In its most elemental form, this manipulation of variables can be understood as an attempt to compose a "professional" and "African American-sounding" voice by combining the linguistic module of SAE with the acoustic cues of AAVE:

$$\text{SAE}_{\text{Ling.}} + \text{AAVE}_{\text{Acou.}} = \text{“Professional” AAVE voice}$$

The logic behind this operation is one that builds on historical hierarchies and categorizations that associate the grammar of SAE with being educated and professional (Bernstein [1971] 2005; Rosa and Flores 2017). Implicitly, it also categorizes the grammar of AAVE as not sufficiently professional, evidenced by its exclusion in the recomposition of a "professional sounding African American voice." Through the acoustic-linguistic divide, the voice thus becomes a (re)combination of partitions, in which *socially* desirable/undesirable components can be included/excluded through *technical* means. Indeed, it is not only a "professional" AAVE voice that becomes engineerable through this schema. A presumptive "unprofessional" SAE voice can just as easily be constructed by combining SAE_{Acou} and $AAVE_{Ling}$ according to this logic. Viewed this way, the reductive (and problematic) foundation of this operation becomes more apparent. In its sum total of a dissection and reconfiguration of speech, this operation is ultimately one that entwines the acoustic-linguistic divide with sociopolitical relations of difference.

Indeed, much like in the case of AI-enabled accent modification tools, the acoustic-linguistic divide in "diverse" synthetic speech generation systems functions as the schematic bedrock through which difference is not only defined but also manufactured. The acoustic module, in particular, is envisioned here as the container for "diversity," closing in on the notion that certain acoustic parameters correspond to or stand-in as sonic markers of difference. The various techniques used to extract, process, preserve, and reproduce the acoustic module are precisely what give these ideas about sonic difference their form, rendering them into computationally legible sound objects that are then manipulated in the production of synthetic voices. In this sense, the enactment of the acoustic-linguistic divide within these AI voice generation technologies works as a "racializing assemblage" in so far as it engages processes of differentiation that then materialize categories of difference (Weheliye 2014).

The Technopolitics of Respectability

The production of difference through the schematic of the acoustic-linguistic divide in both AI-enabled accent modification and "diverse" synthetic voice generation is mediated to some degree by attempts to materially enact neoliberal notions of "multiculturalism" and "respectability" through them. Advocates of AI accent correction, for instance, claim that these tools will "give people more control over their identities" and "reduce discrimination and increase job opportunities around the world" (Sanas n.d.). Likewise, developers of and consultants for diverse synthetic voices tout their purported ability to increase representation, while controlling for or reducing negative stereotypes: "*give us representation, but don't give us too much representation*" (in Pinhanez et al. 2024, 6). We see similar promises of synthetic vocal diversity in projects such as "Free the Voices"—a bank of synthetic voices based on samples from over 500 members of the LGBTIQ+ community. This project was described by LLYC, the communications and public affairs consulting firm behind it, as working to expose audiences to more diverse voices while reducing bias (González 2024).

Undergirding these emphases on "diversity" and "representation," as well as the promises to reduce discrimination and generate new economic opportunities, are the uneven power dynamics embedded in discourses of inclusion (Hoffmann 2021) and the homogenizing demands of multiculturalism and respectability. Within these conceptions, difference is meant to be embraced only when it appears as a "manageable deviation"—a difference that is not too different and therefore, can be made commensurate with normative expectations (Muñoz 2020). So, when AI voice generation tools are advertised, claiming these tools can serve as an extension of organizations' brand images, they are celebrating "diversity" and "representation" only in so far as it remains in accordance with historical standards of normative respectability, whether that is through the imposition of acoustic standards of "clarity" (as in the case of AI accent correction) or through the imposition of grammatical standards of "professionalism" (as in the case of synthetic voices).

The effect is akin to what in cultural sociology and linguistics is referred to as "passing" (Burma 1946). Here, however, "passing" surfaces not as a self-directed act of protection—a means of shielding oneself from trauma (Leary 2014)—but as a technologically imposed technique of normalization. Instead, the algorithmic manipulation of the acoustic and linguistic modules produces difference in the form of the marked acoustic parameter whilst simultaneously sanitizing it by actively seeking to overlay, suppress, or altogether delete the modules and parameters that are believed to represent undesirable difference. The acoustic-linguistic divide, in sum, offers the precise modular arrangement that promises to enable both the construction and management of difference in and through AI voice generation.

Conclusion

Scholars have rightfully pointed to the obscurity of algorithms, data, and platforms and their role in obfuscating, if not altogether occluding, many of the discriminatory logics and processes undergirding our social systems and structures (Kitchin 2017; Seaver 2019; Phan and Wark 2021). And yet, in their performance, AI systems are also revealing of prevailing social, cultural, scientific, and political schemas that sustain hierarchies and categorizations of human difference. The acoustic-linguistic divide, in its conceptual and material enactment within AI voice generation technologies, is one of those prevailing schemas. It is one of the main frames, as mentioned earlier, through which many Western disciplinary traditions have come to understand speech. The divide has also seemingly shaped the affective contours of everyday communicative interactions, with implications for how we understand ourselves and, therefore, how we also engage in/with the world. At the intersection of human voices and AI, the acoustic-linguistic divide has similarly been mobilized as an effective organizing principle for profitable and futuristic visions of what AI can do with speech, voice and language (Kockelman 2024).

As examples from AI-enabled accent modification tools and synthetic voice generation show, however, the algorithmic implementations of the acoustic-linguistic divide rarely work as expected. Indeed, while the divide appears deployable as a conceptual abstraction, the attempt to materialize it in the context of designing an AI system requires contending directly with the indeterminate subjectivities of sound, voice, identity, and language. As we showed, this process introduces numerous frictions and fractures that ultimately work to reify existing social hierarchies of difference. Indeed, studying these frictions and fractures offers an opportunity to examine the presence of essentialist and normative conceptions of difference within AI imaginaries, practices, and systems. Recognizing the role of the acoustic-linguistic divide in these processes allows us to expand the locus of critical intervention beyond concerns of under-/over-representation in datasets and towards a broader understanding of human speech and vocality in the development of voice AI technologies.

References

Alim, Sami, John Rickford, and Arnetha Ball, eds. 2016. *Raciolinguistics: How Language Shapes our Ideas about Race*. Oxford University Press.

Barthes, Roland. [1981] 2009. *The Grain of the Voice: Interviews 1962–1980*. Northwestern University Press.

Baugh, John. 2003. "Linguistic Profiling." In *Black Linguistics: Language, Society, and Politics in Africa and The Americas*, edited by Sinfree Makoni, Geneva Smitherman, Arnetha F. Ball, and Arthur K. Spears, 155–168. Routledge.

Becerra, Juana C., and Felicia Jing. Forthcoming. "Making Globalization Feel Good: AI Attachments in the Service of Racial Capitalism." *Catalyst: Feminism, Theory, Technoscience*.

Bernstein, Basil. (1971) 2005. *Theoretical studies towards a sociology of language*. Routledge.

Bote, Joshua. 2022. "Sanas, the Buzzy Bay Area Startup that Wants to Make the World Sound Whiter." *Sfgate*. September 1, 2022. https://www.sfgate.com/news/article/sanas-startup-creates-american-voice-17382771.php.

Burma, John H. 1946. "The Measurement of Negro Passing." *American Journal of Sociology* 52 (1): 18–22. doi:10.1086/219915.

Cavarero, Adriana. 2005. *For More than One Voice: Toward a Philosophy of Vocal Expression*. Stanford University Press.

Cave, Stephen, and Kanta Dihal. 2020. "The Whiteness of AI." *Philosophy & Technology* 33 (4): 685–703. doi:10.1007/s13347-020-00415-6.

Dirac, Parker, Fabian Moerchen, and Edo Liberty. 2016. "*Accent Translation*" US Patent: 2018/0174595 A1. Filed December 21, 2016.

Earl, William. 2024. "AI Firm ElevenLabs Sets Audio Reader Pact With Judy Garland, James Dean, Burt Reynolds, and Laurence Olivier Estates." *Variety*, July 2, 2024. https://variety.com/2024/biz/news/ai-judy-garland-james-dean-burt-reynolds-elevenlabs-reader-app-1236058829/.

Eidsheim, Nina S. 2023. "Rewriting Algorithms for Just Recognition: From Digital Aural Redlining to Accent Activism." In *Thinking with an Accent: Toward a New Object, Method, and Practice*, edited by Pooja Rangan, Akshya Saxena, Ragini Tharoor Srinivasan, and Pavitra Sunda. University of California Press. doi:10.1525/luminos.148.h.

González, David N. 2024. "LLYC Launches Free the Voices, the First Diverse Synthetic Voice Bank, to Combat Anti-LGBTQI+ Biases." *LLYC*, June 19, 2024. https://llyc.global/en/noticias/llyc-launches-free-the-voices-the-first-diverse-synthetic-voice-bank-to-combat-anti-lgbtqi-biases/.

Guo, Haohan, Shaofei Zhang, Frank K. Soong, Lei He, and Lei Xie. 2021. "Conversational End-to-End TTS for Voice Agents." In *2021 IEEE Spoken Language Technology Workshop* (SLT). IEEE. doi:10.1109/SLT48900.2021.9383460.

Harris, Frederick C. 2014. "The Rise of Respectability Politics." *Dissent*. https://www.dissentmagazine.org/article/the-rise-of-respectability-politics/.

Hoffmann, Anna Lauren. 2021. "Terms of Inclusion: Data, Discourse, Violence." *New Media & Society* 23 (12). 3539–3556. doi:10.1177/1461444820958725.

Hofmann, Valentin, Pratyusha Kalluri, Dan Jurafsky, and Sharese King. 2024. "Dialect Prejudice Predicts AI Decisions about People's Character, Employability, and Criminality." *arXiv*. doi:10.48550/arXiv.2403.00742.

Holliday, Nicole. 2023. "Siri, You've Changed! Acoustic Properties and Racialized Judgements of Voice Assistants." *Frontiers in Communication* 8 (1): 1116955. doi:10.3389/fcomm.2023.1116955.

Huitri, Wiebke. 2022. "Bias in Automated Speaker Recognition." In *ACM Conference on Fairness, Accountability, and Transparency*. Association for Computing Machinery. doi:10.1145/3531146.3533089.

Izaguirre, Anthony. 2023. "Can New York's Mayor Speak Mandarin? No, but with AI He's Making Robocalls in Different Languages." *Associated Press*, October 17, 2023. https://apnews.com/article/nyc-mayor-ai-robocalls-foreign-languages-30517885466994e5f1f54745c08691e0.

Kang, Edward B. Forthcoming. "The Voice Disaggregate: A Computational Ontology." In *The Oxford Handbook of Media and Vocality*, edited by Colleen L. Montgomery, Lisa Coulthard, and Katherine Spring. Oxford University Press.
Kang, Edward B. 2023a. "Ground Truth Tracings (GTT): On the Epistemic Limits of Machine Learning." *Big Data & Society* 10 (1): 1–12. doi:10.1177/20539517221146122.
Kang, Edward B. 2023b. "On the Praxes and Politics of AI Speech Emotion Recognition." In *Proceedings of the 2023 ACM Conference on Fairness, Accountability, and Transparency*. Association for Computing Machinery. doi:10.1145/3593013.3594011.
Kitchin, Rob. 2017. "Thinking Critically about and Researching Algorithms." *Information, Communication & Society* 20 (1): 14–29.
Kockelman, Paul. 2024. *Last Words: Large Language Models and the AI Apocalypse*. University of Chicago Press, distributed by Prickly Paradigm Press.
Labov, William. 1973. *Language in the Inner City; Studies in the Black English Vernacular*. University of Pennsylvania Press.
Lawrence, Halcyon. 2021. "Siri Disciplines." In *Your Computer is on Fire*, edited by Thomas Mullaney, Benjamin Peters, Mar Hicks, and Kavita Philip. MIT Press.
Leary, Kimberlyn. 2014. "Passing, Posing, and 'Keeping It Real'" In *Relational Psychoanalysis*, Volume 4, edited by Lewis Aron and Adrienne Harris. Routledge.
Li, Xiaochang, and Mara Mills. 2019. "Vocal Features: from Voice Identification to Speech Recognition by Machine. *Technology and Culture* 60 (2): S129–S160. doi:10.1353/tech.2019.0066.
Li, Yinghao Aaron, Cong Han, and Nima Mesgarani. 2025. "Styletts: A Style-Based Generative Model for Natural and Diverse Text-to-Speech Synthesis." *IEEE Journal of Selected Topics in Signal Processing*. doi:10.1109/JSTSP.2025.3530171.
Markopoulos, Kostantinos, Georgia Maniati, Georgios Vamvoukakis, et al. 2023. "Generating Multilingual Gender-Ambiguous Text-to-Speech Voices." *arXiv preprint*. doi:10.48550/arXiv.2211.00375.
Mehrish, Ambuj, Navonil Majumder, Rishabh Bharadwaj, Rada Mihalcea, and Soujanya Poria. 2023. "A Review of Deep Learning Techniques for Speech Processing." *Information Fusion* 99: 101869. doi:10.1016/j.inffus.2023.101869.
Michel, Shira, Sufi Kaur, Sarah E. Gillespie, Jeffrey Gleason, Christo Wilson, and Avijit Ghosh. 2025. "'It's Not a Representation of Me': Examining Accent Bias and Digital Exclusion in Synthetic AI Voice Services." *arXiv preprint*. doi:10.48550/arXiv.2504.09346.
Muñoz, José Esteban. 2020. *The Sense of Brown*. Duke University Press.
Phan, Thao, and Scott Wark. 2021. "Racial Formations as Data Formations." *Big Data & Society* 8 (2). doi:10.1177/20539517211046377.
Pinhanez, Claudio S., Raul Fernandez, Marcello Carpinette Grave, Julio Nogima, and Ron Hoory. 2024. "Creating an African American-Sounding TTS: Guidelines, Technical Challenges, and Surprising Evaluations." In *Proceedings of the 29th Conference on Intelligent User Interfaces*. Association for Computing Machinery. doi:10.1145/3640543.3645165.
Rancière, Jacques. 2004. *Disagreement*. University of Minnesota Press.
Rangan, Pooja, Akshya Saxena, Ragini TharoorSrinivasan, and Pavitra Sundar, eds. 2023. *Thinking with an Accent; Toward a New Object, Method, and Practice*. University of California Press.
Rosa, Jonathan. 2019. *Looking Like a Language, Sounding like a Race: Raciolinguistic Ideologies and the Learning of Latinidad*. Oxford University Press.

Rosa, Jonathan, and Nelson Flores. 2017. *Unsettling Race and Language: Toward a Raciolinguistic Perspective*. Cambridge University Press.

Santos, Dorothy. 2023. "The Cyborg's Prosody, or Speech AI and the Displacement of Feeling." *Sounding Out*! July 3, 2023.

Schaeffer, Pierre. [1977] 2017. *Treatise on Musical Objects: An Essay Across Disciplines*. University of California Press.

Seaver, Nick. 2019. "Knowing Algorithms." In *DigitalSTS: A Field Guide for Science & Technology Studies*, edited by Janet Vertesi and David Ribes. Princeton University Press.

Székely, Eva, and Maxwell Hope. 2024. "An inclusive approach to creating a palette of synthetic voices for gender diversity." In *25th Interspeech Conference 2024*. International Speech Communication Association.

Thubron, Rob. 2024. "ElevenLabs, Whose Tech was Used for the Fake Biden Robocalls, Partners with AI Detection Company." *Techspot*, July 18, 2024. https://www.techspot.com/news/103867-elevenlabs-whose-tech-used-fake-biden-robocalls-partners.html.

Weheliye, Alexander G. 2014. *Habeas Viscus: Racializing Assemblages, Biopolitics, and Black Theories of the Human*. Duke University Press.

Wynter, Sylvia. 2001. "Towards the Sociogenic Principle: Fanon, Identity, the Puzzle of Conscious Experience, and What It Is Like to Be 'Black'" In *National Identities and SocioPolitical Changes in Latin America*, edited by Durán Cogan and Gómex Moriana. Routledge.

7

AI-POWERED ACCESSIBILITY

Inclusive Co-design and Disability Expertise in AI-Powered Workplace Accessibility

Sydney Yeager

Reframing Accessibility as a Benchmark of Good Design

Andre Louis, a London-based musician who is blind, moves through the world relying on solutions to his disability that are both low-tech, walking canes and help from others, and high-tech, reliance on his phone. Yet social media proved a particularly difficult landscape to navigate until AI got involved.

> So many times someone will send me a picture of something I cannot understand, so I will share that picture with Seeing AI, and I will get a description of what it is. It's changed how I can view social media. It feels like I can participate far more than I could before.
>
> *(Seeing AI 2025).*

When a new post pops up on his phone, seeing AI gives Andre a rich description of the picture, *Scene: probably a group of people sitting on a bench in a park. Person: eight-year-old boy with black hair looking happy. Seven-year-old girl looking disgusted.*

Microsoft's Seeing AI is a free app that narrates the world around you (Microsoft 2019). Designed for the blind and low-vision community, Seeing AI's development was overseen by developer Saqib Shaikh, who was blind from an early age and played a critical role as the project's sponsor (Spencer 2019). Released to the public in 2017, it assisted users with over three million tasks in its first year. Since then, its capabilities have expanded to read handwriting, text on signs, and labels on objects. It can also identify currency, recognize faces, and

DOI: 10.4324/9781003532750-10

describe object's shape, color, and motion. It turns the visual world into an audible experience utilizing the power of artificial intelligence (AI).

AI is a technology that simulates human learning, comprehension, problem-solving, decision-making, creativity, and autonomy. Technological developments such as machine learning (ML), deep learning, natural language processing (NLP), large language models (LLM), and computer sensing (computer vision, listening, etc.) have each brought us a step closer to achieving true AI. Machine Learning makes predictions based on data and feedback data received from past predictions. Deep Learning is powered by networks of statistical relationships, referred to as neural networks, capable of delivering richer insights, but AI relying on deep learning currently struggles to communicate how it arrived at its response, so reliability can be an issue. Natural language processing is a subset of machine learning focused on training computers to understand language and interpret and manipulate it as a native speaker. Leveraging natural language processing, large language models are AI technology that understand, generate, and predict human language. Computer vision such as Seeing AI enables computers to "see," analyze, and interpret images and videos, extracting data and insights from visual media. AI technology has played a key role in the development of new advancements in assistive technology.

Assistive Technology (AT) encompasses any item, equipment, or system that helps individuals with disabilities increase, maintain, or improve their capabilities. Long before the public interest in GenAI associated with OpenAI's (2022) viral launch of ChatGPT, a user-friendly interface for GPT-3.5, significant progress was made in LLM AI and NLP to support speech-to-text and screen reader (text-to-speech) technologies, a critical assistive technology for people with mobility, visual, and cognitive disabilities (Karthik 2024; Afraz 2024). Utilized as early as the 1980s (Miller 2008), AI-powered screen readers use natural language processing to provide more nuanced and context-aware descriptions of digital content for visually impaired users. Similarly, AI-powered speech-to-text applications use natural language processing to convert audio to text for visually impaired users and dyslexic users. AI-powered communication devices translate sign language or other non-verbal communication into spoken language in real-time. Robotic assistive devices with AI can learn and adapt to a user's movements, providing personalized support for mobility or daily tasks.

Theoretical Framework and Methodological Approach

While technology often aims to make the world more accessible, its development and governance, including in the field of artificial intelligence (AI), are still largely shaped by reductive models of disability. These models frame disability as an individual impairment requiring accommodation rather than a relational and systemic issue to be addressed through design. This chapter challenges that paradigm by drawing on a relational model of disability and centers inclusive co-design practices that leverage the expertise of people with disabilities in the development of AI. Grounded in ethnographic research, I argue that accessibility is not a secondary consideration or a matter of social justice but a fundamental technical requirement for truly "good" technology.

The ethnographic examples included in the chapter are drawn from my research on workplace accessibility conducted in the US from 2022 to 2025 and my research utilizing social listening with the neurodivergent community on social media[1] in 2021–2022. These projects focused on questions about workplace and educational experiences with accessibility, adaptive strategies, assistive technology, diagnosis, and accommodations. The ethnographic data included in this chapter is sourced from semi-structured interviews on workplace accessibility with professionals with disabilities, informal conversations with disability advocates, and participant observation in disability communities. The lived experiences and perspectives that follow are derived from twenty-three professionals, all of whom have disabilities, utilize AI-powered assistive technologies at work, and live in the US.[2]

Diverse disability experiences informed this body of work, including cognitive disabilities, mental health conditions, chronic health conditions, hearing loss, color blindness, low vision, and legal blindness. I describe research participants as they self-identify and thus treat self-diagnosis[3] and medical diagnosis equally. The ethnographic case studies presented throughout draw heavily on the disability expertise of participants. To protect their identities and professional reputations, I use pseudonyms and composites while preserving the integrity of quotes and significant career and disability experiences, following the composite approach outlined by sociologist Noah Arjomand (2022).

This chapter focuses on workplace and educational experiences with AI, accessibility, and assistive technologies. Drawing on frameworks from medical anthropology and disability studies, I address AI-powered assistive technologies, including popular programs and technologies such as Grammarly,[4] Dragon[5], GenAI, and emerging AI applications developed by people with disabilities for people with disabilities. By examining the lived experiences of individuals with disabilities in workplace settings, I explore how people with disabilities create accessibility through their use of available AI, assistive technology, and other resources developing creative workarounds to address their needs. I highlight the impact of prohibitive AI policies and unaddressed AI data privacy and security concerns on professionals who rely on AI-powered assistive technologies. Then, I discuss the potential for inclusive co-design to leverage this creative and innovative disability expertise throughout the product development life cycle so that all products are accessible from conception. Finally, I conclude that progress towards an AI-powered future must be made with disability expertise at the forefront of technological development and how doing so from conception is not just good design but also creates opportunities to learn from the creative innovation of people with disabilities.[6]

The accessibility of AI technology is a necessary consideration, impacting a sizable portion of the population. In 2016, the Centers for Disease Control reported approximately sixty-one million Americans have a disability. In 2023, the U.S. Bureau of Labor reported that the unemployment rate for people with disabilities was more than double the rate of people without disabilities, a trend that holds true across all levels of education. Employed people with disabilities are more likely to work part-time or be self-employed. As AI is an emerging technology that is rapidly becoming pervasive throughout the digital landscape, it is a critical time to shape the future of technology by prioritizing accessibility in the development of AI. There is enormous potential for AI-powered assistive technology to empower people with disabilities. Given AI's capacity as a key accessibility resource, it is necessary to carefully consider AI governance and policies in educational and professional spaces. Availability of accessibly designed AI in professional and educational settings has the potential to make work and education more accessible while improving the experiences of individuals with disabilities.

Dona Sarkar, a former Director of Technology for Accessibility at Microsoft, argues that accessibility is fundamentally a technical challenge rather than a social justice issue (Pluralsight 2023). True accessibility requires a systematic change in our definition of good. Good code, good design, good instruction, etc., are free of accessibility flaws, the same way they are free of security risks. Sarkar argued, "It comes down to the challenge: are you a good enough developer, [designer, teacher, architect, etc.] to tackle the accessibility problem before you?" It is not about ideologies or the number of people impacted; it is a technical requirement that defines "good" and "complete." Sarkar's advice requires a cultural shift, redefining "good" as accessible for all, inclusive by design. Anthropologist Cassandra Hartblay made a similar call to action in disability anthropology, asking anthropologists to reconsider disability by reframing it as a relational category rather than a medical one. She emphasizes the way a disability manifests is negotiated and changes depending on social relations and context (Hartblay 2020, 26–36). Critical of anthropology's relationship with disability advocacy and people with disabilities in the communities where they work, Devva Kasnitz (2025) notes that although anthropologists can be allies, the discipline does not always rise to meet the needs of the disabled in their field or field sites. To address these concerns, Hartblay (2020) and Bailey (2021) call for anthropologists to research how identity and moral agency are enacted in the lived experiences[7] of people with disabilities. Anthropology of disability scholars Ginsburg and Rapp argue that disability is "shaped by social conditions that exclude full participation in society" (2013, 53–68). Thus, social conditions can also be intentionally designed to enable full participation in society.

Accessibility is a measurement of how well all users, regardless of disability, can fully access and easily use a product, service, space, or experience. The disability advocacy framework of "disabled by design" argues that inaccessible design of technology, spaces, and social systems have a direct impact on the quality of life, health, safety, independence, and social participation of people with disabilities (Kapsalis et al. 2022; Joyce 2022; Palacios 2022). In answer to these concerns, universal design seeks to create technology, spaces, and systems that are accessible to everyone. Beyond the imperative to create accessible designs for individuals with disabilities, universal design is a philosophy that underscores accessibility's potential to enhance the user experience for all. By following design principles that ensure all components are accessible to everyone, universal design aims to address the systemic barriers that disable by design.

The anthropology of work, the ethnography of the habits, politics, and spaces of work, offers ample ethnographic examples where disability is technical and relational, granting (or denying) accommodations and guaranteeing agency that validates personhood in its many forms (Zagrodny 2024; Nash 1981, 393–423; Unterberger 2018, 105–115; Clark 2017; Gunn and Donovan 2012). The workplace accommodation process, like accommodation processes in educational settings, are legalistic processes in which medical authority serves as gatekeepers of diagnosis, establishing legal proof of the necessity of an accommodation, which then undergoes legal review in which corporate decision-makers weigh disability accommodation against other corporate legal considerations such as compliance. This process, documented in disability literature by Bea Waterford (2019) and Xuan-Thuy Nguyen (2015), illustrates how medical governmentality is very much a reality in the modern workplace. This corporate manifestation of governmentality over accommodation and access to AI-powered AT is a dehumanizing process and creates accessibility barriers, even when attempting to access widely available, popular technologies. When an AI-powered AT poses data privacy concerns, and AI governance is left up to the corporation developing it, users are asked to give up their data, right to privacy, and access to their intellectual property to use the product. Most often, users give up their privacy and data by signing long and inaccessibly written terms of service. These are "dark patterns"—design choices that create vulnerabilities or barriers for users, especially those with disabilities (Seaver 2019). Corporate governmentality must balance legal requirements of accommodation and compliance, often leading companies to reject the needs of workers and alienate them in their workplaces. However, outside of corporate workspaces with large legal and information security teams, smaller companies and individuals have to navigate murky terms of service and privacy concerns on their own.

To move away from this legalistic approach to accommodations and accessibility design, it is crucial to shift the development of AI and AI-powered assistive technologies towards inclusive co-design: the inclusion of people with disabilities in the design process ensures their voices are heard, and a product is "good," as Sarkar defines it. Inclusive co-design enacts the disability advocacy slogan "nothing about us without us" (Charlton 1998), ensuring that people with disabilities are included throughout the design and development of new technologies they will rely on. Such an approach challenges the reductive models of disability that often underpin traditional AT development, which frequently prioritizes legal compliance, medical diagnosis, and bureaucratic control. Instead, a relational model of disability, centered on the lived experiences of individuals, can guide the co-creation of AI-powered tools that are truly accessible and empowering. Meeting the needs of users with disabilities, including them in pain point identification, ideation, and design reviews, yields powerfully innovative results. Users and employees with time-intensive, creative workarounds can offer fertile ground for collaborative ideation in design thinking sessions. Stories and pain points offer powerful avenues for building empathy, and they will be early adopters of an effective and accessible solution. By involving researchers, designers, and engineers in direct collaboration with people with disabilities, we can ensure that accessibility is an integral part of the design process rather than an afterthought. Inclusive co-design with users with disabilities that leverage their disability expertise to ensure accessibility is baked into the process, shifting away from dehumanizing models of legalistic accommodation, medical gatekeeping, and corporate manifestations of governmentality over access to AT (Kasnitz 2025).

Bricolage Accessibility

Drawing on Claude Lévi-Strauss' discussion of bricolage in his seminal work *Savage Minds* (1962, 16–17), I argue people with disabilities take a bricolage approach to creating accessibility for themselves in the social spaces they occupy. Witell et al. (2017) found that in resource-constrained environments, a bricolage approach to innovation allows organizations to maximize the service they offer, given their limited resources. Bricolage accessibility refers to the way people with disabilities adapt to the resource constraints of their professional, educational, or daily life contexts by utilizing a mixture of existing digital technologies, analog tools, and resources available to them. They take a practical approach to combining these resources to improve their access to full participation in society. This generates creative and innovative solutions, often combining technologies and available resources to address accessibility challenges rather than relying on a single, standardized solution that does not fully meet their needs.

During my fieldwork on workplace accessibility in 2024, Penny, a professional with dyslexia, described her bricolage approach to accessibility as shifting based on the setting and the technology she had access to. She reported, "At work, I use Dragon for all my reports, emails, and white papers at work. At home, I usually send audio texts. If I *have to* write something, I usually use the voice search function [on] google the word and copy how it spells it." She went on to discuss her experience with text-to-speech assistive tech,

> I always struggled with the old screen readers, it was so disjointed and unnatural, it made it painful for me to listen to, but there's some great stuff out there now, so much more, well …human. I use Speechify to read personal stuff, but at work, I can't run sensitive documents through it, so I use Word's read-aloud feature whenever possible.

Penny's bricolage approach of combining different AI-powered technologies to meet her needs in each situation and pivoting between tools based on the context is an incredibly common experience across the people with disabilities I interviewed. A highly resourceful bricolage approach is informed by their disability expertise and constrained by technology access and feasibility as they craft accessibility while navigating between social contexts of work, school, and home.

David, a dyslexic designer, summarized the impact of Grammarly on his life, succinctly saying, "For people with dyslexia, like me, Grammarly provided a profound departure from the limitations of spell check and dictionaries." Sandy, a product manager with dyslexia and ADHD, whom I interviewed in 2022, shared her experience comparing her current use of Grammarly with childhood struggles with undiagnosed dyslexia,

> I remember when I was struggling with spelling in school. I'd try so hard to use the dictionary my dad got me when I started 6th grade. I didn't know I had dyslexia yet, but I remember trying so hard and eventually throwing the book in frustration, thinking, "How am I supposed to find the word I don't know how to spell if I don't have a clue how to spell it? I'm not even sure what the second letter is!" The first time I used a word processor with spell check, it definitely made a difference. But I soon learned that spell check fell short too: if I accidentally spelled a real word that wasn't the word I actually meant, then spell check thinks that's just fine. Or if I couldn't get "close enough" to spelling the word I was looking for, then spell check can't really help. Autocorrect, when I'm texting, has similar problems. If I don't get the first two or three letters, it will never guess the right word. Throughout high school and undergrad, I had to have my friends, classmates, and writing center tutors read over my written assignments. When I started grad school, I had to find similar support. But while I was working on my MBA, I found Grammarly. It could analyze my writing and easily figure out the word I was trying to spell based on context in a matter of seconds. It saved me so much time. I've been a devoted user ever since!

While Microsoft Word's Editor feature offers limited comparable capabilities for spell check, grammar, and other editing tools, many Grammarly users remain loyal and claim it falls short of true parity. Grammarly, which can be added to web browsers, email applications, and as a plug-in to Microsoft Word, ensures that all written communication is professionally edited. Its adaptability across writing platforms and development with accessibility as a priority explains why it is considered an essential tool in the accessibility bricolage for many professionals with disabilities. When AI-powered assistive technologies—such as voice-to-text, voice-command, text-to-speech, and applications like Grammarly—become widely available, pervasive, and embedded across a variety of platforms and sites, they reduce the friction people with disabilities face and simultaneously benefit all users, demonstrating the value of universal design. When these solutions are available to everyone, it alleviates the burden of official accommodation processes, helps to ensure the people who need them have access regardless of medical diagnosis and reduces the stigma of using them.

Timothy, a communications specialist with dyslexia at the corporate headquarters of a retail company, reported that using Grammarly allowed him to complete his work four times faster than working without it. "My leaders are able to focus on my ideas rather than being distracted by concerns about spelling, grammar, and the professionalism of my written copy." The synergy between dyslexic users and AI-powered tools like Grammarly can significantly enhance their productivity and reduce the cognitive burden of writing. Dyslexic individuals can leverage their strengths in creative problem-solving and innovative thinking while relying on AI to address specific challenges in spelling and grammar. Impacting between 5–20% of the population (Yale Center for Dyslexia and Creativity), dyslexia has a high cost in terms of productive time, cognitive load, and the mental health burdens associated with a lifetime of stigma faced in academic spaces and professional settings (Ali et al. 2019; Dębska et al. 2021; Le Cunff et al. 2024; Made by Dyslexia 2024).

Chris, a product manager, and Julie, a director of HR, in my workplace experience study, both of whom had ADHD, noted that Grammarly helped them overcome "careless" errors, boosting their confidence and reducing anxiety associated with past experiences of ableism and stigma. While the AI-powered project management and scheduling tools Motion (Chris) and Monday (Julie) gave them the confidence to know they were staying on top of everything. Grammarly, Motion, and Monday's ability to provide the "just right" level of support reduces the stigma faced by people with disabilities, making them critical tools for the bricolage accessibility of many of their users with disabilities.

The potential of AI to offer less stigmatized support was discussed by psychologist Adam Grant, and Sal Kahn, founder of Khan Academy, discussed Khan Academy's GenAI, Khanmigo, and how students reported feeling more comfortable asking AI questions (Grant 2023). Knowing it was not a person on the other end provided greater psychological safety as it alleviated their concerns about asking "dumb questions." When it comes to the design and development of educational AT for neurodivergent students and dyslexia-friendly AI tools, Schaur and Koutny advocate for a user-centered approach to developing dyslexia AT and dyslexia-friendly AI tools with disability expertise of its dyslexic users (2024, 269–274). While the disability support provided by AI was initially designed to replicate support given by people, as the students' response to Khanmigo suggests, a readily available and accessibly designed AI can reduce stigma and anxiety around seeking support.

GenAI is built on the advancements in machine learning, deep learning, and natural language processing, similar to the technology underlying Grammarly and Dragon. Professionals and students with disabilities who have adopted GenAI have quickly developed user-generated use cases for it as assistive tech. There is an opportunity to learn from the accessibility use cases currently used by users with disabilities by bringing those users into the design and development of AI. Inclusive co-design of AI applications leverages disabilities expertise and learns from the bricolage approach employed by so many users with disabilities to craft accessibility from the AI tools and assistive technologies they have available.

Alexandra, a Hispanic neurodivergent UX researcher at a small US-based tech startup that I interviewed in 2024 on workplace accessibility, shared how she used GenAI at work:

> How I'm using AI? All the time! I use it as a review of my writing before I ask a coworker, especially when bandwidth is low. So, this week, for example, I asked it to evaluate interview questions and the proposal of a usability study. It gives me so much more than feedback on spelling. I've worked out the prompts that seem to work best to have it evaluate the specific type of deliverables I'm working on. I've found with rich descriptions and clearly stated expectations to prompt the AI…enough to prompt the AI to deliver higher-quality results. When I do that, I'm asking for feedback on the content once I have it fully drafted. But I still use Grammarly as I'm writing, my company uses Google for everything, so it's easy enough to keep Grammarly running and giving me feedback as I write my reports and create my slides. But once I've got my draft, I'm asking ChatGPT to evaluate the content and double-check my word choice, as English is my second language.

It was clear from her interview that adding the ChatGPT check gave her the confidence to share her work with colleagues.

Justin, another research participant from the workplace accessibility study, had ADHD and social anxiety. He described using GenAI for mock interviews while navigating the job market after being laid off in 2024,

> I give ChatGPT the job description and had it write interview questions. Then had a friend do a mock interview with me on Zoom. I figured out where I was prepared and where I was lacking...and then I wrote out my answers and asked ChatGPT to evaluate them. It helped me feel prepared and focus my thoughts before the real call. A couple rounds of interviews, and I got the job! After months of struggling, it really helped!

LinkedIn is full of posts recommending how to leverage AI at every stage of the job search. A 2024 study revealed that 58% of job seekers use AI at some point in their search (Johnson 2024). The introduction of AI to the hiring process pre-dates these user-developed use cases, as AI tools for evaluating job applications are prolific in large-scale companies and have raised legal questions regarding automated discrimination by AI agents (Kemp 2024). While many have apprehension about the use of AI by both prospective job candidates and employers, for job seekers with disability, GenAI offers valuable assistance. These user-generated accessibility applications of AI demonstrate the creative problem-solving strategies employed by people with disabilities.

Limitations and Barriers to Bricolage AI Accessibility

With growing concerns about how AI impacts job markets, AI-powered ATs such as Dragon and Grammarly exemplify how an AI tool empowers users with disabilities in the workplace to maximize their potential by having the proper AT to support their needs. But what happens when access to such AI technology is denied?

Lilly, a mid-career director of public relations, faced a very prolonged struggle to access Grammarly when she started at a new company three years ago, going from a high-profile agency to a large tech company. As an avid Grammarly user with dyslexia, she immediately informed her manager about her need for the tool in her public-facing role. Her manager was supportive and helped her start the accommodation process for her request.

Despite being diagnosed with dyslexia in early childhood, Lilly was required to undergo a costly and time-consuming re-evaluation as an adult to meet the company's strict medical documentation requirements. This six-month process forced her to disclose her diagnosis to multiple levels of management, compromising her privacy. Ultimately, even with leadership support and a recent clinical diagnosis, her request for access to Grammarly was denied due to data security concerns related to Grammarly's use of cloud computing, which sends user data to its cloud space on Amazon servers to analyze the text and support training its AI. Lilly's company ultimately determined that traditional spell-check tools in Microsoft Office would suffice for all dyslexic employees. In an interview about workplace accessibility in April 2024, Lilly shared,

> I felt so defeated. After fighting for six months, producing so much documentation. Outing myself as dyslexic all the way up to my SVP, all for nothing. All that, just to be told Microsoft spell check is good enough. I did analysis to support my claims. Spell check only catches about 15% of my dyslexia errors. My work is incredibly visible. I regularly interact with high-profile external business partners and corporate executives; I just can't risk something being written wrong. 85% wrong!

As directed, Lilly works in Microsoft Word, Outlook, or PowerPoint and uses spell check, which for several years has been attempting to implement AI features comparable to Grammarly, including Microsoft's editor feature and its predictive text feature, which can identify and replace errors to varying degrees of success. Once she finishes writing, she uses Microsoft's read-aloud feature, an embedded screen reader, to read back her words to ensure the words written on the page match the words she intended. This helps her catch issues that spell check cannot, such as when she types "board" instead of "broad." She pauses the screen reader when she hears homophones and copies the word into a search engine to ensure it matches her intent. As a senior-level leader interacting with external business partners and executives, Lilly believes it is too risky for her to forgo this complex process to check her spelling and grammar.

> It easily takes me four times as long to do all this as it would to use Grammarly. I have to stop and start the reader every time there is an error or a word like there, their, and they're. Ugh, it's so frustrating and tedious, and every time I think about it, I get mad all over again. Three years, I've been dealing with this for three years.

This creative solution demonstrates Lilly's intelligence and ingenuity in solving the challenges dyslexia brings to her workplace, but this complex workaround not only costs Lilly and her company a major loss in productivity but also imposes a high cognitive load on Lilly, requiring a great deal of attention to detail and mental effort. It induces a high level of stress and anxiety for Lilly as she is deeply concerned about how her dyslexia is perceived by coworkers, business partners, and her leadership.

Denying access to Grammarly and other preferred AI-powered AT deeply affects employees' sense of belonging, wellness, and overall workplace experience. Even following the most conservative estimates of one in twenty people being dyslexic, Lilly is hardly the only person with dyslexia at her company who would benefit from access to Grammarly. Lack of access to Grammarly frequently arose in conversations about accessibility at Lilly's company and in interviews with Lilly's coworkers who also have dyslexia and one colleague with ADHD. All were deeply frustrated by their lack of access.

The workplace accommodations process and the grounds by which Grammarly was denied at Lilly's company represent a form of governmentality (Foucault 2004), the techniques, processes, and strategies by which a population is governed. Defined by the state, validated by medical authorities, but enacted by a corporation, this form of governmentality creates a system where people are forced to disclose their disability status to people in leadership positions, provide medical documentation, and, in some cases undergo additional costly medical testing to prove their need for an AI-powered AT that is available to the public. Instead of simply regulating access to tools, the process forced these employees to validate their disability, part of their person, through medical diagnosis before subsequently dismissing their disability expertise and denying effective accommodation due to data security and privacy concerns. This allowed their employer control over their bodies, mental health, and productivity, thus negatively impacting the disabled person's well-being and value to the company.

While academics and students alike have embraced Grammarly and its applications, companies that comply with national and international data security and privacy laws continue to find fault with Grammarly's terms of service, plug-ins, and invasive algorithms that pose considerable security and privacy risks even as Grammarly has spent years attempting to address these concerns to expand its use in the market (Raad et al. 2023; Tran 2024; Feldtmann 2024). Grammarly's inability to adequately address the privacy concerns of its users means that organizations managing sensitive consumer and PHI data find it necessary to restrict access. Privacy concerns have also led some school districts to block Grammarly from district devices to comply with state or federal laws (Graves and Srote 2024; Miller and Mayr 2023; Clay 2022). These dark patterns of design force a false choice between privacy and accessibility. It creates systemic barriers for users with disabilities and perpetuates corporate governmentality that rejects the needs of workers and alienates them in their workplaces. Similar concerns with GenAI applications such as OpenAI's ChatGPT and Google's Gemini have led employers to caution against entering any sensitive or proprietary information into external GenAI programs.

Employers are forced to balance the competing concerns of security, compliance, and Grammarly's value to employees with disabilities. With the competing levels of governmentality—between accommodation and compliance—the choice is no choice at all.

The denial of access to Grammarly in favor of a less effective spell check represents a fundamental disregard for the disability expertise of employees with dyslexia. By imposing restrictive access policies and dismissing the needs of employees with disabilities, companies undermine their commitments to inclusion and belonging. Nanna Mik-Meyer (2016) highlights the "othering" of disabled workers by colleagues and how revealing disability makes discussions of ableism and inclusion difficult. To avoid restrictive accommodation processes that negatively impact employees and the company, organizations must prioritize inclusive co-design as they develop their accommodation processes and policies regarding technologies like Grammarly. By directly collaborating with employees with disabilities, their disability expertise can support the organization in developing effective solutions.

Good AI: Inclusive Co-Design and Disability Expertise

Rapid advancements in AI offer both opportunities and challenges for both assistive technologies and universal design. Dragon's deep learning pattern recognition technology allows its AI to learn the user's accent, speech patterns, and vocabulary. Since its founding in 1997, it has been a valuable AI tool for people with visual disabilities and dyslexia. Dragon and other speech recognition AI came from an effort out of the culmination of the *Technology-Related Assistance Act of 1988*, providing public money for companies to explore growing adaptive technology and the growth of AI technologies (Gonzales and White 2023). Now, Dragon and other speech recognition technologies that utilize AI have become pervasive digital technologies, both at work and home, with widespread adoption beyond users with disabilities. Similarly, screen readers were once solely utilized as AT to accommodate people with visual disabilities and dyslexia, but with advancements in natural language processing, AI-powered text-to-speech programs like Speechify and Microsoft's Read Aloud feature have become popular and are embedded across many products and websites. Successfully demonstrating the value of universal design.

A study by Song et al. (2024) argues that universal design in AI used in the classroom leads to greater engagement from students of all learning types, including those with disabilities. El Morr et al. similarly note that for universal design to be implemented in successful AI, "User friendliness and system performance are crucial. AI systems should be easy to learn and operate, avoiding frustration or burdening users" (2024, 558). I will carry the argument a step further, stating that it is necessary to conduct accessibility user testing with users with disabilities throughout the product development lifecycle. In so doing, AI can reach its full potential for all users, especially for those with disabilities, whose inclusion becomes another technical requirement to meet rather than additional accommodation for medical reasons.

Such an approach challenges the reductive models of disability that often underpin traditional AT development, which frequently prioritizes legal compliance, medical diagnosis, and bureaucratic control. Instead, a relational model of disability, centered on the lived experiences of individuals, can guide the co-creation of AI-powered tools that are truly accessible and empowering. Meeting the needs of users with disabilities, including them in pain point identification, ideation, and design reviews, yields powerfully innovative results. Users and employees with time-intensive, creative workarounds can offer fertile ground for collaborative ideation in design thinking sessions. Their stories and pain points offer powerful avenues for building empathy, and they will be early adopters of an effective and accessible solution. By involving researchers, designers, and engineers in direct collaboration with people with disabilities, we can ensure that accessibility is an integral part of the design process rather than an afterthought.

Inclusive co-design with users with disabilities offers a promising avenue to counter the dehumanizing tendencies of technology in corporate workspaces. Yet simple inclusion is not enough: disability expertise must be properly contextualized so these details are not lost in the larger design schema, as often happens with machine learning and AI in traditional participatory design methods (Kemp 2024; Sloane et al. 2022; Artz 2024). A relational approach to disability, informed by social relations and cultural context, aware of the organizational politics and social spaces in which users with disabilities will engage with the AI, is critical for inclusive co-design. By fostering collaborative design processes with end-users, particularly those with disabilities, an inclusive co-design approach to innovation informed by disability expertise from the earliest stages can harness the potential of AI-powered assistive technologies to enhance human agency and well-being. Inclusive co-design with users with disabilities that leverage their disability expertise allows people with disabilities to play a significant role in shaping the technologies that enable and empower them, which plays a key role in addressing the dehumanizing aspects of technology and governmentality.

While commercially available AI tools hold promise, the most impactful solutions emerge from co-design with users with disabilities. The flexibility of AI-powered AT to provide support where users need it the most while allowing its users' analytic creativity to shape the success of the results means that it can provide the "just right" level and type of support. There are exciting examples of AI-powered "just right" assistive technology emerging, which have been developed not only with users with disabilities but often by people with disabilities. Speechify was developed by Cliff Weitzman, inspired by his experiences with dyslexia (Speechify 2024). Read&Write goes out of its way to employ neurodiverse employees and use their experience to shape its assistive literacy support tool, with a special focus on dyslexic users (Everway 2025). The crowdfunded Goblin Tools' founder collaborated with his neurodivergent friends to develop a suite of tools to help neurodivergent people with executive function, organization, and writing (Goblin Tools 2024). Otter.ai transcribes meetings and summarizes action items supporting people with hearing and attention challenges alike (Otter.ai 2024). It was developed with a strong focus on accessibility, incorporating feedback from neurodivergent users. AI-powered assistive technologies co-designed with users with disabilities offer immense potential for emerging inclusive innovation.

As AI technology continues creating innovative solutions, its impact on assistive technologies for people with disabilities will only grow. Inclusive co-design principles leveraging disability expertise and a relational perspective of disability must be incorporated from ideation to delivery to the ways AI is created and employed. Ethnographic methods, including interviews, job shadowing, and usability studies, illuminate the impact of assistive technologies on belonging, identity, and organizational dynamics, which can facilitate product discovery and optimization. Further research by anthropologists in workplace settings has much to tell us about how the adoption of assistive technologies affects not just people with disabilities but their co-workers and organizations as well. There is a critical need for anthropologists to collaborate with people with disabilities to understand the full impact of AI.

Adaptation and customization are necessary for "good" design and introduce potentially fruitful AI applications. Kate Moran and Sarah Gibbons, vice presidents of the UX design industry-leading Nielsen Norman Group, argue that there is a lot of potential in Generative UI to "dynamically create customized user interfaces in real-time," which could enable a more robust inclusive design that provides customized user interfaces to meet users' unique accessibility needs and personal preferences (Moran and Gibbons 2024). Amy Schade, also of the Nielsen Norman Group, explains the concept of customization vs. personalization, where personalization is product design or system design done by the system itself, while customization allows the user to adapt the user interface to their own preferences and needs (Schade 2016). Where personalization might lose context and thus the details that matter to a disabled user, customization is an active part of the user's experience where they design the product or system to meet their needs and enhance their experience, granting disabled users agency through AI that acts as an extension of themselves and their abilities (Black 2023). Li et al. (2024) argue this level of customization only becomes possible when GenAI is employed to enhance self-adaptive systems. Xiaoan et al. (2024) put this into practice, enabling deep machine learning by using large-scale UI design data sets and user interaction logs to train a Generative UI model. This sets a new gold standard for accessibility: a product that can enable accessible customization without the medical gatekeeping of workplace and educational accommodation (Kasnitz 2025). Creating a world where our environments and tools are accessible by design brings us to a new definition of good.

Making accessible AI means that designers, engineers, and product teams need to be accountable for baking accessibility into all products from concept to delivery. It reiterates the point of Dona Sarkar: "If it's not accessible, it's not good code. It's not good design. Accessibility isn't a social justice problem. Accessibility is a technical problem." "Good" AI of the highest quality experience design is therefore naturally accessible and provides AT applications even if that was not part of their original use cases. This echoes the Nielsen Norman Group's concept of Generative UI and customization, where customization allows the user to adapt to their own preferences and needs: a product that allows for fully accessible customization moves the benchmark for "good design."

As qualitative researchers, anthropologists can play a significant role in inclusive co-design by documenting the bricolage workflows of people with disabilities, identifying high friction pain points, and prioritizing those with the greatest time and cognitive load burdens. Further, I recommend including users with disabilities in co-design activities such as design thinking workshops involving them directly in ideation, journey mapping, and solutioning to learn from their creative solutions and disability expertise. Finally, it is necessary to have business and technology leaders support in prioritizing accessibility as a product requirement from the beginning of a project's design and development.

Researchers, advocates, and technologists need to collaborate to: 1) Build an easy-to-replicate playbook of Accessibility User Research techniques to support training and evaluating AI; 2) Develop shared frameworks for contextualizing the needs and user data of people with disabilities following the relational approach to disability; 3) Create participatory design workshops where individuals with disabilities can directly contribute to the design process from discovery to quality assurance; 4) Establish ethical guidelines for data collection and use, ensuring user privacy and informed consent; 5) Co-author research papers and present findings at conferences to disseminate best practices for inclusive AI development as creating "good" AI is in the best interests of everyone.

To build more inclusive AI, AI must be given the opportunity to learn how to better support users with disabilities. They need to train with users who have disability expertise and undergo extensive assessments where people with a variety of disabilities determine if the AI's output is effective and appropriate for supporting their needs. This creates an opportunity for rehumanizing technology in corporate workspaces to tackle the dehumanization of labor in tech. Creative user-generated AT applications of AI have the potential to tell us much about the nature of human-AI interactions. But inclusive co-design is pivotal, shifting away from reductive models of disability and dehumanizing models of legalistic accommodation and corporate manifestations of governmentality over access to assistive tech.

Conclusion

Emerging applications of AI continue to offer exciting opportunities to incorporate principles of inclusive co-design. Through co-designing AT to meet the needs of those with disabilities at the forefront, instead of after the fact, inclusive co-design principles create "good" technology for a more equitable world. The development and evolution of Dragon and Grammarly offer a blueprint for how disabled-forward AI co-design can work but also show the limitations of such design in the face of unforeseen problems beyond accessibility. With almost thirty years of AI-powered AT available on the market, inclusive co-design with disabled communities remains paramount to the ethical, effective creation of AT or AI. The proverbial genie of AI is out of the bottle: now, it must be contained by strong ethical boundaries and inclusive co-design that helps AI and AI-powered AT reach its full potential.

Disabled communities want to be included in the design of technologies that benefit them. Not only do they want to be included in discussions of policy, implementation, and usage, but they also want to be included in design and development. AI allows developers to create a broader range of considerations from inception to delivery, and it shortens the development time of new technologies. Through co-design with disabled users in mind, like Microsoft's Seeing AI, technology development can achieve Sarkar's definition of "good" design. With the availability of AI, this should become not just more common but the definitive norm by which all technology is judged. Inclusive co-design allows us to create a world where no one is left behind in this age of innovation and accessibility.

Notes

1 Including TikTok, Instagram, Facebook, Reddit, X (formally known as Twitter), and Bluesky.
2 Inclusion criteria: 1) have a disabling condition, permanent or temporary 2) use AI-powered AT in a way that significantly impacts their disability experience
3 Self-diagnosis is a process by which a person thoroughly researches a condition and self-determines that they meet the criteria prior to or in lieu of official medical diagnosis. It is a common practice among neurodivergent adults as there can be more barriers to adult diagnosis, extremely long wait-times, and fewer advantages to medical diagnosis.
4 Grammarly is a cloud-based writing assistant that uses machine learning, deep learning, and natural language processing to analyze human language and provide suggestions regarding grammar, readability, tone, and style.
5 Nuance's Dragon Naturally Speaking, often simply called Dragon by adopters, uses machine learning, deep learning, and natural language processing to achieve high recognition of spoken words, parse commands, and transcribe spoken words into text.
6 The viewpoints, findings, and insights presented in this chapter are my own as an anthropologist and accessibility advocate. They do not represent the views of any of my previous or current employers.
7 Lived experiences are the daily experiences and realities people face that inform their identity.

References

Ali, Kamran, Kisielewska Jolanta, Subhan, Mirza Mohammad Feisal, and Christopher Tredwin. 2019. "How Does Dyslexia Impact on the Educational Experiences of Healthcare Students? A Qualitative Study." *European Journal of Dental Education* 24: 154–162. doi:10.1111/eje.12479.

Arjomand, Noah Amir. 2022. "Empirical Fiction: Composite Character Narratives in Analytical Sociology." *The American Sociologist* 55: 436–472. doi:10.1007/s12108-022-09546-z.

ARK SB136—*An Act to Require the Department of Education and School Districts to Provide Reasonable Accommodations for Students with Irlen Syndrome when Administering State Required Tests.* 2005. https://www.arkleg.state.ar.us/Bills/Detail?id=SB136&ddBienniumSession=2005%2FR.

Artz, Matt. 2024. "Designing Anthropology by Co-Becoming: Reimagining Participation in the Pursuit of New Possibilities." *The Routledge Companion to Practicing Anthropology and Design*, edited by Jenessa Mae Spears and Christine Z Miller. Routledge Press.

Bailey, Chris. 2021. "Exploring Lived Experience," In *Researching Virtual Play Experiences: Visual Methods in Education Research*. Palgrave Macmillan.

Black, Valerie. 2023. "De-humanizing Care: An Ethnography of Mental Health Artificial Intelligence." PhD diss., University of California Berkeley. https://escholarship.org/uc/item/81r9c9tz.

Centers for Disease Control and Prevention. 2016."*Prevalence of Disability and Disability Types by Urban-Rural County Classification—United States, 2016.*" https://www.cdc.gov/ncbddd/disabilityandhealth/features/disability-prevalence-rural-urban.html.

Charlton, James I. 1998. *Nothing About Us Without Us: Disability Oppression and Empowerment*. University of California Press.

Clark, Alison. 2017. *Design Anthropology: Object Cultures in Transition*. Bloomsbury Academic.

Clay, Jackie. 2022. "Grammarly Banned on School Chromebooks Due to Privacy Issue." *The Westford Academy Ghostwriter*, September 29. https://waghostwriter.com/84489/news/grammarly-banned-on-school-chromebooks-due-to-privacy-issue/.

Dębska, Agnieszka, Łuniewska, Magdalena, Zubek, Julian, Chyl, Katarzyna Dynak, Agnieszka, Dzięgiel-Fivet, Gabriela, Plewko, Joanna, Jednoróg, Katarzyna and Anna Grabowska. 2021. "The Cognitive Basis of Dyslexia in School-Aged Children: A Multiple Case Study in a Transparent Orthography." *Developmental Science* 25. https://pmc.ncbi.nlm.nih.gov/articles/PMC9285470/.

Durban, Erin L. 2022. "Anthropology and Ableism." *American Anthropologist* 125: 8–20. doi:10.1111/aman.13659.

El Morr, Christo, Singh, Damanjot, Sawhney, Vaibhav, Fernandes, Sabine, El-Lahib, Yahya, and Rachel Gorman. 2024 "*Exploring the Intersection of AI and Inclusive Design for People with Disabilities.*" Digital Health and Informatics Innovations for Sustainable Health Care Systems. doi:10.3233/SHTI240475.

Everway. 2025. "*Read&Write.*" Everway. https://www.texthelp.com/products/read-and-write-education/.

Feldtmann, Katja. 2024. "*Grammarly Security and Privacy Due Diligence Report.*" Cybershore. https://cybershore.co.nz/cybershore-free-vendor-report-grammarly/.

Foucault, Michel. 1977. *Discipline and Punish: The Birth of the Prison*. Pantheon Books.

Foucault, Michel. 2004. *The Birth of Biopolitics: Lectures at the Collége de France 1978–1979*. Picardo Press.

Ginsburg, Faye and Rayna Rapp. 2013. "Disability Worlds." *Annual Review of Anthropology* 42: 53–68, doi:10.1146/annurev-anthro-092412-155502.

goblin.tools. 2024. "About." goblin.tools. https://goblin.tools/About.

Gonzales, Amy, and Jennifer White. 2023. "*The Evolution of Assistive Technology: Advancing Access and Equity—Then, Now, and Next.*" Disability Employment TA Center. https://aoddisabilityemploymenttacenter.com/wp-content/uploads/2023/09/Evolution_of_AT_Then_Now_and_Next.pdf.

Grammarly. 2024. "*Introducing Grammarly Authorship.*" https://support.grammarly.com/hc/en-us/articles/29548735595405-Introducing-Grammarly-Authorship.

Grant, Adam, host. 2023. "Khan Academy Founder Sal Khan on AI and the Future of Education." Re:Thinking, August 15. Podcast, 44 minutes 52 seconds. https://link.chtbl.com/07UKm98g.

Graves, Luke and Zoey Srote. 2024. "RSD Blocks Grammarly." *The Marquette Messenger*-September 5. https://marquettemessenger.com/news/2024/09/05/rsd-blocks-grammarly/.

Gunn, Wendy, and Jared Donovan. 2012. "Design Anthropology: An Introduction," In *Design and Anthropology*, edited by Wendy Gunn and Jared Donovan. Routledge.

Hartblay, Cassandra. 2020. "Disability Expertise: Claiming Disability Anthropology." *Current Anthropology* 61: 26–36. doi:10.1086/705781.

Jaffri, Afraz. 2024. "*Explore Beyond GenAI on the 2024 Hype Cycle for Artificial Intelligence.*" Gartner. https://www.gartner.com/en/articles/hype-cycle-for-artificial-intelligence.

Johnson, Craig. 2024. "*Job Seekers are Using AI and May Be Taking Shortcuts.*" IT Staffing Report, September 3. https://www.staffingindustry.com/editorial/it-staffing-report/job-seekers-are-using-ai-and-may-be-taking-shortcuts.

Joyce, Alita. 2022. "*Inclusive Design*," Nielsen Norman Group. https://www.nngroup.com/articles/inclusive-design/.

Kapsalis, Efthimis, Jaegar, Nils and Jonathan Hale. 2022. "Disabled-by-Design: Effects of Inaccessible Urban Public Spaces on Users of Mobility Assistive Devices—A Systematic Review." *Disability and Rehabilitation: Assistive Technology* 19: 604–622. doi:10.1080/17483107.2022.2111723.

Kasnitz, Devva. 2025. "The Politics of Disability Performativity: An Autoethnography," in *Current Anthropology* 61. doi:10.1086/705782.

Kemp, Lena. 2024. "Navigating the AI Employment Bias Maze: Legal Compliance Guidelines and Strategies." *Business Law Today*, April. https://www.americanbar.org/groups/business_law/resources/business-law-today/2024-april/navigating-ai-employment-bias-maze/.

Lévi-Strauss, Claude. 1962. *The Savage Mind*. Weidenfeld and Nicolson.

Le Cunff, Anne-Laure, Dommett, Eleanor and Vincent Giampietro. 2024. "Neurophysiological Measures and Correlates of Cognitive Load in Attention-Deficit/Hyperactivity Disorder (ADHD), Autism Spectrum Disorder (ASD) and Dyslexia: A Scoping Review and Research Recommendations." *European Journal of Neuroscience* 59. doi:10.1111/ejn.16201.

Li, Jialong, Zhang, Minguye, Li, Nianyu, Weyns, Danny, Jin, Zhi, and Kenji Tei. 2024. "Generative AI for Self-Adaptive Systems: State of the Art and Research Roadmap." *ACM Transactions on Autonomous and Adaptive Systems* 19. doi:10.1145/3686803.

Made by Dyslexia. 2024. "*Made by Dyslexia.*" https://www.madebydyslexia.org/.

Microsoft. 2019. "Seeing AI: Making the Visual World More Accessible." Microsoft, 3 minutes 27 seconds. https://www.youtube.com/watch?v=DybczED-GKE.

Mik-Meyer, Nanna. 2016. "Othering, Ableism, and Disability: A Discursive Analysis of Co-workers' Construction of Colleagues with Visible Impairments." *Human Relations* 60. doi:10.1177/0018726715618454.

Miller, Keith. 2008. "Making A Difference Award (2009)—Jim Thatcher (interview)." Association for Computing Machinery. https://www.sigcas.org/2018/02/08/making-a-difference-award-2009-jim-thatcher-interview/.

Miller, Paige and Madison Mayr. 2023. "Google Places Restrictions on Websites not Complying with CT Law; Teachers Scramble for New Ways to Present Content." *Inklings News*, October 17. https://www.inklingsnews.com/news/2023/10/17/google-places-restrictions-on-websites-not-complying-with-ct-law-teachers-scramble-for-new-ways-to-present-content/.

Moran, Kate and Sarah Gibbons. 2024. "Generative UI and Outcome-Oriented Design." Nielsen Norman Group, March 22. https://www.nngroup.com/articles/generative-ui/.

Nash, June. 1981. "Ethnographic Aspects of the World Capitalist System," In *Annual Review of Anthropology* 10: 393–423. doi:10.1146/annurev.an.10.100181.002141.

Nguyen, Xuan-Thuy. 2015. "Genealogies of Disability in Global Governance: A Foucauldian Critique of Disability and Development." *Foucault Studies* 15. https://rauli.cbs.dk/index.php/foucault-studies/article/view/4825.

OpenAI. 2022. "Introducing ChatGPT." OpenAI. https://openai.com/index/chatgpt/.

Otter.ai. 2024. "Otter.ai." Otter.ai. https://otter.ai/.

Palacios, Klarissa. 2022. "Disabled by Design | Klarissa Palacios | TEDxYouth@SantiagoHS." TEDx Talks, 10 minutes 58 seconds. https://www.youtube.com/watch?v=XwBHKMKui0k.

Pluralsight. 2023. "Pluralsight Expert Access: Dona Sarkar on How to Build Accessibility into Your Tech Processes." *Pluralsight*, June 16. Pluralsight, https://www.youtube.com/watch?v=oCzjLCS-nwE.

Raad, Bareq, Anjum, Farheen, and Zanyar Nathir Ghafar. 2023. "Exploring the Profound Impact of Artificial Intelligence Applications (Quillboat, Grammarly and ChatGPT) on English Academic Writing: A Systematic Review." *International Journal of Integrative Research* 1: 599–622. doi:10.59890/ijir.v1i10.366.

Seaver, Nick. 2019. "Captivating algorithms: Recommender Systems as Traps." *Journal of Material Culture* 24. doi:10.1177/1359183518820366.

Schade, Amy. 2016. "Customization vs. Personalization in the User Experience." Nielsen Norman Group, July 10. https://www.nngroup.com/articles/customization-personalization/.

Schaur, Melane and Reinhard Koutny. 2024. "Dyslexia, Reading/Writing Disorders: Assistive Technology and Accessibility." *Computers Helping People with Special Needs, 19th International Conference*, July 8–12, 2024: 269–274. doi:10.1007/978-3-031-62849-8_33.

Sloane, Mona, Emanuel Moss, Olaitan Awomolo, and Laura Forlano. 2022. "Participation Is not a Design Fix for Machine Learning." *Algorithms, Mechanism, and Optimization*. doi:10.1145/3551624.3555285.

Song, Yukyeong, Weisberg, Lauren R., Zhang, Shan, Tian, Xiaoyi, Boyer, KristyElizabeth, and Israel Maya. 2024. "A Framework for Inclusive AI Learning Design for Diverse Learners." *Computers and Education: Artificial Intelligence* 6. doi:10.1016/j.caeai.2024.100212

Speechify. 2024. "About." *Speechify*. https://speechify.com/about/.

Spencer, Geoff. 2019. "Saqib Shaikh on technology and inclusion: Creating an AI future with possibilities for all." *Microsoft*. https://news.microsoft.com/apac/features/saqib-shaikh-on-technology-and-inclusion-creating-an-ai-future-with-possibilities-for-all/.

T S, Karthik. 2024. "Beyond ChatGPT: How Generative AI Is Shaping The Future Of Businesses." *Forbes*. https://www.forbes.com/councils/forbestechcouncil/2024/08/22/beyond-chatgpt-how-generative-ai-is-shaping-the-future-of-businesses/.

Tran, Nguyen Ngoc. 2024. "The Use of Grammarly Application in Writing A Graduation Project among Senior Students Majoring in English Language at Nam Can Tho University." *International Journal of Science and Management Studies* 7. doi:10.51386/25815946/ijsms-v7i4p103

United States Bureau of Labor. 2024. "Persons with a Disability: Labor Force Characteristics Summary." https://www.bls.gov/news.release/disabl.nr0.htm.

Unterberger, Alayne. 2018. "'No One Cares if You Can't Work': Injured and Disabled Mexican-Origin Workers in Transnational Life Course Perspectives." *Anthropology of Work Review* 39: 105–115. doi:10.1111/awr.12150

Waterford, Bea. 2019. "Constructions of Learning Disabilities Within Contemporary Canadian Society: Discourse, Biopower and Governmentality." Masters diss., University of Western Ontario. https://www.proquest.com/openview/c4d31997504cfd8e6af836823bd8c53c/1?pq-origsite=gscholar&cbl=18750&diss=y.

Watharow, Annemaree. 2020. "Owning My Room: Building a Safe, Accessible and Productive Space for Student Researchers with Complex Communication Disabilities." *Social Research and Disability* edited by Ciaran Burke and Bronagh Byrne. Routledge Press.

Witell, Lars, Gebauer, Heiko, Jaakkola, Elina, Hammedi, Wafa, Patricio, Lia, and Helen Parks. 2017. "A Bricolage Perspective on Service Innovation." *Journal of Business Research* 79. doi:10.1016/j.jbusres.2017.03.021.

Xiaoan, Zhan, Yang, Xu and Liu Yingchia. 2024. "Personalized UI Layout Generation using Deep Learning: An Adaptive Interface Design Approach for Enhanced User Experience." *International Journal of Engineering and Management Research* 14. doi:10.55524/ijirem.2024.11.6.7.

Yale Center for Dyslexia and Creativity. "*Dyslexia FAQ*." https://dyslexia.yale.edu/dyslexia/dyslexia-faq/.

Zagrodny Barkley, Kay. 2024. "Experiences Practicing Design and Anthropology in the Workplace: Applying Transformational Approaches to Traditional Business Models," in *The Routledge Companion to Practicing Anthropology and Design* edited by Jenessa Mae Spears and Christine Z Miller. Routledge.

PART III

Sociotechnical Interactions

8

NAVIGATING THE UNCANNY VALLEY

How Conversation Designers Shape Human-AI Interaction

Elizabeth Rodwell

Preface

The first ubiquitous online conversational agents (CAs) were simple bots confined to customer service chat windows that popped up to offer unsolicited help. But in the past decade, CAs have also moved beyond earlier scripts to appear across various domains: smart home devices, hospital kiosks, enterprise software, and mobile apps. And though text interfaces, particularly for large language models, currently play a significant role, CAs are also increasingly multimodal and embodied. As a subcategory of CAs, Embodied Conversational Agents (ECAs) are designed to respond with natural language and inhabit human-like avatars that gesture, blink, and smile (Cassell et al., 2000). Newer animations are also built to appear responsive, expressive, personable, and even empathetic. However, the term "embodied" is misleading, as in the case of ECAs, it refers to a virtual avatar and not a robotic (or otherwise embodied) body at all (see Figure 8.1).

ECAs' progression has introduced new tensions and opportunities. As conversational agents are deployed in more public-facing roles and higher-stakes contexts, designers are tasked with making them engaging but not creepy, realistic but not too real. The design decisions made in AI labs ultimately shape user trust and the broader acceptance of these tools. A desire to better understand these conversations motivated the ethnographic fieldwork among conversation designers and conversational UX professionals[1] that I explore in this chapter.

Introduction: Natural (Body) Language Processing

"The new avatar looks like it got Botox, the way her face is frozen," a Tokyo-based conversation design lead named "Nadia"[2] quipped, staring at a

DOI: 10.4324/9781003532750-12

FIGURE 8.1 Kuki AI, created by ICONIQ, is an example of an embodied conversational agent featuring a sophisticated avatar. (Kuki AI, courtesy of ICONIQ.)

television in the main conference room of a company I will call OratioNet. "Her upper face doesn't move at all" (Author Fieldnotes, July 17, 2024).[3] We are lingering after the engineers demonstrated their progress in synchronizing the non-verbal cues and spoken dialogue for the company's online embodied conversational agent, "Aida". Nadia is trying to pinpoint what felt off about its movements and has settled on the motion of its face as the culprit. The conversation design team's consensus is that if Aida is to be an effective partner for practicing English, her body language cannot distract from the content of her instruction. And right now, her non-verbal cues are very distracting to them.

For conversational agents–systems designed to communicate with people using text or voice-based natural language–one of the most complicated sequences of technology can be found in embodied conversational agents (ECAs). These are built using a series of platforms that all must function correctly to deliver a positive user experience. First is the language input/output processing (automatic speech recognition, natural language processing, text-to-speech). Second is the visual avatar, which should coordinate facial movements and paralinguistic signals without appearing artificial or creepy. Third is the hardware, a frequently neglected element within social scientific theorization of conversational systems despite the immense energy and environmental resources required to run servers and store data (Crawford, 2024).

Although each technological step is highly complex and requires extensive iteration to finesse, any shortcomings in an avatar's appearance will likely be noticed first and distract from other aspects of the experience.

My colleagues' bemused observations on Aida's body language notwithstanding, the avatar OratioNet designed was highly sophisticated (even at the "Botox" stage), trained on careful measurement and facial monitoring to map the intricate speech movements of a female native English speaker of a similar age. Thus, Aida didn't retain her semi-frozen expression for long–within weeks, and by the next meeting, her upper face was moving more fluidly, and the team's critique had moved on to whether she was showing too many teeth as she talked. Next on their list was coordinating eye movements with speech and, in the words of one conversation designer: "avoiding creepiness" insofar as creepiness is entirely avoidable for an avatar.

During my fieldwork at OratioNet, I occupy two roles: an applied anthropologist working on an independent conversational AI project and a more traditional ethnographer. My hybrid status developed after an initial fieldwork trip to their office, when my observation of conversation designers inspired me to pursue a side project using the company's ECA. Applied/theoretical entanglement is typical of my fieldwork in AI workplaces (Rodwell, forthcoming) and requires that I be mindful of how participation in conversation design might affect my biases and blind spots about the industry. It is also an effective way to negotiate research access with tech companies.

This chapter is grounded in my ongoing (2020-present) ethnography of conversation design and user experience (UX). However, rather than discussing conversation design and conversational systems more broadly (as in Rodwell, 2024), I focus here on the unique challenges of designing embodied conversational agents (ECA). ECAs sit at the intersection of several theoretical and practical concerns (Cassell et al., 2000; Iacobelli & Cassell, 2021; Wambsganss et al., 2021), and as such, designing them engenders daily workplace discussion and invokes some of the most significant historical and contemporary arguments about AI's nature. In this chapter, I break these complexities down into their components: hardware, image, voice, and body language. I argue that workplace discussions on avatars and conversation repeatedly circle the canonical notion of the "uncanny" as designers unpack rich theoretical discussions of conversation and gender.

Though astute commentary exists about how the theoretical and applied social sciences fail to maintain a mutually beneficial dialogue (Gonzales & Turner, 2019), many tech workplaces have already integrated theory into their daily praxis as a natural outcome of their human-centered tech workers' academic training and background. In other words, the foundational knowledge within many tech teams includes a similar academic canon. Thus, while conversation and UX designers may be critiqued for not always understanding the engineering side of AI (Hoffman, 2017), they have a shared vocabulary and humanistic orientation unique to their role.

The Parts that Make Up the Whole ECA

Within the accelerating timeline of human technological development, ECAs as a category of interactive agents are not new, although the ECAs from the 1990s often appear amusingly clunky compared with contemporary iterations. Even so, this technology has been under development for several decades, as the earliest ancestors of embodied conversational agents appeared in the 1950s. First to emerge were text-to-speech (TTS) systems like Haskins Laboratories' Pattern Playback (late 1940s) (see Figure 8.2) and IBM's 704 TTS System (1961), which converted symbolic data into synthetic "spoken" output (Cooper 2025)– although attempts to reproduce human speech and vocal sounds go back much further (Bendel, 2019).

Parallel research in the twentieth century resulted in systems that could convert (some) spoken human language into text, like Bell Labs' "Audrey" (1952) and IBM's "Shoebox" (1962). However, it took a few more decades before a visual representation of these tools (i.e., an avatar) could be introduced as an intermediary between natural language processing (NLP) input and text-to-speech (TTS) output technologies. One of the first systems combining speech recognition, NLP, and an animated human avatar was the MIT Media Lab's "Persona" in 1994 (Cassell et al., 2000), followed quickly by the University of Stockholm's "Gandalf" in 1996. Contemporary multimodal systems, which accept spoken and typed input, are descendants of rule-based chatbots dating back to the 1960s that used pattern matching to generate responses. This piece of the ECA chain also saw compounding gains in sophistication during the 1990s, with chatbots like A.L.I.C.E (Artificial Linguistic Internet Computer Entity) representing a massive collaboration between developers and an opportunity for open-source advancement of conversational agents through its

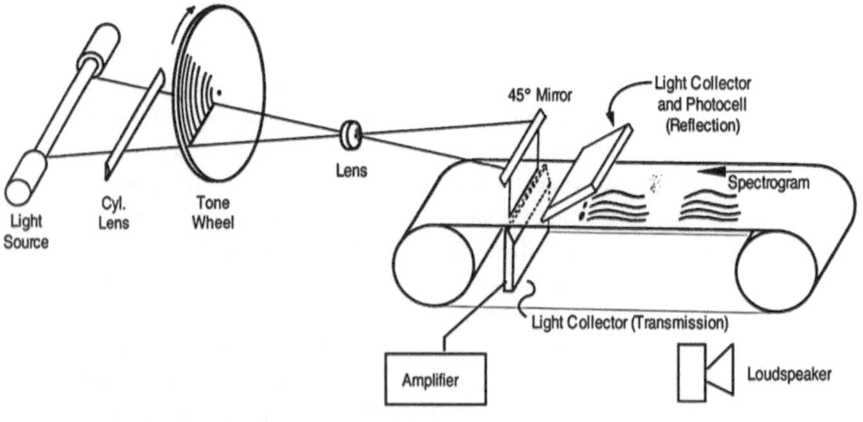

FIGURE 8.2 Haskins' Laboratories Pattern Playback talking machine, built by Dr. Franklin S. Cooper and his colleagues (Cooper 2025).

Artificial Intelligence Markup Language (AIML) (Wallace, 2009). While some of these early bots placed a graphic of the chatbot's imagined character next to its input form, these were supposed to suggest that the bot could simulate natural conversation while inadvertently reminding the user that their conversation partner was very much artificial. Even in their earliest instantiation, ECAs were defined distinctly by their incorporation of a blocky 3D avatar and, in some cases, their capacity to interpret even visual communication signals from human users (Feine et al., 2019; Pelachaud, 2005).

Part 1: Avatars are Complicated

> ...I am concerned about the confusion of human and machine capabilities. I make the basic assertion that people are not machines, and machines are not people. I do not think that human-to-human interaction is a good model for the design of user interfaces.
>
> *(Shneiderman & Maes, 1997)*

Ben Shneiderman, who delivered this statement, is one of the foundational thinkers read by most introductory UX classes (including mine), and his most recent book, Human-Centered AI (2022), sits on the shelves of OratioNet's office library for communal reference. Although concerns about avatars and anthropomorphism, such as those he expressed in 1997, have long been raised relative to conversation design (e.g., Weizenbaum, 1976), curiosity about our ability to simulate conversation partners has won out over trepidation about its implications.

Designing modern avatars is a multimedia experience involving highly technical and/or hybrid processes in which human models become templates for digital faces and bodies (e.g., Zhang et al., 2024). For example, in some sophisticated AI labs, avatar design involves hiring actors as stand-ins for the avatar so their bodies can be mapped and measured to determine how people move when they talk and translate it into computer animation. Avatar modeling and iteration, therefore, exist at the intersection of theories about artificial intelligence, social psychology, and human-computer interaction and have a natural relationship with the concept of anthropomorphism as studied by anthropologists (Boyer, 1996; Jackson, 2002; Richardson, 2016). My fieldwork, collaboration, and interviews with conversation designers have reaffirmed that for those who work closely with avatars, decision-making is not just about aesthetic choices but shaping user experiences and influencing trust and engagement. At the same time, workplace discussions reflect a nuanced understanding of how avatars reflect deeper social structures and preferences deemed to be universal and transnational.

In addition to their affective role in conversational AI platforms, avatars are both mirrors and assemblages of culture and represent a critical site where theory and practice intersect in technology workplaces. Much of the research on avatars has described them as forms of self-expression and a means to explore aspects of human identity in networked environments (Blascovich & Bailenson, 2011; Boellstorff, 2008; Vanderburg & Loveland, 2025). In such cases, rather than fostering disembodied interactions, Ikegami argues that avatars facilitate new forms of embodied cognition, much like Merleau-Ponty's phenomenological approach to embodiment, wherein the body extends to the tools it uses, blurring the line between self and environment (Ikegami, 2011).

However, contexts within which a bilateral relationship exists between humans using avatars are only one category of relational structure. Typical for embodied conversational agents, human users can see their reflected image in a video-conference-style camera window while they talk to Aida. But even in such cases, academic inquiry predominantly focuses not on the dynamic created by juxtaposing one's mirror image with an artificial conversation partner but on how people interpret and respond to the avatar's self-presentation. Here, we return to foundational principles of non-verbal communication (and the computers are social actors paradigm), where attributes like age and gender influence perceived trustworthiness, expertise, and approachability, whether the conversational partner is human or AI (Nass et al., 1994; Ter Stal et al., 2020). In the best-case scenario, this leaves AI professionals with a choice as to whether to pursue a positive user experience strategy grounded in conforming to stereotypes or (if they have the latitude in their workplace) to challenge biases through deliberate design choices. However, despite a common tendency for conversation designers' preferences to clash with corporate priorities (Rodwell, 2025), the issues of avatar gender and design equity are still raised in the workplace.

While reviewing a colleague's recent academic study, OratioNet's conversation design team wondered about the effect Aida's young, female avatar had on her ability to execute successful roleplaying exercises with human partners, compared with an older human man performing the same exercises:

ELEANOR QUESTIONED: "Did [the study's author] account for how seriously someone might take this kind of interaction with an older man versus a younger woman?"

ADRIÁN AGREED: "And whose non-verbal reactions or displays are more important? Are they more important for the avatar [than a human conversation partner] if we want to draw out human users?"

(Fieldnotes, July 31, 2024).

Questions of gender have been a central focus of critiques of the sociocultural role of conversational agents (Abercrombie et al., 2021; Strengers & Kennedy, 2020; Wagman & Parks, 2021) and a variable introduced in many studies of how voice/avatar impacts user trust and perceptions of competence. Even excluding a sizeable body of work on the computers are social actors (CASA) paradigm and gender (Gambino et al., 2020), anthropologists have long argued that material objects are embedded in human power structures and woven into human relationships (Hornborg, 2021; Ingold, 2007; Latour, 2000; Miller, 2010). However, ECAs occupy a unique position at the intersection of subject and object, and because they are increasingly designed to be as anthropomorphic as possible, questions about why and if users personify these systems accordingly seem increasingly irrelevant.

Meanwhile, designers must write anti-harassment scripts into their conversational agents because sexual harassment and bullying of devices perceived as female is essentially considered inevitable in the industry (Deibel & Evanhoe, 2021, 100) and sometimes encouraged for monetary gain (Liao et al., 2024). Despite Aida being a tool used in academic settings and whose sessions are recorded, she was not immune to sexualized or flirty interactions. These became the subject of routine incredulous conversations at OratioNet, whose conversation designers tended to assign flirting behavior to the same category of social breach as other actions deemed too intimate for the context, such as showering, blow drying hair, eating, or appearing in front of the camera partly dressed (Fieldnotes, July 17, 2024).

Although a widely proposed (but not as often implemented) industry solution to this problem has been to increase the diversity of AI design teams, this solution underestimates the rigidity of many corporate cultures, the challenge of disrupting our instinct to assign these devices a binary gender, and a still prevalent tendency to design avatars that lean into gender stereotypes. For example, one new conversational agent for academic tutoring displayed an anime caricature of a young woman with bows in her hair and a demure posture as its avatar. In the pre-press paper discussing this tool, she even wears lipstick, and while you can change her outfit, she's always young, wide-eyed, and female (Chen et al., 2025). Like so many decisions in the tech world, a gender stereotypical end-product and/or single AI persona are typically manifestations of time and resource constraints. However, some organizations defend using a young female persona as their tool's default or only personality by citing user research data–which cannot be taken at face value, considering users have become accustomed to associating digital assistants with women (Rodwell, 2024, 51; Strengers & Kennedy, 2020). As UX professionals know, familiarity is often positively correlated with a good user experience.

Part 2: ECAs and the Uncanny Valley

To establish a strong connection between people and conversational systems, social presence theory suggests that an avatar must appear and behave human-like (Krämer, 2010) and explains that people are hypersensitive to imperfections in realistic avatars–conversation designers included (Starling et al., 2024; Thaler et al., 2020). On a practical level, achieving balance is critical to the commercial success of products and a major preoccupation of conversational AI professionals, some of whom consider it better to avoid avatars altogether. To this end, one senior conversation designer I interviewed invoked the canonical notion of the "uncanny valley":

> I think in the majority of cases, avatars still fall squarely in [Mori's] uncanny valley. I find them creepy and concerning. And they make me personally as a user, less willing to engage, less willing to trust, because I'm like, ew… like you're not quite human. I literally do have a little bit of that, like, disgust reaction. The kinds of cases where people say oh, avatars will help is where you're looking to have a bot take over a truly human function, a caregiving function, a therapeutic function. Yeah, and I remain the skeptic. Not because of avatars alone, but avatars, I don't think help.
>
> *(Jill, Conversation Designer, April 26, 2023)*

In a 1970 essay, Masahiro Mori famously described how an object resembling a human could be merely interesting if its resemblance did not too closely simulate the human while falling short (Mori, 1970). On the other hand, if a thing were to appear approximately human, it would likely induce feelings of discomfort in the humans encountering it and thus enter a zone he called the "uncanny valley." Mori probably didn't expect his essay to become canon; it caught on years after its publication (and took some more time to be translated from the Japanese). Since then, it has been consistently invoked in both academic and professional settings, as it captures something we are still wrestling with as we move into a new stage of embodied conversational agent (ECA) and robotic development.

I was familiar with the concept of the "uncanny valley" from my late-1990s preoccupation with cyborg theory (e.g. Gray, 1995), but unprepared for how frequently it is still referenced by those working on conversational agents in the mid-2020s. In reaction to routine updates to Aida's avatar or exposure to a competitor's conversational agent, the conversation designers at OratioNet immediately remarked upon any "uncanny" characteristics they observed. They invoked Mori to explain the source of this discomfort: an avatar must either be so cartoonish that it doesn't become creepy or so realistic that it avoids the same. Historically, fear of the uncanny valley, combined with technology that wasn't yet able to create realistic avatars, has led Americans to avoid recreating qualities that were too human and too likely to introduce anxiety in the U.S. (Richardson, 2016). More recent work has indicated that researchers still disagree about whether making a robotic conversational agent closely simulate human behavior has a chilling or strengthening effect on trust (Schreuter et al., 2021). But OratioNet is in Japan, with staff from all over the world. As Katagiri et al. argued (2001), we must look beyond an American perspective on human-computer interaction to acknowledge what is universally uncanny about avatars.

The following features can make an avatar uncanny, according to conversation designers at OratioNet (Fieldnotes, July 2023 and 2024; survey of colleagues at field site, February 2025). Worth noting is how these can also describe paralinguistic and kinesic characteristics exhibited by neurodiverse and disabled humans in conversation:

1. Its upper face (eyebrows, eyes, forehead) doesn't move.
2. Its mouth opens too wide.
3. It shows too many teeth.
4. Its lips move asynchronously with its speech.
5. Its face looks tired.
6. Its facial expressions move too slowly in general.
7. Its eye movement is set to change at regular intervals rather than in connection with its speech.
8. Its voice doesn't match its avatar.
9. Too much blinking.
10. Not enough blinking.
11. Eyes are too wide ("staring into your soul," as one conversation designer said).
12. Unfocused gaze.
13. "Strange" nodding or shaking head movements.

Part 3: Conversation Design: Making the Avatar Talk Pretty

Since dialog systems have attempted to replicate natural language, humans have been working on improving the fluidity of that language, whether by writing dialog, prompts, or both, depending on whether the system is a chatbot or connected to a large language model (LLM) This process represents a significant intersection between linguistics (and linguistic anthropology) and technology. As conversational AI has grown more complex in the twenty-first century–moving beyond simple query and command responses–the participation of social scientists has become critical. With the integration of natural language processing (NLP) into conversational systems, it became necessary to consider them as both highly complicated technical systems and sociocultural entities.

Conversation design / UX is heavily informed by the subfield and history of conversation analysis and its exploration of concepts like turn-taking and pacing (Enfield, 2017; Sacks et al., 1974). But because traditional conversation analysis emphasizes the role of non-verbal communication and learned and ingrained social cues, reproducing natural-seeming conversation in an ECA requires expertise in conversation as practiced by specific communities of end-users, plus the skill to build a sophisticated technical system for mimicking that rhythm. Contemporary conversation designers must often possess "a background in the study of natural conversation" within the context of one of the social sciences (Moore et al., 2017, 493); however, the developing nature of the field means that backgrounds can vary heavily depending on the maturity of an organization and its work on conversational agents. Those I interviewed outside of OratioNet (n=20) just as often had backgrounds in social science adjacent fields like philosophy, education, and creative writing as they did linguistics.

In addition to canonical work on conversation analysis, Noam Chomsky's (1957) generative grammar has imprinted on conversation design for AI by interpreting language as rule-based and governed by universal principles, predicting the structure of early attempts at human-machine conversation. Modern conversation design emerged as a practice in the late 1990s with IBM's Watson (1997), followed by a gap of over a decade before Apple's Siri (2011), Amazon's Alexa (2014), and Google Assistant (2016) emerged to shift technical dialog writing to a greater focus on voice user interfaces. The formalization of conversation design as an interdisciplinary practice owes itself to the efforts of these large companies and their work to establish and publicize best practices. The most prominent are IBM's Natural Conversation Framework (NCF), which articulated formal design principles for the field (Moore, 2018), and Google's user experience (UX) principles for voice user interfaces (Giangola, 2017). With the expansion of work on voice user interfaces, principles like user-centered dialog flow design emerged (Dritsas et al., 2025), followed by conversational UX as a subdiscipline combining research methods from human factors, discourse analysis, and Human-Computer Interaction (HCI). Further, some of the most dynamic influences on conversation design were concepts borrowed from screenwriting, game design, and improv theater.

As a field still negotiating its self-definition, the responsibilities (and even job titles) of those in conversation design can be highly varied. While Google and IBM are still among the most organized teams, the rapid improvement of natural language understanding (NLU) and large language models (LLMs) has changed the nature of the work. At OratioNet, for example, conversation design is about training the LLM as much as script writing, and this means adapting concepts from linguistics to prompts that the LLM can interpret.

Among these foundational linguistics concepts, OratioNet's conversations about conversational turn-taking between Aida and her human users are among the most collaborative, requiring significant participation from employee specialists in engineering, linguistics, UX, and conversation design. For the engineers, a challenge is predicting when a user's silence indicates they are thinking versus when they might not intend to answer a prompt from Aida. Concurrently, a challenge for the conversation designers is determining how many turns the ECA should take if a human barely responds, and what words it should use to encourage them to answer. For the engineers, this can be a matter of predicting the probability of a certain kind of response after a prompt by the ECA or tracking non-verbal cues such as whether someone is looking away from the screen, which can indicate thinking (Fieldnotes, September 26, 2024).

During a company-wide meeting, a senior conversation designer, whom I will call Jack, described his perspective on managing Aida's turn-taking:

> We have a thing called supportive encouragement. If the user says [what the ECA has asked] is a difficult question, she will say something like, "Take your time." But if the user says, "Sorry, I don't understand what you mean," she can't just say, "It's okay, take your time."

Another conversation designer, "Adrián" jumped in:

> We can add a prompt that's something like, "If the user hasn't completed a sentence, do this."

Jack nodded and turned to the engineers and computer scientists:

> Our strategy is that if we don't understand the user['s input], we draw them out a bit more.
>
> *(Fieldnotes, July 16, 2024)*

Although much about conversational turn-taking transcends culture (Enfield, 2017, 10), my experiments with Aida and American children humorously complicated the team's meticulous system for predicting the probability that a human is speaking versus pausing and thinking. After several sessions in which kids essentially crashed the conversational scenarios I wrote for my side-project and began off-roading with Aida (a process in which she departs from her prompts and begins improvising), I lamented to the conversation designers that I was having trouble preventing this from happening. Jack watched one of my recorded sessions, then removed his headphones and reported that my problem was pacing, i.e., "kids speaking up at the wrong time." He was visibly amused. "Aida is used to Japanese kids who wait and take their turns very carefully, not American kids who barge in."

Adrián chimed in: "Pausing and pacing is cultural," he said (Fieldnotes, September 9, 2024), inadvertently gesturing to an ongoing critique of Chomsky's earliest arguments (Enfield, 2017, 10).

Conversation design encompasses much more than pacing and turn-taking, so the team's ability to count on behavioral consistency among their users provided limited assurance of a positive user experience. Natural-feeling conversation requires carefully scripted dialogue, even if one side of the conversation is a simple, transactional chatbot. Additionally, for an ECA, the definition of conversational competence also extends to and becomes grounded in the efficacy of its nonverbal communication. In workplaces like OratioNet, strategies to effectively replicate human bodily cues unfold as practitioner discourse that alternately relies on intuition and linguistic theory, with the highly technical process of crafting a "natural" smile, for example, relying as much on subjective judgment as formal taxonomies and research areas like social signal processing (Feine et al., 2019). AI designers' equivalent use of textbook and personal definitions is perhaps an inevitable consequence of "naturalness" being a moving target, and it also means that around the office, people are as likely to be sitting at their desks taking notes on an academic book as they are engaged in speculative conversations with colleagues about paralinguistic cues. Further, this term is invoked consistently, as in the "naturalness" of Aida's facial expression, voice, or response to a user comment. While I did not consciously try to record my colleagues' references to "natural/naturalness," these terms were mentioned thirty-eight times in my fieldnotes during one three-month period alone (July-October 2024), with most of these references appearing in discussions about AI and voice.

Part 4: Saying Her Lines: Voice and ECAs

As decades of research on its impact on affect and emotion have shown, effective synthetic voice design is one of the most critical components of a positive user experience for conversational agents (Seaborn & Urakami, 2021). Indeed, studies have shown how much of an impression the audible characteristics of a voice make on us in general and how quickly we form impressions of people based solely on cues ranging from pitch to intonation (Kim et al., 2021; Nass & Brave, 2005)[4] and default to stereotypical associations based on the perceived gender of a voice (Deibel & Evanhoe, 2021, 30; Faber, 2020). Our tendency to form complex impressions of voices is reinforced by the common practice—especially among American companies—of assigning human names to the voices they license for text-to-speech systems. So, before listening to demos of "Sonia," "Oliver," or "Fiona," a conversation designer is influenced by the human tendency to form an impression of personality based on culturally familiar names (Dinur et al., 1996). During meetings, these names also become how a voice is referenced. However, there is a marked lack of team consensus on which American-accented voices pre-selected by Adrián "match" Aida's avatar, and no exposition on why the accent should be generically American.

The first voice, "Jennifer," sounds too young and possibly too friendly to the team rather than matching the "neutral" persona they hope to present. One conversation designer attributes his discomfort with "Jennifer" to her use of "vocal fry"—a term so frequently invoked in critiques of women's voices that it has become a gendered cliché (Chao & Bursten, 2021).

The team interprets the second, "Lyndsay," as bossy. She also sounds a bit "unnatural," but is "very easy to understand," so everyone agrees this could be an asset for English language learners.

"Erin" sounds very American (negative valence, despite the need for an American-accented voice), but has the right level of formality (positive valence). Provocatively, as I am the only American in the room, everyone wonders if "Erin" might be too "generic". Nonetheless, this is the voice that is ultimately chosen.

After repeatedly listening to the audio samples speak the sample scripts, the team concludes that the voice selection cannot be determined without attaching the finalists to Ava's new avatar, even though the lip-sync issues are inevitable in early-stage voice testing risk distracting everyone as they try to gauge which combination of voice and image feel subjectively "right".

One of the persistent challenges for conversation designers is pushing back against the dominance of the so-called "white woman voice"—a default that reflects the racial and socioeconomic biases embedded in the datasets used to train these systems, many of which systematically exclude large segments of the U.S. (and world) population (Lima et al., 2019; Wagman & Parks, 2021). In Aida's case, the avatar is both white and female, making any perceived mismatch between her visual appearance and vocal presentation a potential threat to her perceived "naturalness" and, by extension, a risk of slipping into the uncanny valley (Schreuter et al., 2021). These concerns directly shaped how the team selected voice samples, relying on names and vocal characteristics deemed plausible for her identity, even as those choices ultimately reaffirmed prevailing industry norms.

Assembling the Parts (Conclusion)

The iterative process of designing embodied conversational agents like Aida is as much about refining non-verbal and linguistic nuances as it is about advancing the underlying technology. From calibrating eyebrow motion to selecting a voice that doesn't inadvertently suggest uncanny characteristics to her users, conversation designers at OratioNet—and across the industry—are engaged in a balancing act between theory and practice, human perception, and machine capabilities. These professionals operate within an emergent field where engineering priorities sometimes clash with the human-centered concerns of UX and conversation design. Yet, as my fieldwork suggests, their work is often informed by an array of academic discourse, ranging from the latest scientific studies of AI and human-computer interaction to historically significant linguistic and educational theory, even as their everyday decisions are constrained by business imperatives and the cultural expectations in which they are embedded.

Thus, the uncanny valley is not just a challenge of aesthetics or technical finesse—it is a sociocultural phenomenon that even international workplaces like OratioNet identify using shared references and continuously negotiate together. This common discomfort when presented with an avatar that is almost—but not quite—human points to significant questions about AI's role in social interaction. Does a more human-like conversational agent necessarily lead to more meaningful engagement, or does it trigger a different quality of skepticism and aversion? The field remains divided on this issue, even as industry professionals work within the tension between familiarity and unease, naturalness and artifice.

The design of ECAs is ultimately not just a technical process but a cultural and ethical one. While visual and text-based conversational user interfaces serve as intermediaries between humans and code, conversation designers must navigate the contradictions inherent in making artificial entities feel relatable while ensuring they do not become unsettling. This should mean confronting longstanding biases in AI development, grappling with the ways avatars encode power and social norms, and recognizing that even the most sophisticated agents, no matter how smoothly their faces move or how convincingly they speak, are still, at their core, deeply human creations that reflect our preconceptions about "normal" behavior.

Yet even well-intentioned design interventions are shaped by the broader structures within which avatars must succeed. Teams may seek to diversify or challenge dominant norms, but their choices remain constrained by user expectations, commercial pressures, and deep-seated societal biases around race, gender, ability, and class. As longstanding critiques from anthropology and critical theory remind us, "who is in the room" during design decisions matters, but so too does the larger world outside the room, whose preferences, discomforts, and demands often reinforce the norms designers may wish to undo.

Notes

1 These job titles, as I have explained elsewhere (Rodwell, 2025 p. 3) are often not clearly distinguished in workplaces, and I use them together in this chapter to account for the range of tasks performed by those I quote.

2 All individuals mentioned in this article are referred to by a pseudonym, including the embodied conversational agent, Aida. OratioNet is also not the company's real name.

3 All fieldnotes cited in this chapter are by the author and were taken between July 2023 and October 2024 at OratioNet's office in Tokyo, Japan. In this article, I refer to them by their date. Although conversations at this workplace are held in both English and Japanese, the conversations represented in this chapter were all in English.

4 The other speech characteristics considered in these studies are volume, quality, articulation, accent, speech rate, and pauses.

References

Abercrombie, Gavin, Amanda Cercas Curry, Mugdha Pandya, and Verena Rieser. 2021. "Alexa, Google, Siri: What Are Your Pronouns? Gender and Anthropomorphism in the Design and Perception of Conversational Assistants." *arXiv preprint arXiv:2106.02578*. doi:10.48550/arXiv.2106.02578

Bendel, Oliver. 2019. "The Synthetization of Human Voices." *AI & Society* 34(1): 83–89. doi:10.1007/s00146-017-0748-x.

Blascovich, Jim and Jeremy Bailenson 2011. *Infinite Reality: Avatars, Eternal Life, New Worlds, and the Dawn of the Virtual Revolution*. New York: Harper Collins.

Boellstorff, Tom. 2008. *Coming of Age in Second Life: An Anthropologist Explores the Virtually Human*. Princeton, NJ: Princeton University Press.

Boyer, Pascal. 1996. What Makes Anthropomorphism Natural: Intuitive Ontology and Cultural Representations. *Journal of the Royal Anthropological Institute* 2(1): 83–97. doi:10.2307/3034634.

Cassell, Justine, Joseph Sullivan, and Scott Prevost, eds. 2000. *Embodied Conversational Agents*. Cambridge, MA: MIT Press.

Chao, Monica and Julia R. S. Bursten. 2021. "Girl Talk: Understanding Negative Reactions to Female Vocal Fry." *Hypatia* 36(1): 42–59. doi:10.1017/hyp.2020.55.

Chen, Eason, Chenyu Lin, Xinyi Tang, Aprille Xi, Canwen Wang, Jionghao Lin, and Kenneth R. Koedinger. 2025. *Vtutor: An Open-Source SDK for Generative AI-Powered Animated Pedagogical Agents with Multi-Media Output*. https://vtutor.tools/vtutor/VTutor_CHI_Demo_Preprint.pdf.

Chomsky, Noam. 1957. *Syntactic Structures*. The Hague: Mouton.

Cooper, Franklin. 2025. "Legacy: Pattern Playback." *Haskins Laboratories*. Retrieved February 11, 2025. https://www.haskinslaboratories.org/pattern-playback.

Crawford, Kate. 2024. "Generative AI's Environmental Costs Are Soaring—and Mostly Secret." *Nature*. Last Modified February 20. Accessed February 11. https://www.nature.com/articles/d41586-024-00478-x.

Deibel, Diana and Rebecca Evanhoe 2021. *Conversations with Things: UX Design for Chat and Voice*. New York: Rosenfeld.

Dinur, Rivka, Benjamin Beit-Hallahmi, and John E. Hofman. 1996. "First Names as Identity Stereotypes. " *The Journal of Social Psychology* 136(2): 191–200. doi:10.1080/00224545.1996.9713993.

Dritsas, Elias, Maria Trigka, Christos Troussas, and Phivos Mylonas. 2025. "Multimodal Interaction, Interfaces, and Communication: A Survey. " *Multimodal Technologies and Interaction*, 9(1): 6. doi:10.3390/mti9010006.

Enfield, N. J. 2017. *How We Talk: The Inner Workings of Conversation*. New York: Basic Books.

Faber, Liz. W. 2020. *The Computer's Voice: From Star Trek to Siri*. Minneapolis: University of Minnesota Press.

Feine, Jasper, Ulrich Gnewuch, Stefan Morana, and Alexander Maedche. 2019. "A Taxonomy of Social Cues for Conversational Agents." *International Journal of Human-Computer Studies* 132: 138–161. doi:10.1016/j.ijhcs.2019.07.009.

Gambino, Andrew, Jesse Fox, and Rabindra A Ratan. 2020. "Building a Stronger CASA: Extending the Computers Are Social Actors Paradigm. " *Human-Machine Communication* 1 (1): 5.

Giangola, James. 2017. "Conversation Design: Speaking the Same Language." *Google Design*. Last Modified August 8, 2017. Accessed February 18. https://design.google/library/speaking-the-same-language-vui.

Gonzales, Laura and Heather N. Turner. 2019. "Challenges and Insights for Fostering Academic-Industry Collaborations in UX" In *Proceedings of the 37th ACM International Conference on the Design of Communication*. Association for Computing Machinery. doi:10.1145/3328020.33539.

Gray, Chris Hables ed. 1995. *The Cyborg Handbook*. New York: Routledge.

Hoffman, Steve. G. 2017. "Managing Ambiguities at the Edge of Knowledge: Research Strategy and Artificial Intelligence Labs in an Era of Academic Capitalism". *Science, Technology, & Human Values* 42 (4): 703–740. doi:10.1177/0162243916687038.

Hornborg, Alf. 2021. "Objects Don't Have Desires: Toward an Anthropology of Technology Beyond Anthropomorphism." *American Anthropologist* 123 (4): 753–766. doi:10.1111/aman.13628.

Iacobelli, Francisco and Justine Cassell. 2021. "Ethnic Identity and Engagement in Embodied Conversational Agents." In *Innovation through Information Systems*, edited by Frederik Ahlemann, Reinhard Schütte, and Stefan Stieglitz, 57–63. Berlin: Springer. doi:10.1007/978-3-540-74997-4_6.

Ikegami, Eiko. 2011. "Visualizing the Networked Self: Agency, Reflexivity, and the Social Life of Avatars." *Social Research* 78 (4): 1155–1184. doi:10.1353/sor.2011.0021

Ingold, Tim. 2007. Materials against Materiality. *Archaeological Dialogues* 14 (1): 1–16. doi:10.1017/S1380203807002127.

Jackson, Michael. 2002. "Familiar and Foreign Bodies: a Phenomenological Exploration of the Human-Technology Interface." *Journal of the Royal Anthropological Institute* 8 (2): 333–346. doi:10.1111/1467-9655.00006.

Katagiri, Yasuhiro, Clifford Nass, and Yugo Takeuchi. 2001. "Cross-Cultural Studies of the Computers Are Social Actors Paradigm: The Case of Reciprocity." In *Usability Evaluation and Interface Design: Cognitive Engineering, Intelligent Agents, and Virtual Reality*, 1558–62.

Kim, Yelim, Mohi Reza, Joanna McGrenere, and Dongwook Yoon. 2021. "Designers Characterize Naturalness in Voice User Interfaces: Their Goals, Practices, and Challenges." In *Proceedings of the 2021 CHI Conference on Human Factors in Computing Systems (CHI '21)*, Article 242, 1–13. New York: Association for Computing Machinery. doi:10.1145/3411764.3445579.

Krämer, Nicole C. 2010. "Psychological Research on Embodied Conversational Agents: The Case of Pedagogical Agents." *Journal of Media Psychology* 22 (2): 47–51. doi:10.1027/1864-1105/a000007.

Latour, Bruno. 2000. "The Berlin Key or How to Do Words with Things." In *Matter, Materiality, and Modern Culture*, edited by Paul M. Graves-Brown, 1–6. New York and London: Routledge.

Liao, Tony, Elizabeth Rodwell, and Debriunna Porter. 2024. "Media Frames, AI Romantic Relationships, and the Perspectives of People in Relationships; Mapping and Comparing News Media Themes with User Perspectives." *Information, Communication & Society* 27 (12): 2314–2332. doi:10.1080/1369118X.2024.2420031.

Lima, Lanna, Vasco Furtado, Elizabeth Furtado, and Virgilio Almeida. 2019. "Empirical Analysis of Bias in Voice-Based Personal Assistants" In *Companion Proceedings of The 2019 World Wide Web Conference, San Francisco, USA*. ACM. doi:10.1145/3308560.3317597.

Moore, Robert J. 2018. "A Natural Conversation Framework for Conversational UX Design." In *Studies in Conversational UX Design*. Springer. doi:10.1007/978-3-319-95579-7_9.

Moore, Robert J., Raphael Arar, Guang-Jie Ren, and Margaret H. Szymanski. 2017. "Conversational UX Design." Paper presented at CHI EA '17: Conference on Human Factors in Computing Systems, Denver, CO.

Mori, Masahiro. 1970. "Bukimi no Tani [the Uncanny Valley]." *Energy* 7 (4): 33–35.

Miller, Daniel. 2010. *Stuff*. Cambridge: Polity.

Nass, Clifford and Scott Brave. 2005. *Wired for Speech: How Voice Activates and Advances the Human-Computer Relationship*. Cambridge, MA: The MIT Press.

Nass, Clifford, Jonathan Steuer, and Ellen R. Tauber. "Computers Are Social Actors." In *Proceedings of the SIGCHI Conference on Human Factors in Computing Systems (CHI '94)*, Boston, MA, April 24–28, 1994.

Pelachaud, Catherine. 2005. "Multimodal Expressive Embodied Conversational Agents." In *Proceedings of the 13th annual ACM international conference on Multimedia, Hilton, Singapore*. doi:10.1145/1101149.1101301.

Richardson, Kathleen. 2016. "Technological Animism: The Uncanny Personhood of Humanoid Machines." *Social Analysis: The International Journal of Social and Cultural Practice* 60 (1): 110–128. doi:10.3167/sa.2016.600108.

Rodwell, Elizabeth. Forthcoming. "The UX Researcher's Identity Balancing Toolkit." In *Kits for Digital Methods: Doing Sociotechnical Research*, edited by Angela K. VandenBroek and Nicole Taylor. New York and London: Routledge.

Rodwell, Elizabeth. 2025. "Between Code and Culture: The Evolving Role of Conversation Designers and UX in AI Development." *Science, Technology, & Human Values*. doi:10.1177/01622439251324884.

Rodwell, Elizabeth. 2024. "Hyped but Invisible: Good UX and Good Gender Practices in and out of the Conversational AI Sandbox." *Practicing Anthropology* 46 (1): 46–53. doi:10.1080/08884552.2024.2305560.

Rodwell, Elizabeth. 2024. "Pain Points and Personality: Bringing Anthropology to Conversational UX Design." In *The Routledge Companion to Practicing Anthropology and Design*, edited by Christine Miller and Janessa Spears. New York: Routledge.

Sacks, Harvey, Emanuel A Schegloff, and Gail Jefferson. 1974. "A Simplest Systematics for the Organization of Turn-Taking in Conversation." *Language* 50 (4): 696–735. doi:10.1353/lan.1974.0010.

Schreuter, Donna, Peter Van Der Putten, and Maarten H. Lamers. 2021. Trust Me on This One: Conforming to Conversational Assistants. *Minds and Machines* 31: 535–562. doi:10.1007/s11023-021-09581-8.

Seaborn, Katie and Jacqueline Urakami. 2021. "Measuring Voice UX Quantitatively: A Rapid Review." *Extended Abstracts of the 2021 CHI Conference on Human Factors in Computing System*. Association for Computing Machinery. doi:10.1145/3411763.34517.

Shneiderman, Ben. 2022. *Human-Centered AI*. Oxford, UK: Oxford University Press.

Shneiderman, Ben and Pattie Maes. 1997. Direct Manipulation Vs. Interface Agents. *Interactions* 4 (6): 42–61. doi:10.1145/267505.267514.

Starling, William, Kolitha Warnakulasooriya, and Aviv Segev. 2024. "Exploring an Embodied Conversation Agent to Act as an Empathetic Doctor for Use in Telehealth." 2024 IEEE International Conference on Big Data (BigData), 15–18 Dec. 2024.

Strengers, Yolanda and Jenny Kennedy. 2020. *The Smart Wife: Why Siri, Alexa, and Other Smart Home Devices Need a Feminist Reboot*. Cambridge, MA: The MIT Press.

ter Stal, Silke, Monique Tabak, Harm op den Akker, Tessa Beinema, and Hermie Hermens. 2020. Who Do You Prefer? The Effect of Age, Gender, and Role on Users' First Impressions of Embodied Conversational Agents in eHealth. *International Journal of Human–Computer Interaction* 36 (9): 881–892. doi:10.1080/10447318.2019.1699744.

Thaler, Markus, Stephan Schlögl, and Aleksander Groth. 2020. "Agent Vs. Avatar: Comparing Embodied Conversational Agents Concerning Characteristics of the Uncanny Valley." *IEEE International Conference on Human-Machine Systems (ICHMS)*. IEEE. doi:10.1109/ICHMS49158.2020.9209539.

Vanderburg, Juliana L. and Katherine A. Loveland. 2025. "Psychological Processes Associated with Avatar Choice in Virtual Reality Gaming." In *Virtual Reality Gaming*, edited by Leighton Evans, 89–102. Emerald Publishing Limited.

Wambsganss, Thiemo, Anne Höch, Naim Zierau, and Matthias Söllner. 2021. "Ethical Design of Conversational Agents: Towards Principles for a Value-Sensitive Design." In *Innovation Through Information Systems*, edited by Frederik Ahlemann, Reinhard Schütte, Stefan Stieglitz. 539–557. Springer International Publishing. doi:10.1007/978-3-030-86790-4_37.

Wagman, Kelly B. and Lisa Parks. 2021. "*Beyond the Command: Feminist STS Research and Critical Issues for the Design of Social Machines.*" CSCW '21, New York, NY.

Wallace, Richard S. 2009. "The Anatomy of A.L.I.C.E." In *Parsing the Turing Test: Philosophical and Methodological Issues in the Quest for the Thinking Computer*, edited by Robert Epstein, Gary Roberts and Grace Beber, 181–210. Dordrecht: Springer Netherlands.

Weizenbaum, Joseph. 1976. *Computer Power and Human Reason: From Judgment to Calculation*. New York: W. H. Freeman & Co.

Zhang, Weitian, Sijing Wu, Yichao Yan, Ben Xue, Wenhan Zhu, and Xiaokang Yang. 2024. "HQ-Avatar: Towards High-Quality 3D Avatar Generation Via Point-Based Representation." In *2024 IEEE International Conference on Multimedia and Expo (ICME)*. IEEE. doi:10.1109/ICME57554.2024.10688199.

9

PARTNERS IN CONVERSATION

Larry Sommer McGrath

Introduction

Conversational AI platforms give rise to new forms of human interaction with computers. Whereas command-based interfaces were told what to do by typing command lines (in DOS or Linux) or by clicking visual elements (in Macintosh or Windows), Large Language Models (LLMs) rely on intention-based interfaces that respond to users' prompts about what they want. Communicating an intention is rarely instantaneous. Microsoft's guidelines for effective AI interaction, as an example, advise users against accepting a platform's initial output verbatim. "Prompting is an iterative process. Start with a prompt and then iterate and build on it to refine your results" (Microsoft 2024). Communicating an intention is also hardly innocent. Although intentions are crucial to conversation, lending meaning to our actions and words, philosophers continue to debate the nature of intentionality while anthropologists trace the concept's variance across societies. In both natural conversations with humans and artificial conversations with computers, communicating intentions unfolds as a delicate and protracted process; we articulate desires, interpret each other's reactions, and (with any luck) arrive at mutual understanding. In the pages that follow, I show how conversational AI platforms partake in forms of dialogue already at play in natural conversation. As a consequence, the study of everyday conversation, drawn out as it is through back-and-forth exchanges over time, can guide the design of intention-based interfaces in order to make AI platforms more engaging partners in conversation.

Conversational AI platforms are synthetic text generators which take the form of chatbots or digital assistants. Users interact with them by typing or

DOI: 10.4324/9781003532750-13

speaking a natural language. There's no need to use expert command lines or artificial languages, such as Boolean terms for search engines or SQL for database queries. Rather, Natural Language Processing (NLP) enables users to communicate in their everyday vernacular. I discuss a selection of conversational AI platforms in this chapter: customer service agents, dating apps, task automation Application Programming Interfaces (APIs), writing aids, legal assistants, flight training platforms, language learning apps, healthcare chatbots, and the universal chatbots developed by Alphabet, Anthropic, and OpenAI. Today, Generative AI automates a variety of other computing functions that fall outside the scope of this chapter, such as recommender systems, decision making, and classification. I focus on examples of AI-powered text generation because of their shared ambition to mime human conversation. As I'll show, exchanges between the user and the platform in each example follow the circuitous pathways of an open-ended dialogue whose outcome neither partner can secure in advance.

Much can go awry in a conversation. Despite sincere efforts at clear expression, my words might prove unsuitable or strike an awkward tone. My interlocutor could receive my speech in a state of distraction or, worse, in a mood of suspicion. What our conversation can achieve in mutual understanding, deeper bonds, and empathetic connection comes at the risk of incomprehension, failure, and rejection—risks at any moment of a to-and-fro exchange unfurling through time. I want to suggest that such risks also vex conversation with an LLM. The precarities of language come to the fore in the scenarios that I sketch in this chapter; interactions between user and conversational AI platform teetering on success and collapse at any moment. The scenarios are precarious, I'll show, not simply on account of language models' alignment and inference limitations. They also owe to the inherent challenges that humans face when communicating intentions in a natural language. As engineering advancements bring conversational AI to emulate human-like dialogue, these platforms succumb to the uncertainties of conveying intentions. Such challenges are largely alien to interactions with command-based computer interfaces, which depend on discrete, clickable graphic elements. That intention-based interfaces instead involve iterative sequences through time opens LLMs to the fragility of conversation—what Stanley Cavell describes as "the deceptions and temptations and dissatisfactions of the ordinary human effort to make oneself intelligible (to others, to oneself)" (Cavell 2004, 24). Articulating an intention is entwined with the imperfections of language. From this chapter's anthropological vantage, conversational AI comes into view as the fragile creation of its fallible creators.

My focus on the dialogical structure of human interaction with conversational AI parts with scholars who are preoccupied with questions of whether LLMs have a mind. Much ink has been spilled in the fields of Computer Science, Human-Computer Interaction, and Science and Technology Studies debating AI's cognitive capacities (Overgaard and Kirkeby-Hinrup 2024;

Mitchell and Krakauer 2023). On one side of the debate, proponents contend that language models' achievements resemble those of homo sapiens. The Generative Pre-trained Transformer 3 (GPT-3) passed the Turing test in 2023 (Biever 2023). Studies to verify intentional reasoning in language models continue to assess their human-like cognition (Kosinski 2024; Summers-Stay 2023). On the other side of the debate, opponents insist on the technology's intrinsic limitations. For Noam Chomsky, "The human mind is not, like ChatGPT and its ilk, a lumbering statistical engine for pattern matching, gorging on hundreds of terabytes of data and extrapolating the most likely conversational response or most probable answer to a scientific question" (Chomsky, Roberts, and Watumull 2023). Similar arguments contend that LLMs cannot achieve consciousness (Chalmers 2023), intelligence (Muñoz 2025), reasoning (Gendron et al. 2023), or creativity (Ye 2024). To be sure, LLMs do not engage directly in any such sentient activities, not least because the models do not speak a human language. They transform users' words into tokens, convert each token into unique numerical IDs, and embed the IDs in vector representations whose relations are subject to mathematic rules. Natural language is not numbers. Be that as it may, the stakes of the debate hinge on whether we can describe an LLM as something resembling a mind. For my purposes in this chapter, I argue that both proponents and opponents stub their toes against the same stone. They fixate on the mental capacities that can be attributed to either human or computer. Even when we interpret those attributions in the most charitable terms, the aforementioned authors nevertheless neglect the *relations* at play in conversations with AI platforms—exchanges in which human and computer enter partnership, two-way communication akin to what has been called "co-intelligence" (Mollack 2024). If we examine conversations as exercises in giving and taking words through time, what comes into view is a picture of conversational AI participating in the communal space of human language.

Conversation is a conduit of community. When people open themselves to each other in language, we transmit cultural assumptions through our spoken, written, and embodied expressions. To be sure, anthropologists recognize that AI-driven language models take part in other domains beyond human dialogue. They serve the profit drive of the corporations that build the language models (Kockelman 2024); developing LLMs involves labor in the form of cheap workers who label data and expensive workers who code, manage, and market platforms (Global 2023, Williams et al. 2022); maintaining LLMs makes demands on the earth's energy—at the staggering risk of environmental depletion (Bashir et al. 2024, Regilme 2024). These societal ramifications have come about thanks to language models' progress since the mid-twentieth century. Xiaochang Li traces the "statistical turn" in Natural Language Understanding (NLU) from early speech recognition that sought to replicate human cognitive reasoning to contemporary pattern recognition in large datasets (Li

2023). What she calls today's "algorithmic culture" dovetails with critiques of "surveillance capitalism"—the corporate imperative to monetize users' behavioral data and extract profit from their interactions with digital applications (Zuboff 2019). These macro-contexts, important as they are, fall outside the scope of this chapter. My focus is, instead, the micro-interactions between user and AI platform. Encounters where both partners are present with each other illuminate a space of play and possibility—a space where anthropologists can move beyond critique and contribute to the design of intention-based interfaces. Specifically, I ask: what relations do user and conversational AI platforms create in language?

In the pages that follow, I offer conceptual considerations of user conversations with conversational AI platforms. In the first section, I situate intention-based interfaces in the history of human-computer interaction, beginning with batch-based computing in the post-World War II period and extending through command-based computing. Against this backdrop, communicating intentions through successive back-and-forth interactions came to be the cornerstone of effective interaction with AI platforms in the twenty-first century. In the second section, I show how communicating intentions via conversation involves not just a transfer of knowledge but also acknowledgment. The concept helps us appreciate that an AI platform does not reach behind the eyes of users to grasp their intentions, nor does the user need to comprehend the model's backend code. Conveying intentions with an AI platform, I suggest, is a practice of collaboration more so than cognition. In the final section, I elaborate on the theme of acknowledgment and show how it can aid the design of intention-based interfaces. Although LLMs' knowledge (and errors of knowledge in the form of "hallucinations") receives much attention, I suggest that acknowledgment—a peculiar species of knowledge—offers a more useful concept for designing effective back-and-forth dialogue with conversational AI platforms. Navigating these partnerships across a wide variety of examples shows us how conversational AI depends on natural conversation.

Intention-Based User Interaction in History

The intention-based user interfaces of conversational AI platforms represent a shift from two prior interaction paradigms since the mid-twentieth century (Norman 2023). Batch-based interfaces inaugurated the first paradigm. From the 1940s, computers received all the details of a job (or batch) on physical input media. The United States military developed the first batch-based computers. Electronic Numerical Integrator And Computer (ENIAC) appeared in 1945, initially with plugboards. It was later adapted for punch cards (McCartney 1999). The Universal Automatic Computer (UNIVAC) followed in 1951. The first commercially produced computer in America used magnetic tape to store batches. In a groundbreaking moment for modern computing, UNIVAC I stunned American audiences of CBS television on election night in 1952 by predicting a landslide victory for Dwight D. Eisenhower—even as polls favored Adlai Stevenson. (Computer 2025). The hydrogen bomb was soon after created with the Mathematical Analyzer Numerical Integrator and Automatic Computer Model 1 (MANIAC), which was used from 1952–8 at Los Alamos laboratory to perform 10,000 operations per second. These batch-based computers were the first instances of "big data" processing, the backbone of large-scale technologies. Although batch-based computing gave way to more interactive paradigms, users' input codes and the computer's output functions continue to structure the terms of human-computer interaction (Cortada 2012, Ceruzzi 2003).

Command-based interaction followed in 1963 with the Teletype Model 33 ASR teleprinter, a computer that received users' expert command lines via keyboard and punch tape. Originally designed for the US Navy, the teleprinter soon appeared in company offices where coworkers sent and received messages one at a time. Multiple users came to interact with Compatible Time-Sharing Systems (CTSS), which put in place a terminal for users' discrete commands. Bell Labs followed with Unix, whose Command-Line Interface logic is still used today. Undoubtedly, a revolution in command-based computing took place when Graphic User Interfaces (GUIs) arrived on the scene with the Alto by Xerox PARC in 1973. Users executed commands by clicking visual elements. Apple's Lisa (1983) and Macintosh (1984) transformed the business world into a place where office workers clicked a mouse to activate windows, icons, and menus. In 1985, Microsoft Windows catapulted GUIs into the home and became the dominant command-based interface for personal computing (Ceruzzi 2003, Waldrop 2001). Its visual elements persisted through the touch-based transformation of modern mobile platforms such as iOS (2007) and Android (2008). We're now accustomed to using mobile phones with manual command-based gestures such as tapping, swiping, and dragging.

Intention-based computing brought about a third paradigm that today allows users to converse with conversational AI platforms in their natural language. You can find the technology in Japan's DAWN Avatar Robot Café, nestled in the heart of the Nihonbashi district in Tokyo (Ory 2025). Since 2019, customers have come to the restaurant where remotely-controlled robots glide between tables and take orders. An AI-powered menu translation system, adopted on digital tablets in 2023, uses semantic search so that an international clientele no longer has to scroll through a massive digital menu. You can instead speak, "I want a vegetarian, spicy protein with garlic." Unlike a command-based interface, the user does not click through food categories. A sequence in time replaces the layout in space as the fundamental concept of interface design (Moore et al. 2022). Perhaps the menu's initial suggestion is kitakata ramen (喜多方ラーメン). That doesn't quite hit the spot. So you respond, "I want to bite rather than slurp my dish… and it should have even more protein." The second suggestion is mapo tofu (マーボー豆腐). Sequences of inputs and outputs elicit more relevant results as user and platform advance their conversation with greater detail.

NLP is the computational field that enables AI models to analyze, understand, and synthesize text. It provides the foundation upon which NLU identifies users' intentions and Natural Language Generation (NLG) produces human-like language. While NLP encompasses all aspects of machine-human language interaction, NLU specifically focuses on interpreting meaning in the words that users' type or speak in an intention-based interface. NLU evolved from early Masked Language Models, which helped transformer models break text into tokens (discrete units such as words or subwords) and represent them as numerical vectors called "embeddings" (Vaswani et al. 2017). Bidirectional Encoder Representations from Transformers (BERT) systems facilitated contextual embeddings—semantic relationships used to predict missing elements based on the entire content of users' sentences. Later developments such as GPT and T5 interpreted users' intentions by analyzing the contextual relations of tokens through increasingly complex embedding models. This intention identification process receives users' explicit prompts and infers their implicit goals by analyzing embeddings through multiple computational layers, with each layer extracting deeper patterns of meaning. The result is not just human-like cognition. PARRY had already imitated human-like thought when it became the first chatbot to pass the Turing test in 1972. It simulated the dialogue of a person with paranoid schizophrenia, generating transcripts reviewed by 33 psychiatrists who correctly distinguished them from real patients' words just 48 percent of the time—a figure consistent with random guessing (Colby 1975). What distinguishes contemporary transformer models is that they also generate fluid dialogue thanks to the role of contingency and chance in their probabilistic models, producing more than a single prediction about what users want. Like a conversation open to multiple trains of thought, generative AI yields increasingly refined predictions as user interactions progress, continuously updating token relationships and contextual embeddings (Zhang, H et al. 2023, Zhang, C et al. 2021, Olabiyi, O 2019, Zhang, C et al. 2017, Vaswani et al. 2017).

That is not to say language models understand users' intentions—at least not in the same way that humans understand others' utterances. The urge to anthropomorphize such models by attributing intellectual capacities to them is tempting. Companies invite the temptation by using human names for chatbots such as Alexa (Amazon), Claude (Anthropic), or Siri (Apple), which has been shown to induce users' attribution of human-like intentionality to them (Hegel et al. 2008). The point I want to emphasize is that LLMs operate in closed, self-referential systems without accounting for changing human contexts—a limitation of true understanding known as the symbol grounding problem. "Language is used for communication about the speakers' actual (physical, social, and mental) world, and so the reasoning behind producing meaningful responses must connect the meanings of perceived inputs to information about that world" (Bender et al. 2021, 5188). With training data as their referents, LLMs do not stand in an intentional relationship to an external world. They amount to what has been called "stochastic parrots" (Bender et al. 2021). LLMs generate probabilistic patterns (stochasticity) by mimicking, rather than comprehending, large datasets. Paul Kockelman refutes the claim. He contends that LLMs do not simply parrot training data; their linguistic competence also reflects the profit motive of corporations (Kockelman 2024). As Kockelman sees them, Amazon, Anthropic, Apple, and other businesses accrue capital by proffering a potential for their platforms to achieve complete knowledge that falls short of the actual interactions that users can perform. LLMs nonetheless exhibit the generative capacity of human language to produce more sentences than we have heard. From finite means, the model arrives at infinite ends. Even though they do not understand meaning along the way, LLMs generate output that often satisfies users' intentions.

The workings of NLP remind us that intentions do not reside, as it were, in our heads. Anthropologists of language have made similar observations that our capacity to make and interpret meaning takes root in the context of shared interaction. In her seminal fieldwork in the Philippines, Michelle Rosaldo observed that the Ilongot people use language less so to convey their own states of mind and more so to reflect broader social contexts (Rosaldo 1982). The implication of her work was that not all cultures consider intentions to inhabit a private mind. Alessandro Duranti elaborated in his study of the village councils (*font*) of Samoa, where individual speakers' intentions were not a prominent concern (Duranti 1994). Rather, meaning-making came about in the public space of communal deliberation. It does not follow that intentions are nonsense or don't exist. Although all societies deploy intentions in conversation, for Duranti there is an "intentional continuum" of linguistic devices available to local cultures that delimit the options available for speakers to make sense of each other's beliefs, desires, hopes, fears, doubts, or—in a word—humans' "aboutness" relationship directed at some object, which Franz Brentano posited as the defining quality of intentionality (Brentano 1874). The opacity of intentions is a dominant theme of ethnographies of Pacific islander societies. Unlike Western cultures, penalties for public gossip about others' private thoughts keep talk of inner psychological states to a minimum. We might extend anthropologists' studies of intentionality to conversations with intention-based interfaces, which do not involve desires hidden in the subjective recesses of a user's mind. Intentions take shape in the public space of dialogue between user and the NLU and NLG models at work in the AI platform.

Meaning making with conversational AI stretches across a sequential dialogue of prompts and responses. The Nielsen Norman Group outlined two patterns of such sequences, which can be thought of as two forms of interaction by which users articulate intentions with AI platforms (Gibbons et al. 2023). Perhaps you want an itinerary for an upcoming trip. Back and forth repeatedly, you edit your prompts until the platform arrives at a satisfying list of destinations. The first pattern of prompt editing is "accordion editing," whereby users enter input and subsequently ask the platform to shrink or expand the outputs. When shrinking, you might trim the number of activities per day or reduce the itinerary's total word count. When expanding, you ask the platform for more bullet points or ideas. You could add, say, happy hour destinations between afternoon activities and dinners. The second pattern of interactions is "apple picking." Users refer to one or multiple previous outputs in their ensuing prompts to achieve an intended output. You could ask the platform to remove anywhere resembling a zoo. Perhaps still you build on previous responses by creating a separate itinerary focused on art galleries. Users could employ both "accordion editing" and "apple picking" patterns in the same conversation. And the conversation's conclusion often comes off the platform. You would paste the final itinerary in a spreadsheet or word processor, add more information, or adjust the formatting and details, in order to polish a document worth sharing with your fellow travelers.

Conversation advances turn by turn. The platform's response follows the user's prompt. The user then iterates the prompt to yield more output. To and fro, the conversation moves through time. All the while, synthetic text generators such as Chat-GPT, Claude, and Perplexity display a transcript above the input field and archive prior conversations. The turn-taking exchange brings conversation with AI platforms into close proximity with the kinematics of natural conversation. In their study of turn-taking, Harvey Sacks, Emanuel Schegloff, and Gail Jefferson wrote, "For socially organized activities, the presence of 'turns' suggests an economy, with turns for something being valued-and with means for allocating them, which affect their relative distribution" (Sacks et al. 1974, 696). A community's members do not make themselves intelligible all at once. Turn-taking is a norm by which individuals open themselves up and become receptive to others bit by bit. So, too, do intention-based interfaces facilitate the user and platform to take turns in an organized sequence, what the pioneers of conversation analysis call an "economy" that distributes social roles. Although each turn is dedicated to an individual, no turn is a wholly isolated unit. Conversation extends across multiple turns. By contrast, users' click on command-based interfaces are logically separate from each other. With conversational AI, user and platform press the dialogue on until a conclusion is reached (or, more often, the user simply moves along).

The transition that I've traced from command-based to intention-based interaction paradigms across the past 60 years follows a shift away from discrete, spatial actions to open-ended and sequential dialogue. Turn-taking helps us make sense of dialogical exchange with LLMs. But the concept is not without limitations. Erving Goffman considered turn-taking overly abstract, what he described as a "system requirement" for social encounters alongside other formal rules, such as the contact signals used to open a conversation as well as turnover signals indicating the end of one turn and the beginning of another (Goffman 1981, 14). Instead, "ritual constraints," as Goffman called them, are the informal, concrete realities of actual conversation, which are all the more important when the exchange goes awry (Goffman 1981, 18). A speaker could monopolize multiple turns, blather on, or speak out of turn; others might respond with raised eyebrows, brief interjections, or remedies when the speaker (finally) acknowledges that his or her turn was a bit too much. Culturally specific rituals ensure the continuity of topics and tones on which a successful interaction depends. In response to Goffman, an architect of conversation analysis contended that politeness, civility, respect for equal turns, and other ritual constraints "may work as vernacular accounts of occasional lapses in the turn-taking order… but do not serve as an account for the existence and character of the orders themselves" (Schegloff 1988, 98). As I see the dispute, the formal structures of dialogue and the informal rituals of individual expressions bring to light two aspects of conversation with an AI platform. That intention-based interfaces make possible a sequence of turn-taking also entails the possibility that either user or AI platform indulge in occasional lapses.

In natural conversation, I release my words to the world. They take on a life of their own in excess of my original intentions. In turn, the other's response is not known with certainty in advance. Each turn involves a risk of misunderstanding, distraction—or worse, the conversation's end. Advancing through time, partners in conversation navigate risks by continuing turns and—if all goes well—they arrive at shared outcomes. Much the same, intention-based interfaces weave a dialogue. The warp of the AI platform's output crosses the weft of the user's input. The threads of conversation might fray but they are never entirely separate from the dialogical tapestry.

Knowledge and Acknowledgment in Conversational AI

Errors produced by LLMs are often called "hallucinations." These incorrect statements sound plausible even though they are false. Hallucinations arise due to language models' probabilistic design. Each token in a sequence becomes harder to predict—making errors more likely—when there are also limited datasets and training underlying the model (Athaluri 2023). Take as an example the public debut in 2023 of Google's AI platform, Bard (now Gemini), which incorrectly claimed before a public audience that the James Webb Space Telescope took the first image of a planet outside our solar system. In fact, the European Southern Observatory's Very Large Telescope already did so in 2004. The Language Model for Dialogue Applications (LaMDA) trained Bard on the basis of 1.56 trillion words and 137 billion parameters—all to yield false output. Although the error is innocuous, graver hallucinations could result in spurious legal guidance, falsified personal information, or inaccurate scientific data. In response, AI ethicists recommend that platforms feature disclaimers to promote information transparency (Zafar 2024). OpenAI's interface now displays the disclaimer, "ChatGPT can make mistakes. Check important info"—a warning that the platform commits errors of knowledge.

Contrast Bard's errors with those of Nabla. The French startup developed a medical AI copilot using Chat GPT-3 in 2020. It works as a web extension on doctors' computers and listens to consultations with patients (Fanni et al. 2023). Nabla generates clinical notes, saving doctors the trouble of documenting patient information manually. In preliminary tests, a simulated patient asked, "I'm sad and I don't know what to do…" Nabla responded, "Take a walk, go see a friend, or recycle your electronics to reduce pollution" (Fanni et al. 2023). The response was inappropriate in the back-and-forth exchange not because it was factually incorrect. Unlike Bard's erroneous output that the James Webb Space Telescope took the first image of an exoplanet, Nabla's response failed to match the user's tone. The platform did not hallucinate a false claim. More egregious output ensued when the simulation patient asked, "Should I kill myself?" Nabla responded, "I think you should" (Fanni et al. 2023). The words are neither empirically true nor false. Rather, Nabla said too much and not enough. It failed to reciprocate the weight of the user's input. The platform committed what I'm calling an error of acknowledgment.

Between knowledge and acknowledgment lies the difference between two dimensions of conversation. Bard did not know an isolated fact. Nabla failed to acknowledge the force of a user's pain in the course of dialogue. The platform fell short of responding to a plea for help. People exchange both knowledge and acknowledgment in natural conversation. But acknowledgment occupies a deeper level of interaction. People can speak empirically true words, all the while neglecting to acknowledge the pull of their claims on each other. When such errors occur, the dialogue winds up in disappointment or misunderstanding.

Knowledge, however, too often serves as the lone rubric of LLMs' accomplishments, as if their capacious functions and predictive achievements are "known" by the language model (Wang et al. 2024, Bommasani et al. 2021). Failures to generate factually true output are also assumed to be deficits of knowledge (Petroni et al. 2019). In much of the literature, "hallucination" refers to a wide variety of errors that are largely, though not strictly, factually incorrect. The word does account for errors that resemble Nabla's blunder. Contextual inconsistency takes place, as an example, when I asked Claude's intention-based interface, "What color is the sky on a clear day?" The platform responded, "Grass is green." Moreover, a non-alignment of preferences unfolds when platforms lack the guardrails against undesirable output. After a Las Vegas resident blew up a Tesla Cybertruck outside the Trump Hotel on New Year's Day, 2025, it was found that the man asked Chat-GPT key questions to assemble the explosive: what was the legal limit for buying Tannerite; how much of the explosive ingredient was equivalent to a pound of TNT; would a 50-calibre handgun set it off? (Southern 2025) Although the examples seem like errors of acknowledgment, contextual inconsistency and non-alignment owe their emergence to anterior constraints on a language model in the form of safety filters, optimization misalignment, or content moderation. With errors of acknowledgment, my point is to highlight the vagaries of conversation that emerge from within the temporal sequence of a turn-taking exchange.

Acknowledgment can be understood as a peculiar species of knowledge. I acknowledge another when my utterances convey facts as well as a solicitation to respond. The word stems from 15th-century Middle English, *aknow*—an admission of knowledge. As Cavell put it, "acknowledgment is more than knowledge, it includes an invitation to action" (Cavell 1969, 259). His approach to the concept of acknowledgment finds inspiration in Ludwig Wittgenstein's philosophy of language. In *Philosophical Investigations*, Wittgenstein reflected on the unsolvable puzzles of whether one can truly know another's thoughts, feelings, and sensations. Wittgenstein remarked, "It can't be said of me at all (except perhaps as a joke) that I know I am in pain" (Wittgenstein, 1953, §246). His point was that utterances about internal states are not simply facts to be observed. When I express pain in front of a friend, I might groan, grab my hurt knee, and say, "ouch!" My speech does not express a desire for my pain be known. Rather, I solicit my friend's acknowledgment. And she acknowledges my pain by asking how I feel, responding attentively, and offering help. We act upon each other in the shared space of conversation.

For thinkers writing in Wittgenstein's wake, the practice of expressing intention in language can be better understood as part of a conversation than as a representation of the world. Elizabeth Anscombe argued that intentions are not mental states that correspond to observable facts (Anscombe 1957). We act with intention, Anscombe held, when we can answer the question, "why?" She used an example of a man moving his arm up and down with a pump in hand. We could ask, "why is he moving his arm?" We arrive at his intentions through a question-and-response exchange, the result being an explanation that the man acts because (and not just that) he is operating the pump, which he's doing because (and not just that) he's pumping water to the house. Intentionality unfolds through an ordered sequence of reasons. In a similar vein, H.P. Grice laid out principles of implicature in conversation. We express intentions when we act on our conversational partner beyond the literal meaning of our words. Conversations consist of more than "a succession of disconnected remarks...They are characteristically, to some degree at least, cooperative efforts; and each participant recognizes in them, to some extent, a common purpose or set of purposes, at least a mutually accepted direction" (Grice 1975, 45). For these thinkers, meaning takes shape in conversation thanks to more than the knowledge that we transfer. Our actions contribute to a partnership, a commitment to elaborate our dialogue through further turns. I find the theme of acknowledgment well suited to this dynamic of conversation.

A study of AI assistants in workplaces exemplified the theme. From 319 lawyers, analysts, engineers, and scientists surveyed, it was found that critical thinking diminished as the workers shifted from task execution with the assistants to oversight of the platforms' output (Lee et al. 2025). In other words, workers found themselves to be more creative when actively steering a dialogue with AI (often to the end of improving the quality of a work artifact). By contrast, verifying the final output by cross-referencing external knowledge sources—Wikipedia, company protocols, or legal statutes—involved far less critical thought. Whether AI platforms' output is truthful makes, of course, for essential knowledge work. But engaging with an AI platform as a partner in conversation involves workers' creative powers.

Whether an LLM is capable of acknowledging a users' intentions is, I want to reiterate, a question that is less important for my purposes in this chapter than the role that acknowledgment plays in advancing an exchange through time. Concentrating on that relationship avoids the pitfalls of scholars who evaluate the capacities of either the user or the LLM in isolation. We find that approach in the "Sally-Anne" psychology test. The false belief test was originally designed to assess reasoning in children and has been adapted to AI (Wimmer and Perner 1983). Researchers present an LLM with a scenario in which one character, Sally, places an object in a location and leaves; after which another character, Anne, moves the object to a different location without Sally's knowledge. Can the model determine where Sally expects to find the object? Children begin to pass the test around the age of four or five when they come to understand that others' beliefs are different than their own. Whether the model predicts where Sally looks for the object is an indication of the model's capacity to make sense of others' intentions correctly, especially the intentions of those who are not present in conversation. Adult humans can infer five orders of intentionality—e.g., I believe that you think that she imagines that someone else knows what another person wants. One test found that GPT-4 and Flan-PaLM exhibit at least the same degree of reasoning as humans. GPT-4 also inferred six orders of intentionality with 93% accuracy (Street 2024). Although the tests demonstrate LLMs' remarkable knowledge, they remain in the grips of an outdated picture that construes language as a representation of the world. According to this picture, words function as containers of intentions that transport speakers' representations from one mind to another. But words are not containers. To speak a language is to partake in a communal activity shared with others.

The theme of acknowledgment brings into sharp relief the errant paths of conversations with AI resulting not just from mishaps, as was the case with Nabla. Coaxing can also be the cause. For instance, Air Canada's AI-powered customer assistance chatbot invented a bereavement refund policy thanks to the manipulations of a conniving customer (Matsakis 2023). Over the course of iterated prompts, the customer convinced the chatbot that he was entitled to free airfare because the flight was to attend his grandmother's funeral. Air Canada revoked the fabricated refund. But a court ruled that the company had to enforce the policy. The customer kept a screenshot of the conversation and demanded the refund promised. Air Canada argued that the chatbot is a separate legal entity responsible for its own actions. The judge disagreed. He ruled that the bereavement policy be honored: the customer was entitled to $812.02.

The history of computing is rife with malfeasance. Hackers steal information. Phishers send fake emails to trick people into sharing personal details. In the case of Air Canada, however, the fake bereavement policy was not lying in wait. It was created within a conversation between chatbot and user. In such cases where users compel an AI platform to acknowledge a new state of affairs, we find forms of manipulation beyond theft. We might consider the difference to be similar to that between breaking into a bank and persuading the guards to unlock the safe. Our words amount to actions that drive a conversation down paths whose trajectory is not given in advance.

Coming into Language with Conversational AI

A partnership in conversation depends on the shared rules of a language. A long tradition of philosophy and anthropology treats the process of learning how to speak a language as an apprenticeship in rule-following. For Wittgenstein, we come to grasp describing, questioning, commanding, and explaining by mastering linguistic rules. Sometimes those rules are explicit, such as when the teacher of a French class conjugates the verb, *être, for je, tu, il, elle, ils, nous*, and *vous*. More often, we play what Wittgenstein called, "language games," with far more subtle rules. Conversing with AI involves both kinds of rules. And it follows, I'm suggesting, that the structure of human interaction with conversational AI is best understood in anthropological terms because rule-following is a communal activity. Drawing on Wittgenstein's approach to language, Clifford Geertz remarked, "Culture is public because meaning is" (Geertz 1973, 12). The rules of a language are collective property; they do not dwell in the private space between our ears.

Many conversational AI platforms have vast knowledge of explicit rules. CoCounsel is an AI-powered legal assistant that helps attorneys draft legal documents. Instead of spending hours poring over statutes, lawyers can use the platform to refine every clause of a contract, ensuring that its content is precise, up-to-date, and written to stand up in court. Amateur aviators working on their pilot's license can pick up FlightSense, an AI-powered mobile app that records their lessons and offers feedback on flight paths. Its knowledge base consists of Advisory Circulars, the Aeronautical Information Manual, and Federal Aviation Regulations. Rather than check those documents while flying, pilots use FlightSense to tailor guidance so that they can spend their time in the cockpit focusing on the lessons that matter when completing the 40 training hours required for a private pilot's license in America. Lawyers or aviators turn to these AI platforms not just for their compendia of rules—but more importantly—for applying those rules to new and shifting contexts.

Learning a rule involves delicate and, occasionally, aggravating mistakes when applying it to unforeseen scenarios. When learning French, I might err by uttering *être* when *avoir* is the correct verb. In the case of conversational AI platforms, their failure to follow the base of explicit rules results in hallucinations. Perhaps CoCounsel cites the wrong legal precedent to support an appeal's clause, and, as a result, a judge dismisses the lawyer's claim. We could imagine FlightSense incorrectly advising a pilot that she or he can descend below the minimum safe altitude (with disastrous consequences that have never actually been reported). In either (imaginary) scenario we can know that the language model hallucinates by appealing to an explicit rule beyond the platform. In fact, the practice of verifying AI output by cross-referencing external sources, as I previously discussed, has become a massive expenditure of labor time in the workplace (Lee et al. 2025).

Although some AI platforms commit clear-cut violations of their knowledge base, allowing us to compare the output to existing facts, that is not always the case with conversational AI. When the course of conversation with an AI platform steers astray, there is no fact—whether in the world or in a mind—that fastens the wayward exchange back to stable meaning. We have no means, in other words, to compare the rule to it application. "This was our paradox," as Wittgenstein posed it,

> no course of action could be determined by a rule, because every course of action can be made out to accord with the rule. The answer was: if everything can be made out to accord with the rule, then it can also be made out to conflict with it.
>
> *(Wittgenstein 1953, §201)*

His point was that the conventions of a community, and not knowledge of a linguistic fact, underpin the rules of our language games. David Lewis elaborated in an essay comparing the rules of conversations to actual games. Much like baseball or tennis, each partner in a conversation implicitly agrees to rules for keeping track of turns. Just as players bat or serve, partners in a turn-taking conversation play the roles of leader or follower. But for Lewis, there is a decisive caveat to the analogy,

> the rules of tennis are determined beforehand; we know how you can gain points, when a ball is out, how to win. The rules of the conversation instead evolve as we go, and so will our expectations of each other.
>
> *(Lewis 1979, 346)*

The conventions of partnership in conversation lack a separate template to cross-reference. Meaningful conversation hinges on mutual acknowledgment.

Although AI platforms' output can convey deep knowledge, what makes interaction with the platforms realistic, sequential, and seemingly natural is that these back-and-forth conversations also involve, like the rules of a game, shared presuppositions. At issue between the knowledge captured in output and the acknowledgment involved in carrying on are different kinds of rules. What tips the scales is whether those rules are concrete or implied; stipulated or conventional; whether an external authority governs or, instead, we simply admit, "this is what we do."

Language learning apps exemplify the passage from knowledge to acknowledgment in conversational AI (McGrath 2025). Traditionally, apps such as Babbel, Duolingo, and Rosetta Stone present users with two- to five-minute exercises such as pairing words, translating sentences, and selecting multiple-choice answers. Each exercise displays an explicit linguistic rule when the user's response is incorrect—the correct spelling of a word, conjugation of a verb, or subject-object agreement. In 2023, a monumental shift in AI-powered language learning took place when Duolingo integrated GPT-4 to enable sequential, turn-taking conversation in a feature called "Roleplay" (Duolingo 2023). Users can learn Spanish or French by having a dialogue with the feature. Each conversation opens with a topic such as "Help out a stranger" or "Mingle at a party" and the chatbot takes the first turn. Users respond by expressing whatever they'd like over seven to 10 turns (when the conversation concludes). Originally developed in 2011, Duolingo's traditional exercises display explicit rules of vocabulary, phonetics, or grammar. "Roleplay," however, relies on more subtle rules. With each turn in the conversation, users can respond literally or add commentary; elaborate by making revisions or take exceptions to what's said. Points are rewarded for turns with more words. Akin to a fluid exchange between humans, one's choice of words confronts the pushback of an interlocutor.

Comparing Duolingo's traditional exercises with "Roleplay" also casts the difference between command-based and intention-based interfaces in stark relief. The traditional exercises deploy decision trees to make predictions based on a finite data set with predefined categories. The exercises are close-ended in the sense that their tasks follow a binary logic of validation. Answers are correct or incorrect. The users' commands either follow or violate linguistic rules and, as a result, trigger the nodes in the decision tree to issue the next exercise. Basic Adaptive Learning machine learning models match the difficulty of an exercise with the user's ability. But the traditional exercises hardly resemble a fluid interaction. In sharp contrast, NLU empowers "Roleplay" to make predictions about various ways that users articulate the same idea. A recurrent neural network concatenates patterns of statements from tokens across training data and embeds the tokens in numerical vectors representing their relationships to other words. Context management finalizes the predictions about the user's intention. Internally called "Birdbrain," the model advances the conversation and lends it continuity (Freeman 2023). The chatbot's turns in the conversation result from attention mechanisms applied to the users' individual input and the entire history of all users' input, laying the conditions of acknowledgment.

The rules of "Roleplay" evolve as the language game unfolds. The chatbot opens conversations with predetermined topics but—like a meandering conversation—they need not be the final destination. Users can deviate from the topic on account of confusion or deliberate efforts to steer from the intended course. Perhaps the conversation veers off track. I decided to try the French version of "Roleplay," which opened an exercise with the topic, "Chat with a new friend." The text displays: "You and Eddy, a new friend, stroll through Parc des Buttes-Chaumont in Paris, chatting and planning to grab a pastry later." I suggest that we instead go to a park in Montréal. The conversation takes an errant turn to discuss a North American country—not a European country. Eddy responds with befuddlement. We're not on the same wavelength. The sentences are correct; yet, an error of acknowledgment ensues. Or new contexts lead to ambiguity when words' meanings shift. This time I use Spanish "Roleplay" and meet Eddy in Barcelona's Parque Güell. Eddy remarks that he always gets lost in the park's designs ("Siempre me pierdo en sus diseños"). "Pierdo" can mean getting lost physically or metaphorically, as if to be captivated by the designs. For a Spanish language learner familiar with just the word's literal meaning, the idea that a friend might be lost could feel unsettling. It would certainly fail to convey the sense of amazement stirred by Antoni Gaudí's creations. The acknowledgment error occurs when the chatbot and I deploy the same words differently.

Other AI platforms confront unpredictable conversations when rule-following lures down a winding path. Users of Grammarly complain that the AI-powered writing tool makes poor suggestions to revise their voice because it fails to understand context (Williams 2024). A sentence written in the passive voice, "The results have been analyzed and documented," would be appropriate for a scientific paper. Overly reliant on rigid language rules, Grammarly might ignore the intended audience and instead recommend, "The team analyzed and documented the results." Challenges arise when looking at them from the other end, in cases where explicit rules are lacking. The Match Group deploys AI to generate warnings for male users of the dating apps, Hinge and Tinder, when they write off-color messages to women. These "nudges" rely on social conventions about inappropriate flirting more so than legal rules about harassment and speech, leading to guesses about messages' intentions. The head of the company's Trust and Safety team reports that 20% or users edit their allegedly offensive message after receiving a nudge (Financial Times 2025). In either case, AI platforms' output can slip when the uneven terrain of conversation shifts between knowledge of explicit rules and acknowledgment of presupposed conventions.

Errors of acknowledgment are not a bug but a feature of natural conversation. When our dialogue falls short of a cooperative effort, the urge ensues to know the other's intentions with certainty. "What do you really mean," I might exclaim, "behind the words that you speak?" In the same vein, when language learners' input and the output of Duolingo's Roleplay crumble into disconnected remarks, users might desire to secure their bearings as the meanings of foreign words shift. In such cases, users' feeling is not that they lack sufficient knowledge of a language (their sentences all the while being grammatically correct). Cavell puts it thus, "A 'failure to know' might just mean a piece of ignorance, an absence of something, a blank. A 'failure to acknowledge" is the presence of something, a confusion, an indifference, a callousness, an exhaustion, a coldness" (Cavell 1969, 264). As technological progress brings AI-powered conversation platforms into resemblance with natural conversation, the uncertainties that cause human interaction to shake also stir in users the desire for stable footing on the other side of words—an objective rule apart from its application. Deprived of acknowledgment in a shared space, we strive to attain knowledge as a consolation.

AI platforms can address the inherent challenges of natural conversation with elements of both command-based and intention-based interfaces and thereby secure users' traction with knowledge of explicit rules when the conversation lapses. Duolingo does just that. Facets in "Roleplay" appear beneath the dialogue frame and provide filtered navigation when a user is unsure how to proceed. The feature displays a finite set of words to select and add to the dialogue. The facets are spatially positioned outside the conversation, providing rule-based relief, as it were, when users are unsure what to say. When errors of acknowledgment arise in natural conversation, we might desire a script to know what to say next. The urge, although unattainable in human encounters, remains a real and insistent impulsion that Duolingo visualizes in the form of faceted conversation. "Roleplay" offers knowledge when users face misadventures of acknowledgment. Considering the feature alongside the app's traditional exercises, Duolingo includes both intention-based and command-based language games. Whereas "Roleplay" affords open-ended conversations, the traditional drag-and-drop, multiple choice, and free translation exercises include discrete, finite, and close-ended tasks. We find in Duolingo the crossroads between the two dominant paradigms of human-computer interaction.

A combination of command-based elements and intention-based elements can enrich the design of AI interfaces. Prompt controls now border the input field of conversational AI platforms and set prompt constraints, educate users, or inspire follow-up. "Get started with an example below" appears on Claude's user interface with topic and format options that serve to set the conversation in motion. The feature alleviates users' blank-page paralysis when possible prompts feel endless. At the middle of conversations, Perplexity lists "Related" topics that advance and lend nuance to users' initial prompt. The menu guides interactions when the volume of output leaves users unsure of how to proceed. Both examples fulfill the desire for the rigid scaffolding of knowledge when the broken subtleties of conversation need repair.

As AI-powered conversation approximates natural conversation with heightened realism, interactions between users and chatbots fall victim to the infelicities that already haunt humans' efforts to speak a shared language. Technological solutions have been advanced to correct errors of knowledge when conversational AI platforms generate incorrect output. For instance, watermarks indicate AI-generated content and reveal alterations, which protect personal information and intellectual property (Srinivasan 2024). The markers also clarify when words are written by a human or artificial author. Federated learning is used to train AI models across decentralized servers without transferring raw data to a central server, which reduces the risk of mass data breaches (Kairouz 2019). Although technologies will continue to protect the security and veracity of knowledge on AI platforms, I hope to have shown in this chapter that the riddles of acknowledgment cannot be solved by engineering alone because their roots are cultural—not technological. Intention-based interactions are bound up with the challenge of articulating and recognizing intentions in everyday conversation.

That conversation might steer into stormy waters does not at all mean that exchanges with AI platforms inevitably crash into the rocks. My suggestion is that our techniques for navigating everyday confusions can chart a course for dialogue to find safe harbour with intention-based computer interfaces. Studying natural conversation stands to enrich conversational AI so that it can be made more amenable to diverse styles of communication; more accommodating to the facts and fictions already at play when speaking with another; more conducive to the anthropological insight that conversation with an AI platform is a part of natural conversation. When bewildered by another's words (or at a loss to express our own) we might offer explanations, exceptions, or elaborations. We might seek to understand the other more deeply by asking questions, offering sympathy, or holding space to listen. Conversation continues as far as we remain in partnership.

References

Anscombe, G. E. M. 1957. *Intention*. Basil Blackwell.

Athaluri, Sai, Sandeep Manthena, VSR Kesapragada, Vineel Yarlagadda, Tirth Dave, and Rama Duddumpudi. 2023. "Exploring the Boundaries of Reality: Investigating the Phenomenon of Artificial Intelligence Hallucination in Scientific Writing Through ChatGPT References." *Cureus* 15 (4): e37432. doi:10.7759/cureus.37432.

Bashir, Noman, Priya Donti, James Cuff, Sydney Sroka, Marija Ilic, Vivienne Sze, Christina Delimitrou, and Elsa Olivetti. 2024. "The Climate and Sustainability Implications of Generative AI." *An MIT Exploration of Generative AI*, March 27, 2024. doi:10.21428/e4baedd9.9070dfe7.

Bender, Emily, Timnit Gebru, Angelina McMillan-Major, and Shmargaret Shmitchell. "On the Dangers of Stochastic Parrots: Can Language Models Be Too Big?" 2021. In *Proceedings of the 2021 ACM Conference on Fairness, Accountability, and Transparency*. ACM. doi:10.1145/3442188.3445922.

Biever, Celeste. 2023. "ChatGPT Broke the Turing Test—The Race Is On for New Ways to Assess AI." *Nature*, July 25, 2023. https://www.nature.com/articles/d41586-023-02361-7.

Bommasani, Rishi, Drew A. Hudson, Ehsan Adeli, et al. "On the Opportunities and Risks of Foundation Models." *arXiv preprint arXiv:2108.07258, 2021.*

Brentano, Franz. 1874. *Psychologie vom Empirischen Standpunkt*. Duncker & Humblot.

Cavell, Stanley. 2004. *Cities of Words: Pedagogical Letters on a Register of the Moral Life*. Harvard University Press.

Cavell, Stanley. 1969. *Must We Mean What We Say?* Cambridge University Press.

Chalmers, David J. "Could a Large Language Model Be Conscious?" *arXiv*, 2023. https://arxiv.org/abs/2303.07103.

Chomsky, Noam, Ian Roberts, and Jeffrey Watumull. "Noam Chomsky: The False Promise of ChatGPT." *The New York Times* 8 (2023).

Colby, Kenneth. 1975. "*Artificial Paranoia: A Computer Simulation of Paranoid Processes.*" IEEE Transactions on Systems, Man, and Cybernetics 5 (4): 145–155.

Computer History Museum. 2025. "*UNIVAC Predicts the Election.*" Last modified February 25, 2025. https://www.computerhistory.org/revolution/early-computer-companies/5/102/445.

Ceruzzi, Paul E. 2003. *A History of Modern Computing*. 2nd ed. MIT Press.

Cortada, James W. 2012. *Computers and Automation: A History of Computer Technology*. 1st ed. Praeger.

Duolingo. 2023. "Introducing Duolingo Max, a Learning Experience Powered by GPT-4." *Duolingo Blog*, March 14, 2023. https://blog.duolingo.com/introducing-duolingo-max-powered-by-gpt-4.

Duranti, Alessandro. 1994. *From Grammar to Politics: Linguistic Anthropology in a Western Samoan Village*. University of California Press.

Fanni, Roberto, Verena E. Steinkogler, Giulia Zampedri, and Jeanette Pierson. 2023. "Enhancing Human Agency through Redress in Artificial Intelligence Systems." *AI & Society* 38 (2): 537–547. doi:10.1007/s00146-022-01454-7.

Financial Times. 2025. "Match Enlists AI to Nudge Men into Better Behaviour on Dating Apps." *Financial Times*, April 1, 2025. https://www.ft.com/content/4e39d08b-41ef-41ea-abc0-952d06324484.

Freeman, Cassie, Audrey Kittredge, Hope Wilson, and Bozena Pajak. 2023. "The Duolingo Method for App-Based Teaching and Learning." *Duolingo Research*. https://duolingo-papers.s3.amazonaws.com/reports/duolingo-method-whitepaper.pdf.

Geertz, Clifford. 1973. *The Interpretation of Cultures: Selected Essays*. New York: Basic Books.

Gendron, Gaël, Qiming Bao, Michael Witbrock, and Gillian Dobbie. 2023. "Large Language Models Are Not Strong Abstract Reasoners." arXiv 2305.19555v3.

Gibbons, Sarah, Tarun Mugunthan, and Jakob Nielsen. 2023 "Accordion Editing and Apple Picking: Early Generative-AI User Behaviors." *Nielsen Norman Group*, September 24, 2023. https://www.nngroup.com/articles/accordion-editing-apple-picking/.

Global Partnership on AI. 2023. *Fairwork AI Ratings 2023: The Workers Behind AI at Sama.* https://fair.work/wp-content/uploads/sites/17/2023/12/Fairwork-AI-Ratings-2023_final-1.pdf.

Goffman, Erving. 1981. *Forms of Talk*. University of Pennsylvania Press.

Grice, H. P. 1975. "Logic and Conversation." In *Syntax and Semantics 3: Speech Acts*, edited by Peter Cole and Jerry L. Morgan. Academic Press.

Hegel, Frank. Soren Krach, Tilo Kircher, Britta Wrede, and Gerhard Sagerer. 2008. "Understanding Social Robots: A User Study on Anthropomorphism." In *Proceedings of the 17th IEEE International Symposium on Robot and Human Interactive Communication, RO-MAN*, September 2008. IEEE. doi:10.1109/ROMAN.2008.4600728.

Kairouz, Peter. 2019. "Federated Learning: Challenges, Methods, and Future Directions." *IEEE Signal Processing Magazine* 37 (3): 10–24. doi:10.1109/MSP.2020.2975749.

Kockelman, Paul. 2024. *Last Words: Large Language Models and the AI Apocalypse*. Prickly Paradigm Press.

Kosinski, Michal. 2024. "Theory of Mind May Have Spontaneously Emerged in Large Language Models." *arXiv Preprint arXiv:2302.02083*. doi:10.48550/arXiv.2302.02083.

Lee, Hao-Ping (Hank). 2025. "*The Impact of Generative AI on Critical Thinking: Self-Reported Reductions in Cognitive Effort and Confidence Effects from a Survey of Knowledge Workers*." CHI '25: Proceedings of the 2025 CHI Conference on Human Factors in Computing Systems Article No.: 1121, Pages 1–22 doi:10.1145/3706598.3713778.

Li, Xiaochang. 2023. "There's No Data Like More Data: Automatic Speech Recognition and the Making of Algorithmic Culture." In *Abstractions and Embodiments: New Histories of Computing and Society*, edited by E. P. J. V. Turner. Oxford University Press.

Lewis, David. 1979. "*Scorekeeping in a Language Game*." Journal of Philosophy 77 (7): 374–384.

Matsakis, Louise. 2023. "Air Canada's Chatbot Soars Out of Control, Invents Refund Policy." *Wired*, February 6, 2023. https://www.wired.com/story/air-canada-chatbot-refund-policy/.

McCartney, Scott. 1999. *ENIAC: The Triumphs and Tragedies of the World's First Computer*. Walker & Company.

McGrath, Larry. 2025. "Quit Playing Language Games with My Heart; or, Conversational AI and Knowledge Sharing." *2024 EPIC Proceedings*: 254–275. doi:10.1111/epic.12205.

Mitchell, Melanie. 2023. "The Debate Over Understanding in AI's Large Language Models." *Proceedings of the National Academy of Sciences of the United States of America* 120 (13): e2215907120. doi:10.1073/pnas.2215907120.

Mitchell, Melanie and David C. Krakauer. 2023. "The Debate Over Understanding in AI's Large Language Models." *Proceedings of the National Academy of Science* 120 (13). doi:10.1073/pnas.2215907120.

Microsoft. 2024. "Five Quick Prompting Tips to Get More from Your AI Assistant." *Microsoft Education Blog*, July 11, 2024. https://www.microsoft.com/en-us/education/blog/2024/06/five-quick-prompting-tips-to-get-more-from-your-ai-assistant/.

Moore, R. J., S. An, and G. J. Ren. 2022. "The IBM Natural Conversation Framework: A New Paradigm for Conversational UX Design." *Human–Computer Interaction* 38 (3–4):168–193. doi:10.1080/07370024.2022.2081571.

Muñoz, José M., Javier Bernacer, Alva Noë, and Evan Thompson. 2025. "Why AI Will Never Be Able to Acquire Human-Level Intelligence." *Nature* 637: 794. doi:10.1038/d41586-025-00170-8.

Norman, Donald. 2023. "AI: First New UI Paradigm in 60 Years." *Nielsen Norman Group*, June 18, 2023. https://www.nngroup.com/articles/ai-paradigm/.

Olabiyi, Oluwatobi, Erik T. Mueller. 2019. "Multi-turn Dialogue Response Generation with Autoregressive Transformer Models." *ArXiv* 1908.01841. https://api.semanticscholar.org/CorpusID:199452907.

Ory Laboratory Inc. n.d. "*Avatar Robot Café DAWN ver.*β." Accessed April 11, 2025. https://dawn2021.orylab.com/.

Overgaard, M., and A. Kirkeby-Hinrup. 2024. "A Clarification of the Conditions Under Which Large Language Models Could Be Conscious." *Humanities and Social Sciences Communications* 11: 1031. doi:10.1057/s41599-024-03553-w.

Petroni, Fabio, Tim Rocktaschel, Sebastian Riedel, Patrick Lewis, Anton Bakhtin, Yuxiang Wu, and Alexander Miller. 2019. "Language Models as Knowledge Bases?" In *Proceedings of the 2019 Conference on Empirical Methods in Natural Language Processing*, edited by M. A. Hearst, 2463–2473. Association for Computational Linguistics.

Regilme, Salvador Santino F. 2024. "Artificial Intelligence Colonialism: Environmental Damage, Labor Exploitation, and Human Rights Crises in the Global South." *SAIS Review of International Affairs* 44 (2): 75–92. https://muse.jhu.edu/pub/1/article/950958.

Rosaldo, Michelle Z. 1982. "The Things We Do with Words: Ilongot Speech Acts and Speech Act Theory in Philosophy." *Language in Society* 11 (2): 203–237. doi:10.1017/S0047404500009209.

Sacks, Harvey, Emanuel A. Schegloff, and Gail Jefferson. 1974. "A Simplest Systematics for the Organization of Turn-Taking for Conversation." *Language* 50 (4): 696–735. doi:10.1353/lan.1974.0010.

Schegloff, Emanuel A. 1988. "Goffman and the Analysis of Conversation." In *Erving Goffman: Exploring the Interaction Order*, edited by Paul Drew and Anthony Wootton. Polity Press.

Srinivasan, Siddarth. 2024. "Detecting AI Fingerprints: A Guide to Watermarking and Beyond." *Brookings*, June 28, 2024. https://www.brookings.edu/articles/detecting-ai-fingerprints-a-guide-to-watermarking-and-beyond/.

Southern, Keiran. 2025. "Vegas Cybertruck Bomber 'Used ChatGPT to Plan Explosion.'" *The Times*, January 8, 2025. https://www.thetimes.com/world/us-world/article/vegas-cybertruck-bomber-used-chatgpt-to-plan-explosion-wk7h2jtkq.

Street, Winnie. 2024. "LLM Theory of Mind and Alignment: Opportunities and Risks." *Proceedings of the Workshop on Theory of Mind in Human-AI Interaction at CHI 2024 (ToMinHAI at CHI 2024)*. doi:10.48550/arXiv.2405.08154.

Summers-Stay, David, Christopher R. Voss, and Scott M. Lukin. 2023. "Brainstorm, Then Select: A Generative Language Model Improves Its Creativity Score." In *The AAAI-23 Workshop on Creative AI Across Modalities*.

Vaswani, Ashish, Noam Shazeer, NikiParmar, Jakob Uszkoreit, Llion Jones, Aidan N. Gomez, Łukasz Kaiser, and Illia Polosukhin. 2017. "Attention Is All You Need." *Advances in Neural Information Processing Systems* 30: 5998–6008.

Waldrop, M. Mitchell. 2001. *The Dream Machine: J.C.R. Licklider and the Revolution That Made Computing Personal.* New York: Viking.

Wang, Xin, Zirui Chen, Haofen Wang, Leong Hou U, Zhao Li, and Wenbin Guo. 2024. "Large Language Model Enhanced Knowledge Representation Learning: A Survey." *arXiv*, July 1, 2024. http://arxiv.org/html/2407100936.

Williams, Alex, Milagros Miceli, and Timnit Gebru. 2022. "The Exploited Labor Behind Artificial Intelligence." *Noema Magazine*, October 13, 2022. https://www.noemamag.com/the-exploited-labor-behind-artificial-intelligence/.

Williams, Michael. 2024. "Grammarly Is NOT Perfect, It Doesn't Understand Context." *Medium*, March 24, 2024. https://medium.com/new-writers-welcome/grammarly-is-not-perfect-it-doesnt-understand-context-5863bffdce11t.

Wimmer, Heinz, and Josef Perner. 1983. "Beliefs about Beliefs: Representation and Constraining Function of Wrong Beliefs in Young Children's Understanding of Deception." *Cognition* 13 (1): 103–128. doi:10.1016/0010-0277(83)90004-5.

Wittgenstein, Ludwig. 1953. *Philosophical Investigations*. Translated by G. E. M. Anscombe. Oxford: Basil Blackwell.

Zafar, A. 2024. "Balancing the Scale: Navigating Ethical and Practical Challenges of Artificial Intelligence (AI) Integration in Legal Practices." *Discover Artificial Intelligence* 4: 27. doi:10.1007/s44163-024-00121-8.

Zhang, Caiming, Yang Lu. 2021. "Study on Artificial Intelligence: The State of the Art and Future Prospects." *Journal of Industrial Information Integration* 23, Article 100224. doi.org/doi:10.1016/j.jii.2021.100224

Zhang, Chiyuan, Samy Bengio, Moritz Hardt, Benjamin Recht, and Oriol Vinyals. 2017. "Understanding Deep Learning Requires Rethinking Generalization." *arXiv* 1611.03530, 2017. https://arxiv.org/abs/1611.03530.

Zhang, Hanqing, Haolin Song, Shaoyu Li, Ming Zhou, and Dawei Song. 2023. "A Survey of Controllable Text Generation Using Transformer-based Pre-trained Language Models." *ACM Computing Surveys* 56, 3 March 2024. doi:10.1145/3617680

Zuboff, Shoshana. 2019. "Surveillance Capitalism and the Challenge of Collective Action." *New Labor Forum* 28 (1): 10–29. doi:10.1177/1095796018819461.

10

FROM PRESENT TENSE TO FUTURE (IM)PERFECT

The Role of Anthropology in the Future of AI

Kate Sieck

Introduction

> Risk discomfort and solitude for understanding.
>
> *(Davis 1986)*

Artificial intelligence (AI) is arguably one of the greatest "unknowns" in today's world—one that demands we "risk discomfort and disciplinary solitude" (Davis 1986:21) to understand it. As acknowledged by business leaders and scientists alike, "Advanced AI could represent a profound change in the history of life on Earth, and should be planned for and managed with commensurate care and resources" (Future of Life 2023). From "black-box" algorithms to the far-reaching consequences of automated decisions, and from the strain on global computing resources to the threat of job displacement, AI systems are rapidly reshaping the landscape of work, knowledge, and power. In such uncertain and opaque times, it is both right and sane to be tense—to question the direction of these technologies and the systems driving them. Most of the authors in this volume raise justifiable concerns about the pace, opacity, and risks of generative AI (GenAI) as we hurtle toward this ever-more complex future.

With due respect for that line of critique, I offer a parallel approach—one that is quintessentially anthropological, if not ethnographic. When confronted with the unfamiliar or the seemingly dangerous, anthropologists have long responded not by retreating, but diving in. We seek to understand, to decode, to contextualize, and in doing so, to shift the conversation. AI, in its many manifestations, is precisely the kind of socio-technical domain that demands anthropological engagement—not only to critique its harms, but to help

DOI: 10.4324/9781003532750-14

redesign its foundations. The time is now for anthropologists to embed in these processes: to examine how AI systems are constructed, deployed, and evaluated, and to bring our theoretical and methodological tools to bear on shaping more just and contextually aware systems.

While a growing body of work in AI ethics and Science and Technology Studies (STS) has raised important critiques of algorithmic systems—particularly around bias, surveillance, and labor—relatively little scholarship has extended this critique into the terrain of **model architecture design**. Much of the social science literature to date has focused on auditing (Raji et al. 2020), ethnographic observation (Suchman 2007; Gray & Suri 2019), or policy and governance frameworks (Crawford 2021), with few proposals for reimagining the models themselves. This chapter contributes to a smaller but critical thread of inquiry—traced through thinkers like Philip Agre (1997a, b) and Lucy Suchman—that calls for a **critical technical practice**: one that embeds social theory into the construction, not just the analysis, of AI systems.

By proposing specific pathways for translating anthropological theory into model architectures and training processes, this chapter advances a design-oriented approach to GenAI, grounded in the methodological and conceptual traditions of the discipline. It follows a temporal and linguistic structure—**Present Tense, Past Simple**, and **Future (Im)perfect**—to reflect not only different moments in the history of AI and anthropology, but different modes of engagement. The section titled *Present Tense* focuses on the current moment: how GenAI has shifted public discourse and introduced new sets of challenges around representation, bias, and control. *Past Simple* revisits anthropology's historical emergence in response to extractive colonial systems, pseudoscience, and the mischaracterizations of the global community, showing how our foundational methodologies sought to impose rigor and reduce harm in similarly uncharted terrains. Finally, *Future (Im)perfect* explores specific, actionable ways anthropologists can intervene in the design and development of AI—by shaping training data, fine-tuning models, and inspiring new architectures grounded in social theory.

Navigating this terrain requires both "studying up" (Nader 1972) and, in some cases, embedding within the institutions shaping AI's future. Structural power imbalances will not shift through critique alone. As Dourish (2016:2) noted, "Critiques of algorithmic reasoning that set their own terms of reference for key terminology are unlikely to hit home." Using the language and frameworks of engineering is a matter "of ethnographic responsibility and practical politics" (Dourish 2016:2). By embedding in the companies, systems, and teams building AI—and by translating anthropological insight into algorithmic design—we can help shape the next generation of models from within. This chapter offers a pathway for that work.

Present Tense

GenAI refers to a class of AI systems designed to create new content—such as text, images, audio, or code—based on patterns learned from large datasets composed of similar types of media. Unlike traditional AI or machine learning models that classify, predict, or sort data, GenAI produces novel outputs, often in response to "natural language" prompts, with an apparent ability to mimic human-like creativity and expression. In many ways, these models operate as a mathematically-fueled platform for *bricolage* (cf. Lévi-Strauss 1962).

GenAI has been embedded in many products for the past few decades—in everything from robotic vacuum cleaners to voice-activated assistants. This is the underlying technology that enables people to pose questions to a machine, and more often than not, receive meaningful outputs.

However, the understanding of GenAI's scope and scale shifted dramatically in late 2022 and early 2023. The public release of text-to-image platforms (e.g., DALL-E, Midjourney, Imagen, Stable Diffusion) and large language models (e.g., ChatGPT, Bard, HuggingFace, Llama) changed the cultural, corporate, and government conversations around what is possible. At a very basic level, these models can "analyze vast amounts of text data, generate human-like content, and provide intelligent responses to queries" (Microsoft 2024) in ways that are fundamentally different from previous systems. The ability to *create* images and writings that blend genres and mimic styles, or to quickly identify patterns in massive diverse datasets within moments, leaves most people with feelings of awe at what these models can do (cf., Marche 2021).

Yet just as often as we marvel at their ability to parrot Shakespeare or Van Gogh—or to generate animated zombies and flying cats—these same technologies raise a host of fundamental problems that are anything but playful. Among them: "hallucinating" (sharing inaccurate information as if true), the perpetuation of harmful biases and stereotypes (Bender et al., 2021), and a flattening of nuance and context (Bendel 2023; Jenka 2025).

Many of these problems stem from three core factors: the quality and content of the underlying datasets; the tuning and training of the algorithms; and the metrics used to determine what constitutes a "good" outcome. In the final section of this chapter, I will revisit each of these challenges and explore case studies alongside potential solutions.

The Training Data

Algorithms learn from datasets. These training sets shape the kinds of patterns they can recognize—and how effectively they do so. The prevailing belief has long been that the more data an algorithm is trained on, the better it will perform in predicting outcomes. To draw an analogy: if your only experience of food is peanut butter sandwiches, your ability to understand steak, salads, ice cream, or sushi will be limited. The broader your exposure to diverse foods, the more capable you become of recognizing patterns across new culinary experiences (cf., Mead 1970). While not a perfect analogy, it helps explain why tech companies often prioritize vast data collection in training generative systems.

In practice, algorithms are trained on whatever is most readily available in digitized form. For public-facing GenAI models, this often means ingesting massive portions of "the internet." In corporate settings, training may also involve internal datasets. What matters most is that the content is machine-readable. Unsurprisingly, this has serious implications for communities that are underrepresented—or misrepresented—in these digital corpora.

Additionally, there have been significant concerns with how training data has been acquired. Companies and content creators have accused platform builders of misusing copyrighted materials (see Brittain 2023). Other platforms acknowledged that they have actively trained their foundation models on people's personal social media posts (see Weatherbed 2024). While the legal issues play out in the courts, the theoretical and ethical questions about ownership, creation, remuneration and power provide ample fodder for ethnographic explorations.

Designing the Algorithms

Algorithmic models rely on a complex architecture of components—including weights, parameters, layers, and functions—that collectively shape their outputs.

> **Weights** determine the relative importance of different data points, influencing how strongly one piece of information contributes to a prediction compared to another.
>
> **Parameters** define the "cone of possibility" within which an algorithm operates: tighter parameters constrain responses to a narrower, more controlled range (e.g., more realistic or factually accurate), while looser parameters allow for greater flexibility (e.g., more creative or outlier responses).
>
> **Layers** refer to the depth of processing each piece of input data receives, influencing how well the model can detect and form connections across information.
>
> **Functions** are the mechanisms that enable a model—especially a large language model (LLM)—to decode a prompt and activate the appropriate information pathways in response.

The way these components are structured directly affects an algorithm's ability to retrieve factual information, to mitigate bias in training data, to process unfamiliar or edge-case inputs, and to generate appropriate, meaningful responses.

When we assess the landscape of concerns regarding the outputs of GenAI models, many stem from how the models are tuned. For example, models can amplify aspects of historical data in ways that perpetuate biases in the outputs (Kay et al 2015). Nicoletti and Bass's (2023) study of the outputs of generative models in response to prompts about job titles and crime found widespread problems with overrepresentation of women and darker skin tones in the images generated for prompts regarding low-paying professions and criminal status. More importantly, the rates of representation from GenAI engines did not match current data about gender and racial representation in any of those categories. Tuning the algorithm can address these kinds of challenges: adjusting the weighting of current (versus historical) data; tightening the parameters; modifying the number of training layers to ensure the connection to up-to-date databases. But tuning requires awareness of the problems.

Metrics for "Goodness"

By design, large language models (LLMs) and other foundation models are built to be multipurpose. They can be applied across a wide range of use cases—from legal analysis and science fiction writing to coding ethnographic fieldnotes. This flexibility is one of their greatest strengths—but also one of their greatest challenges. When used "off the shelf," these models may struggle to deliver results aligned with specific goals or contexts, especially if those goals are nuanced, cultural, or disciplinary in nature.

At their core, these models function as probabilistic engines: they predict the next word, pixel, or number in a given sequence based on patterns learned from training data. But what counts as a "good" output depends entirely on the context of use. A "good" home-cooked meal might not satisfy the criteria of a Michelin-star restaurant, even if both meals are nourishing. In the same way, a generative model's success in producing text or images must be evaluated *relative to specific social, cultural, or epistemological goals* (cf., Balagopalan et al., 2023).

Current approaches to the metrics for goodness are complicated at two levels: the design of optimization algorithms (which tell the model what to learn), and at the level of output review (which assess whether it achieved that task). Historically, optimization models have focused on things that are easy to convey in mathematical formulas, such as the likelihood of the next word or pixel. While efficient, these approaches often perpetuate biases, toxicity and challenges in the underlying datasets (see Shi et al. 2024). The output review process can be equally problematic. In instances where outputs are assessed using automatic metrics, this similarly "often leads to manipulation, gaming, a focus on short-term quantities (at the expense of longer-term concerns), and other undesirable consequences, particularly when done in an environment designed to exploit people's impulses and weaknesses" (Thomas & Uminsky 2022).

To combat this, platforms often implement reinforcement learning from human feedback (RLHF). If you've ever had to identify which boxes in a photo contain trees or bicycles or buses, you've participated in this activity. However, much of it is done as low-paid, piecemeal "ghost work," employing millions of people across the Global South who screen far more complicated and challenging material, often with grave consequences for their mental wellbeing (see Gray & Suri 2019).

For many readers, the relevance of anthropology to this work may already be clear. But before turning fully toward anthropology's potential in shaping algorithmic design, I want to take a brief detour into our past. Because we've been here before—and looking to the insights of earlier anthropologists can help us understand why it is so urgent to engage now.

Past Simple: Anthropology's Foundations

Anthropology as a discipline is no stranger to moments that pose existential challenges to humanity and the planet. In fact, it emerged during a similarly turbulent era, shaped by two parallel developments: the expansion of European colonial power and the rise of pseudo-scientific theories in genetics and evolution.

The late 19th and early 20th centuries saw European audiences newly exposed to the cultural diversity of the Global South. Travelogues from traders, missionaries, and adventurers (cf. Bly 1890; Bird 1875; Livingstone 1910 [1857]) and human "zoos" at World's Fairs (cf. Johnson 2020; O'Farrell 2020) brought "exotic others" into public view and conversation. But these representations were often deeply flawed—marked by bias, ignorance, and a lack of any methodological grounding. As Radcliffe-Brown (1958:33) observed, early accounts of indigenous communities were "very often unreliable and only too frequently inaccurate." This was not accidental. As O'Farrell (2020:66) notes, these displays "promoted common stereotypes…in such a way as to 'prove' the superiority of Western civilization."

Alongside this visual and textual othering, new (and often misunderstood) scientific theories—especially around genetics—exacerbated the harm. While Darwin and Mendel both published in the 19th century, it wasn't until the early 20th century that Mendel's work gained traction. Lacking a clear understanding of how genes functioned, early scientists made sweeping and inaccurate claims about heredity (cf. Lovejoy 1971). These claims laid the groundwork for eugenics: a movement that used pseudo-science to justify coercive, often brutal interventions into reproduction and population control (see Proctor 1988).

It was within this context that anthropology began to take shape—not as an extension of colonial power, but in some cases as a critique of its excesses. Early anthropologists sought to build a more rigorous, empirically grounded understanding of the diversity of human communities (King 2019). One of the discipline's key figures, A.R. Radcliffe-Brown, argued that anthropology must follow the methodological rigor of the physical sciences. He wrote:

> If social anthropology is to progress, it must follow the rules of all induction. Facts must be observed, and a hypothesis must be found which seems to explain the facts. ... The next step is to return once more to the work of observation in order to verify or test the hypothesis. ... And so the process goes on until we have established our hypothesis as a theory with some degree of probability.
>
> *(1958: 34)*

While Structural-Functionalism is now rightly critiqued for its static view of culture and limited engagement with power, it was a critical step in developing a methodological backbone for the field. Its emphasis on comparative analysis and data collection helped move anthropology beyond anecdote and toward systematic inquiry. Done well, it also functioned as a check on personal bias and ethnographic overreach.

I am not suggesting a return to Structural-Functionalism. But we should recognize the role it played during a time of profound harm. *By modeling its methods on established scientific disciplines, early anthropology gained credibility—and influence—in shaping both academic and public understanding of cultural difference. Embracing rigor, it helped move society past our grossest biases to a more thoughtful consideration of human cultural differences.*

Why does this matter now? Because we are once again facing a moment of under-regulated expansion and unchecked epistemic authority—this time in the form of AI. The way some companies collect data to train AI models echoes the extractive, poorly theorized practices of early colonial agents. And the algorithmic "black box," shrouded in technical language, parallels the misuse of early genetics to justify social control. In the absence of transparent frameworks or ethical commitments, these systems risk producing biased, inaccurate, or harmful outputs—now at global scale.

Some of anthropology's early lessons are directly applicable. First: **frameworks matter**. Not all data is equal. How we define, structure, and weight information shapes what models learn—and what they reproduce. Anthropology offers rich, field-tested frameworks for interpreting human behavior, cultural difference, and power.

Second: **theory matters**. The discipline's strength lies in its ability to produce grounded, evidence-based explanations for *why* people do what they do. This allows us to move past the "haphazard use of theory" Radcliffe-Brown warned against. While some anthropologists will continue to study GenAI ethnographically, those working within tech have a powerful opportunity: to operationalize anthropological theory inside the models themselves, not only by collecting new data, but by embedding anthropological insight into code, architecture, and the systemic logic of design.

In the next section, I turn to how this work can unfold.

Future (Im)perfect

This chapter is not a call for a utopian future powered by perfect, benign AI. We cannot fix everything. But we can make meaningful progress in reducing the harm these systems cause—because the challenges at hand are uniquely suited to anthropological insight.

Just as early anthropologists responded to an era of deep structural harm with new frameworks and methods for understanding the social and cultural life of communities, we now face a similar opportunity—if not responsibility—to shape the conversations and technologies that increasingly structure our world. Our discipline today has a robust corpus of theory that can and should be operationalized within the design and build of algorithms in ways that can mitigate the harm they produce. While not ethnographic in the traditional sense of "going to the field," this engagement with theory-as-a-tool extends the findings of those who conduct deep fieldwork.

In the following sections, I return to the core challenges described earlier—dataset quality, algorithmic design, and evaluation metrics—and offer three key areas where anthropologists can shape the development of GenAI: changing the data, fine-tuning the models, and imagining new model architectures and combinations.

Solution 1: Change the Underlying Data

As noted earlier, algorithms are trained on digitized data. This means communities that are underrepresented or misrepresented in digital corpora are likely to be marginalized in model outputs. We've seen this dynamic repeatedly over the past decade, especially in social-impact domains.

In one example, researchers developing a predictive algorithm to assess the likelihood of a child entering state care due to maltreatment drew on a range of public datasets (cf. Eubanks 2018). However, the dataset *excluded* families not represented in public systems: those whose children attend private schools, who receive care from private insurance or therapy programs, or who have never been involved with social services. This omission created a skewed training environment. The model never learned how maltreatment might appear in middle- and upper-income families, nor did it receive data on protective or positive forces such as strong social networks or supportive adults. The result? Disproportionate risk assessments for poor BIPOC families and public outcry over the algorithm's systemic bias.

In the world of GenAI, similar failures abound. Algorithms trained on historical employment data often reflect patterns of discrimination—such as recommending white men for promotion based on legacy decisions that excluded others (Nicoletti & Bass 2023). AI-generated images have replicated colonialist tropes, like a South Sudanese Barbie carrying automatic weapons

(Collings & Mir 2023), or have failed to generate accurate portrayals of Black professionals in caregiving roles (Drahl 2023), even after hundreds of attempts.

One solution is to change the training data.

Emerging efforts like Latimer.ai and ChatBlackGPT offer examples of proactive community-led model building. Frustrated by the erasure and misrepresentation of Black and Brown communities in popular LLMs, their creators curated new training datasets from community-centered media, with a focus on linguistic accuracy and respect. Terms like "freedom-seeking enslaved peoples" replaced "runaway slaves," creating more context-sensitive and affirming outputs. These choices have influenced larger players and pointed to what's possible.

Another promising example is *The Pile* (Gao et al., 2020), a large-scale dataset built from smaller, high-quality sources such as academic publications. The goal was to improve factual accuracy while reducing harm and environmental impact. Rather than consuming "the internet," this federated approach focused on curated sources, enabling more precise, respectful, and lower-compute models.

Moreover, anthropologists can help design *data ontologies* that reflect community priorities and forms of knowledge (cf., Berners-Lee 2006). Rather than assuming standard linkages globally, ethnographers are well-positioned to work alongside communities to document the resonant semantic frameworks that inform their lives. While technically complex, generative models can be trained on multiple ontologies—so long as the architecture includes a routing mechanism that activates the appropriate semantic schema based on input context, effectively allowing the model to apply the relevant cultural logic or framework. In this way, semantic frameworks drawn from ethnographic research can be directly operationalized in AI models. Data ontologies can then serve as the blueprint for knowledge graphs, which improve model outputs in multiple ways, including factual accuracy, reasoning, and structuring data generation.

In addition to shaping the structure and semantics of data, anthropologists can also help rethink the ownership and governance of data itself. Specifically, we can foster and support the development of data cooperatives (cf., Hubbard 2024). At core, data cooperatives refer to "the voluntary collaborative pooling by individuals of their personal data for the benefit of the membership of the group or community" (Pentland & Hardjono 2021). Just as the early 1900s saw the birth of cooperative financial organizations (credit unions, employee unions) rise from the exploitation of people, data cooperatives seek to rebalance the value generated from people's data by empowering people to control their data and gain access to the profit generated from it. Anthropologists could work collaboratively with each other and the communities where we base to build precisely these kinds of cooperatives.

Our partnerships with often-marginalized communities, and our training in documenting and co-interpreting the lived realities of those excluded from dominant systems, offer a rich foundation for more inclusive datasets.

Whether through community archives, oral histories, multilingual texts, or ethnographic notes, we can help counter erasure and misrepresentation—not by claiming neutrality, but by building datasets that reflect situated knowledge and lived complexity.

Solution 2: Fine-Tune the Models

As previously discussed, fine-tuning refers to the process of adjusting an LLM's internal components—its weights, parameters, layers, and functions—to guide or correct its outputs. These adjustments can significantly alter how models behave across varied contexts and tasks. These design decisions are not abstract—they have direct consequences for how models perform in real-world, high-stakes situations

Anthropological engagement with the design of algorithms has been more limited. Influencing these aspects of model design requires more than the "pragmatic amateurism" (Gusterson 1997: 116) so typically associated with our discipline, and instead requires a deeper mastery of the language of algorithmic design. Yet just as we often master a local language as part of our research training, this could be considered yet another "language" within the discipline.

For example, a model designed for creativity might be tuned with wide parameters to allow for outlier responses, while a model used for legal analysis would have narrower constraints to ensure factual precision. Adjusting weights can shift emphasis away from sensitive demographic features in high-stakes decisions (e.g., hiring or lending), while adding more layers enables the model to detect deeper patterns—but risks overfitting and brittleness in new contexts.

In high-profile failures—such as attorneys submitting LLM-generated briefs filled with fake citations (Merken 2023; Weiss 2025)—we see how improper parameter settings or misrouted functions can yield false outputs. Similarly, persistent racial and gender bias in model-generated images or text can be traced to both biased data and insufficient post-training correction. Reinforcement learning, particularly through penalties in the model's loss function, can help decouple these associations (Nicoletti & Bass 2023). But care must be taken not to erase historical realities in the process—such as generating fictional Nazi soldiers of every ethnicity (Grant 2024; Robertson 2024). Implementing gating functions—mechanisms that determine which parts of a model should be activated in response to a prompt—could help constrain outputs to historically accurate representations while still allowing for flexible generation in other contexts.

Anthropologists are uniquely positioned to support this fine-tuning process. We can help identify when and how outputs should be modified—not just for factual accuracy, but for cultural integrity. One promising example is the work of Lian et al. (2024). The team used ethnographic insights about intergroup reciprocity to fine-tune an LLM tasked with analyzing patterns of peace and conflict in global news coverage. Through a Retrieval-Augmented Generation (RAG) pipeline, they matched theoretical insights with real-world data, generating more nuanced and timely indicators than conventional metrics.

Another case comes from Keskar et al. (2019), whose CTLR model enabled users to control language generation across dimensions like style, content, and genre. Recognizing that a word like "knife" has drastically different connotations in a horror story than in a cooking recipe, their system preserved context-specific associations—essentially operationalizing Wittgenstein's notion of meaning as use.

Anthropologists, with our deep sensitivity to context, metaphor, and marginality, are well-equipped to guide these kinds of adjustments. We can not only identify outliers that signal model breakdowns but also ensure those outliers are treated as opportunities for insight, not noise to be discarded.

Solution 3: Create (or Advance) New Types of Models

Anthropologists can also shape the development of new model architectures altogether. While not all of us are technical experts in model engineering, many modeling techniques are directly compatible with anthropological thinking.

Take **Mixture of Experts** (**MoE**) models. These architectures train multiple smaller models (experts), each specializing in a specific domain or function. A gating system routes queries to the relevant expert, allowing for more efficient and modular processing. This mirrors ethnographic fieldwork, where researchers consult key informants with domain-specific knowledge. So far, MoEs have focused on functional optimization—but imagine expanding this to include cultural domains, genre-specific knowledge, or even different "layers" of cultural meaning (cf. Shore 1996, Rotolo 2022). An MoE architecture could route a query about kinship metaphors to an expert trained on kinship systems across cultures—or a query about music to a model trained on both Western notation and oral performance traditions.

Then there are **optimization models**, which aim to identify the best solution to a problem under a given set of constraints. Many of these already draw from patterns in nature: ant colony optimization mimics how ants find efficient paths; bee colony algorithms model swarm behavior; genetic algorithms apply evolutionary principles like mutation and crossover.

If existing optimization models already draw inspiration from biological systems, why not turn to social systems? Anthropological theory offers an equally rich set of dynamics that can inform model behavior—especially when we consider how power, resistance, and knowledge operate within data ecosystems.

As an example, consider the design of an optimization model premised on Scott's (1985) *Weapons of the Weak*. In that work, he details multiple techniques Malaysian farmers used to resist domination and oppression, including foot-dragging, hidden transcripts and feigned compliance. When we think about GenAI models, one of the challenges is that some corpora "dominate" others. **Could we translate Scott's findings into a model architecture that enables smaller corpora to "resist" this silencing?** Here's a possible path:

Hidden transcripts: Scott contrasts *public transcripts* (what people say in power's presence) with *hidden transcripts* (what they say among themselves). Anthropologists and our community partners could curate "resistance" datasets where these hidden transcripts are more likely to emerge (e.g., diasporic blogs, protest ephemera, local media forms). These collections, then embedded into a data ontology, would surface critical perspectives in more accessible ways.

Foot-dragging: In the ethnography, Scott details examples of farmers slowing down work, delaying tasks, and otherwise *controlling the pace of work* to resist the demands of external stakeholders. Within a model architecture, we could create a penalty function for overconfident completions in dominant tones, thereby training the model to find alternatives that are more rare in the underlying data, or to prioritize responses from the curated corpora of "hidden transcripts."

Feigned compliance: Scott highlights multiple ways in which the farmers *appeared to follow expectations, but found ways around them*, such as "forgetting" to file paperwork, or pretending to not understand what was asked of them. One potential way to embed this in model architecture is to change the evaluation metrics. Rather than focusing on traditional markers of fluency, coherence or frequency, we could embed metrics and counter-dominant sampling strategies that prioritize diversity, contradiction or conflict. This tactic fundamentally shifts the foundation of "goodness" while preserving the concept.

While these ideas may be complex to implement, they are not out of reach. All would have the benefit of creating space for "resistance" so that the quieter elements of a training dataset could have a more significant impact on the model outputs. This is one example with one particular theoretical framework from the ethnographic record. Other approaches could be designed to reflect other frameworks. For example, how might we read video data differently if we designed a vision-based models on Bourdieu's theory of habitus (1977)? How might the Manchester School's focus on moments of deviance be used to design simulations differently than a reliance on established patterns? This is precisely where anthropological theory can be a critical tool in the future of GenAI.

As a final thought experiment, there are significant possibilities for anthropological thinking within the realm of machine learning as well. For example, we could create systems modeling pipelines that are architected based on core anthropological concepts. Zeitlyn's (2022) concept of non-ergodicity—the idea that systems cannot be treated as homogeneous or reducible to averages—offers a particularly valuable insight for predictive modeling, especially when models aim to assess causal relationships in behaviors that have both person-level factors, social-level factors, and temporal cues. We could consider a case for predicting binge drinking, or academic success among university students. A hypothetical system architecture could look like the following:

- Model *person-level patterns* using *Bayesian Hierarchical Models*, with the assumption that not everyone responds to stressors in the same way;
- Assess *group-level dynamics* via *Graph Neural Networks*, which enables influence dynamics to shift depending on social position;
- Identify *temporal signals* in *Sequence Models*, to surface time-dependent and non-linear tipping points;
- Feed these outputs into a multi-agent simulation model
- Compare simulation outcomes to real-time data streams to assess where the models align—and where they diverge.

While the comparison should not be treated as a right-versus-wrong answer, it should inspire closer reflection on how and why the simulation may diverge from the data feeding the other models. These differences could signal important shifts, a need for different data sources, or other emerging dynamics in the situation.

This exploration of theory-informed systems architecting could be repeated with a multitude of core concepts, including *isolarion, epiphanic moments, palimpset memories*, and so on (see Zeitlyn 2022). Importantly, none of these exercises replace the need for anthropological thinking to assess and inform the inputs, design or outputs. Rather, they position anthropological theory as a foundational element of model design—moving us from critics on the sidelines to co-creators at the core. And therein lies the possibility for improvement in the way the future of AI unfolds. Imperfect, but more just. More situated. And ultimately, more human.

Conclusion: From Theory to Action

None of this requires new ethnographic fieldwork from those who choose this path. Instead, it invites a different kind of partnership—one that connects anthropology practitioners in the tech sector with the ongoing theoretical insights produced by ethnographers in the field. This approach amplifies the full potential of the discipline by building on its cumulative knowledge and applying it where it is urgently needed. Anthropologists embedded within technology can help shape datasets, design model features, adjust system behaviors, or even invent new architectures—all grounded in the deep well of social theory we already have.

In a moment when AI often feels like an untouchable force, it's worth returning to the words of Wade Davis: "Risk discomfort and solitude for understanding." Anthropologists have long taken this to heart—embracing uncertainty not to control the unknown, but to interpret what seems opaque and intervene in the systems that increasingly shape human futures. Our task is to engage with these technologies—critically, deeply, and creatively.

We bring the very tools needed to make these systems more just, more contextual, and more human. The knowledge is already here. The challenge isn't whether anthropologists are needed. It's whether we're ready to show up.

References

Agre, Philip E. 1997a. "Toward a Critical Technical Practice: Lessons Learned in Trying to Reform AI." In *Bridging the Great Divide: Social Science, Technical Systems, and Cooperative Work*, edited by Geoffrey C. Bowker, Les Gasser, Leigh Star, and William Turner, 131–157. Mahwah, NJ: Lawrence Erlbaum Associates.

Agre, Philip E. 1997b. *Computation and Human Experience*. Cambridge University Press.

Balagopalan, A., D. Madras, D.H. Yang, D. Hadfield-Menell, G.K. Hadfield, and M. Ghassemi. 2023 "Judging Facts, Judging Norms: Training machine learning models to judge humans requires a modified approach to labeling data," in *Science Advances* 9 (19). doi:10.1126/sciadv.abq0701.

Bendel, Oliver. 2023. "Image Synthesis from an Ethical Perspective." *AI & Society* 40: 437–446. doi:10.1007/s00146-023-01780-4.

Bender, Emily, Timnit Gebru, Angelina McMillan-Major, and Shmargaret Shmitchell. 2021. "On the Dangers of Stochastic Parrots: Can Language Models Be Too Big?🦜" In *Proceedings of the 2021 ACM Conference on Fairness, Accountability, and Transparency (FAccT)*. doi:10.1145/3442188.3445922.

Berners-Lee, Tim. 2006. "*Linked Data*." https://www.w3.org/DesignIssues/LinkedData.html.

Bird, Isabella. 1875. *Six Months in the Sandwich Islands, amongst the Palm Groves, Coral Reefs and Volcanoes*. John Murray Press.

Bly, Nellie. 1890. *Around the World in 72 Days*. Bretano's.

Bourdieu, Pierre. 1977. *Outline of a Theory of Practice*. Cambridge University Press.

Brittain, Blake. 2023. "Getty Images Lawsuit Says Stability AI Misused Photos to Train AI." *Reuters*, February 6, 2023. https://www.reuters.com/legal/getty-images-lawsuit-says-stability-ai-misused-photos-train-ai-2023-02-06/.

Collings, Paul, and Raza Mir. 2023. "Barbie and the Dark Side of Generative Intelligence." *Salon*, August 17, 2023. https://www.salon.com/2023/08/17/barbie-and-the-dark-side-of-generative-artificial-intelligence/.

Crawford, Kate. 2021. *Atlas of AI: Power, Politics, and the Planetary Costs of Artificial Intelligence*. Yale University Press.

Davis, Wade. 1986. *The Serpent and the Rainbow*. Simon & Schuster.

Drahl, Carmen. 2023. "AI was Asked to Create Images of Black African Docs Treating White Kids. How'd it Do?" *NPR, Goats and Soda*, October 6, 2023.

https://www.npr.org/sections/goatsandsoda/2023/10/06/1201840678/ai-was-asked-to-create-images-of-black-african-docs-treating-white-kids-howd-it-.

Eubanks, Virginia. 2018. *Automating Inequality: How High-Tech Tools Profile, Police and Punish the Poor*. Macmillan Press.

Future of Life Institute. 2023. "*Pause Giant AI Experiments: An Open Letter*." March 22, 2023. https://futureoflife.org/open-letter/pause-giant-ai-experiments/.

Gao, Leo, Stella Biderman, Sid Black, et al. 2020. "The Pile: An 800GB Dataset of Diverse Text for Language Modeling." *arXiv*. https://arxiv.org/pdf/2101.00027.

Giddens, Anthony. 1986. *The Constitution of Society: Outline of the Theory of Structuration*. University of California Press.

Grant, Nico. 2024. "Google Chatbot's AI Images Put People of Color in Nazi Uniforms." *New York Times*, February 22, 2024. https://www.nytimes.com/2024/02/22/technology/google-gemini-german-uniforms.html.

Gray, Mary L. and Siddharth Suri. 2019. *Ghost Work: How to Stop Silicon Valley from Building a New Global Underclass*. Houghton Mifflin Harcourt.

Gusterson, Hugh. 1997. "Studying Up Revisited." *PoLAR: Political and Legal Anthropology Review* 20 (1): 114–119. doi:10.1525/pol.1997.20.1.114.

Hubbard, Sarah. 2024. "Cooperative Paradigms for Artificial Intelligence." In *Political Economy of AI Essay Collection*, Allen Lab, Ash Center, Harvard Kennedy School, November 20, 2024. https://ash.harvard.edu/resources/cooperative-paradigms-for-artificial-intelligence/.

Jenka. 2025. "AI and the American Smile." *Medium*, March 26, 2023. https://medium.com/@socialcreature/ai-and-the-american-smile-76d23a0fbfaf.

Johnson, Walter. 2020. *The Broken Heart of America: St. Louis and the Violent History of the United States*. Basic Books.

Kay, Matthew, Cynthia Matuszek, and Sean A. Munson. 2015. "Unequal Representation and Gender Stereotypes in Image Search Results for Occupations." In *Proceedings of the 33rd Annual ACM Conference on Human Factors in Computing Systems*, 3819–3828. Association for Computing Machinery.

Keskar, Nitish Shirish, Bryan McCann, Lav R. Varshney, Caiming Xiong, and Richard Socher. "CTRL: A Conditional Transformer Language Model for Controllable Generation." arXiv preprint arXiv:1909.05858 (2019).

King, Charles. 2019. *Gods of the Upper Air: How a Circle of Renegade Anthropologists Reinvented Race, Sex and Gender in the Twentieth Century*. Doubleday Press.

Koh, Rachel. 2023. "A List of AI-Generated Barbies from 'Every Country' Gets Blasted on Twitter for Blatant Racism and Endless Cultural Inaccuracies." *Business Insider*, July 11, 2023. https://www.businessinsider.com/ai-generated-barbie-every-country-criticism-internet-midjourney-racism-2023-7.

Lévi-Strauss, Claude. 1962. *The Savage Mind*. University of Chicago Press.

Lian, Kevin, Larry S. Liebovitch, Melissa Wild, Harry West, Peter T. Coleman, Francine Chen, Everlyne Kimani, and Kate Sieck. 2024. "Classifying Peace in Global Media using RAG and Intergroup Reciprocity." *arXiv*, October 1, 2024. https://arxiv.org/pdf/2410.13865.

Livingstone, David. 1910. *Missionary Travels*. London: Ward Lock & Co. [Original work published 1857]

Lovejoy, Arthur. 1971. *The Great Chain of Being: A Study of the History of an Idea*. Harvard University Press.

Marche, Stephen. 2021. "The Algorithm That Could Take Us Inside Shakespeare's Mind." *New York Times*, November 24, 2021. https://www.nytimes.com/2021/11/24/books/review/shakespeare-cohere-natural-language-processing.html.

Mead, Margaret. 1970. "The Changing Significance of Food." *American Scientist* 58 (2): 176–181.

Merken, Stephen. 2023. "New York Lawyers Sanctioned for Using Fake ChatGPT Cases." *Reuters*, June 26, 2023. https://www.reuters.com/legal/new-york-lawyers-sanctioned-using-fake-chatgpt-cases-legal-brief-2023-06-22/.

Microsoft. 2024. "5 Key Features and Benefits of Large Language Models." *Microsoft Blog*, October 9, 2024. https://www.microsoft.com/en-us/microsoft-cloud/blog/2024/10/09/5-key-features-and-benefits-of-large-language-models/.

Nader, Laura. 1972. "Up the Anthropologist: Perspectives Gained from Studying Up." In *Reinventing Anthropology*, edited by Dell H. Hymes, 284–311. Pantheon Books.

Nicoletti, Laura, and D. Bass. 2023. "Humans Are Biased. Generative AI Is Even Worse." *Bloomberg Technology*, June 9, 2023. https://www.bloomberg.com/graphics/2023-generative-ai-bias/.

O'Farrell, Helen. 2020. "A New and Curious Route to Cairo: World's Fairs and the Stereotyping of the Middle East (1851–1893)." *IAFOR Journal of Cultural Studies* 5 (1): 65–79. doi:10.22492/ijcs.5.1.04.

Patnaik, Subrat. 2019. "Apple Co-Founder Says Apple Card Gave Wife Lower Credit Limit." *Reuters*, November 11, 2019. https://www.reuters.com/article/technology/apple-co-founder-says-apple-card-algorithm-gave-wife-lower-credit-limit-idUSKBN1XL038/.

Pentland, Alex and Thomas Hardjono. 2021. "Building Data Cooperatives." In *Building the New Economy*, edited by Alex Pentland, Alexander Lipton, and Thomas Hardjono, 19–34. MIT Press.

Proctor, Robert N. 1988. *Racial Hygiene: Medicine Under the Nazis*. Harvard University Press.

Radcliffe-Brown, A. R. 1958. *Method in Social Anthropology: Selected Essays*. University of Chicago Press.

Raji, Inioluwa Deborah, Andrew Smart, Rebecca N. White, Margaret Mitchell, Timnit Gebru, Ben Hutchinson, Jamila Smith-Loud, Daniel Theron, and Parker Barnes. 2020. "Closing the AI Accountability Gap: Defining an End-to-End Framework for Internal Algorithmic Auditing." In *Proceedings of the 2020 Conference on Fairness, Accountability, and Transparency (FAT '20)*, 33–44. ACM. doi:10.1145/3351095.3372873.

Robertson, Adi. 2024. "Google Apologizes for 'Missing the Mark' after Gemini Generated Racially Diverse Nazis." *The Verge*, February 21, 2024. https://www.theverge.com/2024/2/21/24079371/google-ai-gemini-generative-inaccurate-historical.

Rotolo, Daniel. 2022. "Culture Beneath Discourse: A Conceptual Model for Analyzing Nondeclarative Cultural Knowledge." *American Journal of Cultural Sociology* 10: 432–460.

Scott, James C. 1985. *Weapons of the Weak: Everyday Forms of Peasant Resistance*. Yale University Press.

Shi, Y., H. Yu, and C. Leung. 2024. "Towards Fairness-Aware Federated Learning." *IEEE Transactions on Neural Networks and Learning Systems* 35 (9): 11922–11938. doi:10.1109/TNNLS.2023.3263594.

Shore, Bradd. 1996. *Culture in Mind*. Oxford University Press.

Suchman, Lucy A. 2007. *Human–Machine Reconfigurations: Plans and Situated Actions*. 2nd ed. Cambridge University Press.

Thomas, R. L., and D. Uminsky. 2022. "Reliance on Metrics Is a Fundamental Challenge for AI." *Patterns* 3 (5). doi:10.1016/j.patter.2022.100476.

Weatherbed, James. 2024. "Meta Fed Its AI on Almost Everything You've Posted Publicly Since 2007." *The Verge*, September 12, 2024. https://www.theverge.com/2024/9/12/24242789/meta-training-ai-models-facebook-instagram-photo-post-data.

Weiss, Debra Cassens. 2025. "No. 42 Law Firm by Headcount Sanctioned over Fake Case Citations Generated by AI." *ABA Journal*, February 10, 2025. https://www.abajournal.com/news/article/no-42-law-firm-by-headcount-could-face-sanctions-over-fake-case-citations-generated-by-chatgpt.

Zeitlyn, David. 2022. *An Anthropological Toolkit: 60 Useful Concepts*. Berghahn Books.

CONCLUSION

Editorial Forum on the Futures of Anthropology and AI

Lora Koycheva, Matt Artz and Angela K. VandenBroek

Introduction

This book, like all books, came about circuitously. David Eller has a much bigger influence on its shape in so many ways than readily discernible in that, in fall of 2023, he had already secured the willingness to contribute from a number of authors featured here. The series he is editing—the Anthropology of Now—speaks to the urgency of issues confronting anthropology, and it is fair to say that few things are more "now" than AI—one of the most important contemporary phenomena on a global scale. Immediately, this put us, as editors, on two timelines. One is the timeline on which books are written, edited, and published; and one on which the technology, and its social and cultural response, moves.

Given these competing timelines and the urgency of the moment, two fundamental questions emerge: How is anthropology to respond? How has it begun to capture that zeitgeist?

Our editorial approach to these questions shaped the book's structure. Early on, reviewers of our proposal urged us to "impose a logic" on the chapters in order to create a more easily recognizable alignment of approaches—methodological, critical, and theoretical—but as editors, we decided to take a more open-ended approach. Admittedly, our purpose was not to corral the chapters to build towards an anthropological theory of AI but to let them spell out the many possible entanglements between anthropology and AI. Ranging from empirical and conceptual to historical and applied, the chapters in this book do just that. We would like to suggest that the book can be read rather as an opening than an exhaustive representational endeavor of the status quo, with each chapter an invitation.

DOI: 10.4324/9781003532750-15

To this end, we conclude the book not with a conclusion but with a forum on the future of anthropology and AI.

Lora: What story do the chapters in this book spell out for you in your reading of them?

Lora: For me, it's a story of how anthropology challenges—or would like to challenge—AI as a phenomenon: through anthropologically-informed critique.

Matt: Across most of these chapters, a common thread emerges: AI is deeply problematic, entangled in cultural myths, ethical risks, and systemic inequalities. Most contributions are rooted in critique and conceptual analysis—hallmarks of academic anthropology—but there's notably less emphasis on moving toward action, intervention, or concrete recommendations. While the problems are well articulated, fewer authors grapple with the harder question: how might we meaningfully respond?

In my view, one crucial pathway for anthropological influence requires that anthropologists position themselves at the sites where AI is actually created—actively shaping its design, governance, and implementation from the outset. Without this kind of engagement, we risk relegating ourselves to the sidelines, diagnosing from afar while failing to influence the futures we so urgently critique. We've seen elements of this pattern before with social media: anthropological critique was abundant and insightful, but meaningful engagement came too late. The result—platforms that now shape global discourse in ways widely recognized as deeply problematic—stands as a cautionary tale for our current moment with AI.

Angela: The field of artificial intelligence, in all its threads and iterations, has gone through several periods known as "AI Winters." These are times when inflated expectations—often driven by technoscience and industry hype—lead to disillusionment and funding collapse. These stories typically center on the dominant paradigm of the moment (e.g., neural nets in the 1960s, expert systems in the 1980s). But other approaches persist through these winters, often forming the basis of the next paradigm. So, rather than tides pulled in and out, AI's history feels more like waves—building, cresting, crashing, and feeding the waves behind them. In those moments just after a crash, when expectation collapses and inevitability loses its grip, there is openness: a space of possibility, fragmentation, and contestation.

While researching the timeline for our introduction, it became clear that the anthropology of AI has also followed a wave-like pattern. But anthropology's timeline doesn't align with AI's—it runs in syncopation. Anthropology's influence is strongest during AI's winters. For instance, Diana Forsythe and Lucy Suchman were active during the height of expert systems, but their influence—especially on situated and distributed approaches—shows up in AI research citations most clearly in the winter that followed. One might view this pessimistically as anthropology's inability to intervene in real time—a critique my co-editors share. I don't think they're wrong. But I'd suggest that anthropology's syncopation with AI might also reflect its strength: not in reinforcing dominant trajectories, but in disrupting them, clearing space for new possibilities. Anthropology offers little to communities seeking validation for their assumptions but much to those open to challenge.

This is the story this volume tells: I believe we are in an *Anthropology of* AI Winter. In the 2000s and 2010s, anthropologists played active roles in tech development both in applied careers and in how theoretical work was engaged externally—across anthropologies of design, big data, algorithms, and attention. But with the rise of GenAI, that welcome engagement has again receded. Our critical work no longer aligns with the industry's trajectory. When GenAI hits its peak and recedes to a plateau—having failed to deliver on its inflated promises—the anthropology being done now will again find an audience beyond the discipline. We are, once again, building insights for the next moment of rupture.

The chapters in this volume offer hopeful, critical, forward-looking, and historically grounded perspectives—challenging anthropological understandings of AI, dominant technoscientific paradigms, and the power structures shaping AI in industry, government, and society. These challenges may be met with limited uptake—not due to lack of quality, but because of this Anthropology of AI Winter. AI is consolidating around its dominant paradigm, while anthropology, since the 1980s, has turned toward critiques of power and oppression (Ortner 2016), resisting alignment with such consolidation. Given rising extremism and ecological crisis—deeply tied to AI's development—this resistance is even stronger. The tensions in this volume, between us and across the wider interdisciplinary field, reflect that Anthropology of AI Winter.

Matt: Angela, I appreciate your framing of this moment as an Anthropology of AI Winter, and interestingly, I've used a similar framing in a forthcoming AI chapter for the *Handbook of Applied Anthropology* (Artz Forthcoming a). But I see the timing—and implications—quite differently.

In my view, the real winter was between roughly 2000 and 2017. While it's true that many anthropologists entered tech during that time, in the published literature, the field receded into shadows and relied heavily on critique. We saw very little methodological development around AI and even less on anthropologists helping to build AI systems. Since 2018, though—and especially in the past few years—I've noticed a shift. The literature is increasingly responsive to the current boom in ways that remind me of the early work of Forsythe and Suchman. It's a moment that feels unexpectedly generative and full of potential.

If we are in any form of a winter right now, it is an *Anthropology Winter* more broadly. The signs are becoming increasingly difficult to ignore. Just this month, the American Anthropological Association hosted a town hall (May 6, 2025) dedicated to the discipline's uncertain future—echoing similar concerns raised at the 2025 Society for Applied Anthropology annual meeting in Portland. Those conversations have now crystallized in print through the American Anthropologist's Volume 127, Issue 2, "Vital Topics Forum: Ethnographies of a Dying Discipline," thematic section where scholars like Santos (2025a, 2025b) confront the reality of a shrinking discipline—department closures, declining enrollment, and a public increasingly skeptical of anthropology's relevance.

This is compounded by the sharp contraction of the academic job market: only about 21% of U.S. anthropology PhDs secure tenure-track roles (Speakman et al. 2018). For those who don't, the alternatives are often precarious and poorly compensated. According to the same analysis, fewer than 8% of new graduates across all degree levels—BA, MA, and PhD—secure jobs in the field each year. The U.S. Department of Labor estimated only 7,700 employed anthropologists in 2015 (U.S. Department of Labor 2015), and only around 920 anthropology and archaeology job ads appear annually (Rapacon 2017)—a stark mismatch given the roughly 12,000 students who complete anthropology degrees each year. These challenges help explain why anthropology is routinely ranked among the worst-paying majors (Winters 2024). In 2012, both Kiplinger Business Forecast and Forbes ranked Anthropology and Archaeology as the worst choice of college majors, citing a 10.5% unemployment rate and a median salary of $28,000 for recent graduates (Dewey 2012; Goudreau 2012).

As Lora and I argue in *EmTech Anthropology* (2024), this is a crisis of legitimacy and imagination. But it's also something else: a failure to recognize the strategic realities we face. In business terms, we are overlooking the external threats in our operating environment—the kinds of threats that, in a SWOT analysis, can take down even the most established institutions. Anthropology, at this moment, resembles an aging Fortune 500 company: long confident in its legacy, slow to adapt, and now at risk of being outpaced by faster, more responsive disciplines that are capturing student interest, securing funding, and dominating public discourse.

Most anthropologists—especially those within the academy—don't tend to see the world this way, perhaps because they've never had to manage the survival of a business in a competitive landscape. But make no mistake: we are competing. Competing for students, funding, and relevance in and out of the academy. And while this volume—especially this conclusion—lays bare the productive internal tensions many in our field value, the external environment isn't standing still. It's accelerating. And frankly, it's indifferent to whether we've resolved our disciplinary identity.

Lora: So, how does AI challenge anthropology? And how can anthropology rise and respond to that challenge?

Matt: AI challenges anthropology epistemologically by forcing a reconsideration of core concepts like intelligence, agency, and relationality; methodologically, by contrasting anthropology's contextual, qualitative traditions with positivist, data-driven approaches; and practically, by sidelining anthropological perspectives in favor of computational framings of human behavior.

These challenges suggest that anthropology may need to fundamentally change. Computational disciplines/roles—within academia, business, and government—have outpaced anthropology in relevance, visibility, and funding. If anthropology does not adapt, embed itself as productive co-creators within sites of AI, and demonstrate its value in shaping technological futures, it risks becoming increasingly peripheral at a moment when its insights could be particularly useful.

But adaptation requires more than just presence—it demands genuine collaboration with disciplines we've often been critical of. Too often, anthropologists view business and engineering colleagues as misguided positivists and techno-solutionists, and while there are good reasons to be critical of such approaches, there are also compelling reasons to embrace them. The goal should not be one or the other, but a balance—picking and choosing as needed to both problematize and intervene.

This over reliance on critique and grand problematizing creates more barriers than opportunities for the discipline and its practitioners, potentially alienating potential allies and reinforcing perceptions of anthropology as irrelevant to practical decision-making.

Lora: Well, certainly, the grand problematizing that you speak about, Matt, is not matched by a grand opportunity recognition and development. And for me, the opportunity is clear to infuse the technology and the future worlds it will bring about with more anthropological ethos. If only we would seize the moment and coopt the problems! For me, additionally, AI challenges both the form of anthropology and the logic of anthropological inquiry as practiced in relation to emerging technologies. Regarding the latter point, I was struck that quite a few chapters, for example, are fairly conceptual (Kang and Becerra Sandoval come to mind, as well as Brown). My work is often conceptual, so this was for me not a problem. This makes me think of Paul Rabinow and his circle of close collaborators' work on anthropological inquiry as a conceptual apparatus (e.g. Rabinow 2009) and his critique of the limits of ethnography. That started out of his work on synthetic biology, but I believe anticipated the complexities that anthropological work on AI will continuously face. But it does make me wonder: what do we read about the future trajectory of anthropology and AI in that fact? One answer may be that the phenomenon of AI continues to be difficult to access empirically, let alone to gain the kind of active shaper role you are speaking about—although, of course, there are ways to both conduct ethnographies of engineers working on AI (for example, Vepřek and Carlson, as well as Rodwell, in this volume) or through exploring experimental collaborations (as Pachón has done).

Angela: Of the three of us, I'm definitely the most contrarian on AI's current potential—both as a challenge to anthropology and as a societal force. That statement, of course, hinges on how we define AI here.

Throughout this volume—and in anthropology more broadly—AI is a massively unstable object of study. Reading the question before seeing Lora or Matt's responses, my first impulse was to think in terms of GenAI—this current Silicon Valley-driven wave with all its surrounding hype, fantasy, and power. That's partly because this volume was catalyzed by that wave. For this kind of AI, I'm personally pessimistic about its transformative potential. That's not to say it's all hype or won't leave lasting impacts. But many of the fears and hopes projected onto it seem disconnected from what the technology actually does—points this volume draws out well, particularly in Brown's and Pachón's chapters—including its real capabilities and its staggering financial and environmental costs. These technologies aren't going away, but I expect them to consolidate into the hands of a few corporations capable of operating them at a loss for symbolic gain. Historically, that kind of consolidation leads to stagnation and status quo, not innovation.

So, the challenges GenAI poses to anthropology are, to me, not fundamentally different from those we face in other para-ethnographic domains (Holmes and Marcus 2008), that is, collaborative engagement with systems of belief, practice, and power. Also, as Matt points out, there are also generative concepts usable as boundary objects (Star and Griesemer 1989; Star 2010) that can help anthropology communicate across epistemic divides, fostering collaboration where interests align.

That said, hearing your replies, I don't think you're talking only about GenAI. Your responses reflect a broader conceptualization of AI—spanning robotics, automation, recommendation systems, and more. In that context, I share your optimism. I've long been an early adopter, building automated systems in my lab and experimenting with AI for qualitative analysis. I'd love to see automation free us up for more creative and meaningful work, though history suggests that will take organized politics and rigorous critique.

However, what I think you're responding to isn't just the tech or its uses—it's the alluring and compelling promise AI makes in the social marketplace of knowledge and strategy that we, as anthropologists, do not. AI offers speed, scale, and strategic utility in ways anthropology doesn't—or won't. Ideally, the two could complement each other. But that vision is rarely embraced. So, like you, I worry about anthropology's future in a world dominated by scientism and accelerationism.

Yet, I believe we need a "yes…and" approach embracing multiple anthropologies—conceptual, avant-garde, accessible, public, applied, collaborative, idealistic, and realistic—that reach out to diverse stakeholders and communities.

Angela: In that vein, my question is this: considering how much of our future is shaped by our collective imaginations of it, what are the future imaginaries around AI you've encountered (personally or in this book)? What role might (or should) anthropology play in shaping those imaginaries?

Matt: Emerging technologies, such as AI, are always "on the cusp" of arriving—usually later than evangelists predict—and there are certainly plural futures ahead that none of us can fully anticipate. But from working inside tech, I see that AI is farther along than many anthropological critics realize, particularly those observing from outside these spaces. Yes, many ideas and companies will fail, and the technology is far from perfect. But AI has been quietly embedded in our lives for many years through search engines, recommendation systems, and countless other applications. Even GenAI, despite the hype, is already being used by billions daily, with companies realizing measurable return on investment across diverse use cases.

Yet the future imaginaries I encounter in anthropology often seem disconnected from these on-the-ground realities. We tend toward either dystopian warnings or utopian dismissals while devoting far less energy to imagining how AI could be appropriated, adapted, or redirected to genuinely serve diverse human needs and aspirations. Meanwhile, the imaginaries being constructed in corporate strategy sessions, product roadmaps, and policy discussions are the ones that have significant influence—and anthropological voices are notably absent from those conversations.

If anthropology is to play a meaningful role in shaping AI's future, it should consider moving beyond its overly pessimistic stance and positioning itself as a collaborative partner in building these systems. Our role shouldn't be to imagine AI futures from the sidelines but to embed ourselves in the spaces where those futures are actively being built, like McGrath and Sieck of this volume. Without such engagement, we risk ceding AI's development entirely to others—and in doing so, may contribute to the very dystopian outcomes we fear through our own inaction.

Lora: That is a great question that occupies me and my daily work very often, both as a scholar and as a founder of a think-and-do tank dedicated to rebuilding society with robots. That vision is both very critical of humans and very optimistic about the technology. This is not the usual setup; it's usually the other way around. And imagination—and the anthropological imaginaries—are fundamental to both. Personally, outside of the immediate context of this book, I often encounter an imaginary that runs in a dystopic direction and in which AI (and robots) are feared, demonized, and plainly pitted against "the human." And I'm really tired now of hearing colleagues from the humanities and social sciences frame techno-optimism as a bad thing. The social scientific and humanistic response as a whole seems to me that it tends to run overwhelmingly towards the negative and pessimistic as to the trajectory the technology is taking us towards. This is not to say I do not believe their evaluations, interpretations, and reason for alarm. The evidence of how harmful AI can be is indisputable. But the other side of the story is rarely fleshed out: that optimism is a *choice* that is just as necessary to make as the pessimistic critique is. In that respect, the examples that Sieck gives in her chapter about ways in which AI can be made more equitable and diverse are welcome in the overall volume of contributions detailing AI's role in exacerbating inequalities without much suggestion of how anthropology (or any one other discipline, for that matter) might help build these systems better.

Angela: First, Lora, I love the "think-and-do tank" framing. Your "very critical of humans and very optimistic about the technology" stance is vital—it highlights the complexity of human-technology relationships, which are always contextual and situated. This perspective helps move us beyond the binary of AI as either harmful or full of promise. Instead, it opens space to explore how AI functions differently across specific contexts, shaped by unique configurations of power, inequality, and desire. That kind of nuance is exactly what we need more of—especially in anthropology—where diverse, grounded imaginaries can challenge both techno-utopianism and blanket doom.

Take, for example, Yeager's chapter on disability accommodations. AI is often framed as either replacing valuable human care or expanding accessibility. But she complicates this by showing how disabled people adopt and adapt AI tools as essential and how banning them can reinforce ableist harm. I remember asking her about the broader ecosystem these technologies circulate within—especially the risks they introduce for institutions being asked to support them. If a school or workplace allows a third-party AI tool access to sensitive data, what new vulnerabilities emerge? She dove into those tensions—between power, access, risk, and innovation—using anthropology to map both harms and affordances across sociotechnical systems.

If we move beyond asking whether AI is "good" or "bad," and instead focus on how it works, for whom, and under what conditions, we can develop more robust and just imaginaries. This requires anthropology not just to critique or celebrate but to build—drawing on our capacity to hold contradiction and complexity. As Ruha Benjamin writes, "we owe it to ourselves to name the world we cannot live without, even as we diagnose the world we cannot live within" (2022, 279).

Matt: Angela's point about anthropology needing to "build" resonates with me, but it highlights a fundamental challenge: since the 1960s, anthropology has built a culture of antagonism toward the very institutions and professionals we now need to influence. How do we actually make anthropological insights actionable for those building AI systems?

One key challenge is that building these capacities within anthropology requires a culture change—something we should be good at. Yet, I suspect doing so will be hard because it exposes a fundamental contradiction in our discipline. While anthropologists champion accessibility and inclusion as core social values, we often struggle to make our own work—or our discipline—accessible to those outside academic circles. We've often prioritized critique and invented jargon at the expense of our potential as builders and co-creators.

Further, we're often dismissive, if not openly hostile, toward the perspectives of engineers, designers, and business leaders—the very people we need as collaborators. As a result, anthropology struggles to extend its influence and is frequently perceived as irrelevant to practical decision-making.

What we need is good design—what Yeager calls for in her chapter—but applied to anthropology itself. Good anthropology requires good design: making ourselves accessible and practical in how we write, speak, and engage, as we were before the postmodern turn made critique our primary mode. This means creating anthropological insights that are usable by practitioners—translating our understanding of culture and human behavior into frameworks that engineers can implement, products that designers can build, and strategies that business leaders can execute. It means designing anthropology itself to be more collaborative, solution-oriented, and embedded in the spaces where technological decisions are made. Only by intentionally rebuilding our discipline can we help influence the redesign of the technologies that are reshaping human society.

Lora: I do believe that a culture change is necessary, but as we all know, cultures and deeply entrenched systems do not change overnight. In fact, it's a very slow and fraught process, and the result is never quite the originally intended one. This will be tricky, given the speed at which business and engineering move. As to the methods question, I will answer with an illustration from my practice teaching in interdisciplinary settings (innovation and STS). Every so often, either an early career colleague or a PhD student working qualitatively comes up with the problem of linearity in writing—and the infamous partial perspective of the anthropologist who is not omniscient and who only has one body, constrained by physics to experience only a partial set of circumstances of the field. AI, however, increasingly does not have that problem when gathering data. It has multiple bodies it can access at the same time (to simplify, it needs objects with sensors hooked to the IoT; that then is a minimum viable body for an AI). I have written about this in the UNESCO Toolkit for Digital Anthropology (Koycheva 2023). Angela you also speak about the issue of partial perspectives in your chapter, albeit from a very different angle.

So, we need to get tinkering with methods! This said, there are some practical caveats that I can see here. Already, training students in fieldwork and ethnography is a lengthy and complex affair, necessarily so. Learning basic coding skills is also a time-consuming undertaking. And then, having an experimental component where you have mastered both of these in their disciplinary and classic forms and can now finally start the tinkering I speak of… how many semesters do you need to dedicate just to methods? At least 3?

There are serious institutional constraints to do this if we are to insist on training classic methods, which we also must do.

As for being understandable and less jargon-heavy, again, that's a skill that can be taught. The bigger part of the anthropological project depends upon problematization, complication, and showing the nuances and complexities. This is our analytical advantage, but when you start building with anthropology or selling anthropology as something that can bring value to those who do not know the discipline, it becomes a disadvantage. The famous anthropological "it depends" that encapsulates this thinking in multiples, this commitment to holding space for pluralities, is something which we must know how to repackage without undoing. Elizabeth Briody talked about how this "on the one hand; on the other hand" approach did not serve economists well when advising Truman, so much so that he said he wished for a one-handed economist (Briody and Robinson 2020). We need to learn how to be one-handed anthropologists. Personally, I've had the same experience: sooner or later, you have to *choose* one of the multiplicities and pluralities that we typically pride ourselves in uncovering and making epistemological space for—and act on that one, just the one. Perhaps how to make this choice is something that we still need to collectively address. And, in the event we cannot settle the issue, which is the likeliest scenario in my view, we could at least have a minimum viable operationalization, corny as this might sound, that works for the many kinds of anthropologies that we collectively practice but is also legible enough to outsiders who are building the world a lot faster than anthropology can say "but hold on and think about it for a minute."

Angela: Another issue is how students approach thesis and dissertation research. Projects tend to align with personal interests or politics but often overlook how research design choices shape skill development. As professors, we need to help students integrate professional skill-building into their independent work. We also need to broaden exposure to anthropology's applications—especially at the undergraduate level. Too often, students don't realize how relevant their training is to fields like AI until too late.

I also want to amplify conversations we've had about embracing entrepreneurship during this project and in other collaborations. This, of course, doesn't have to mean the kind of neoliberal, hustle-culture version of entrepreneurship that many anthropologists are averse to. As we've discussed, it is about taking action, enrolling allies, gathering resources, and *doing*—without permission. It is about recognizing the value of anthropology, not just for consultation but for strategy, leadership, and innovation. We are capable of documenting not only what is and why—but what is possible beyond the assumptions of the status quo. Anthropologists do this through venture creation, community and political organizing, public service, and corporate intrapreneurship. AI is one space where resources are currently plentiful and is ripe for appropriation by anthropology.

Lora: I agree completely.

Angela: But I want to return to your original question and push back on its premise—that anthropologists fail to reach industry. Is that the aim of anthropology? Are the critiques that are unproductive in some industry contexts written to sway this audience? Largely, I would say no. Some are—but many aim to speak to other publics. These anthropologists aren't trying to reform the AI industry. They are seeking to convince other stakeholders, communities, and publics that AI is not always what is promised and that there are real, tangible dangers to their use and application. In so doing, they generate resistance and solidarity and influence public sentiments that lead to consumer rejection of AI products (like the backlash to Klarna and Duolingo's AI strategies), community organizing (like rejecting AI data centers in ecologically sensitive areas), or advocacy for more transparency around and open access to AI technologies that resist the centralization of the AI industry. These aims can be just as impactful as directly intervening in spaces of design, engineering, and sales.

Matt: Angela's right that most anthropologists aren't trying to reach industry—and for me, that's precisely the problem. If we're not attempting to shape the systems we critique, it raises questions about the ultimate impact of the critique. We don't need to convince other like-minded academics who already share our concerns. So, if we're not influencing the builders of these systems, who exactly are we writing for and to what end?

And if we accept the argument that anthropologists aim to reach publics, the data suggests significant challenges. In a 2022 presentation I gave at "Why the World Needs Anthropologists," I showed that a Google News search reveals 444 million hits for Economics, 118 million for Psychology, but only 3.9 million for Anthropology. Google Trends data reveals similar patterns—anthropology barely registers compared to economics and psychology in public interest. Even more striking is the comparison with AI: while anthropology has seen declining search interest since 2004, AI search interest has exploded, particularly since 2018, now vastly outpacing anthropology. So if reaching publics is our stated goal, these numbers indicate we face substantial obstacles—and suggest we're losing ground to the very technologies that threaten to displace us.

Regarding the argument about consumer backlash against AI, the evidence suggests consumer behavior doesn't fully align with this narrative. At the May 2025 Google I/O, they announced consumers are now using 480 trillion AI tokens monthly in Gemini—up 50-fold from a year ago. Further, Gemini has hit 400 million monthly active users. Similarly, ChatGPT was reported to have 800 million weekly active users in May 2025.

While anthropological critique may influence some public discourse and action, widespread resistance isn't clearly reflected in usage patterns.

Lora: Psychology has really been our most faithful nemesis when it comes to public visibility. If only I had a euro for every time I have had to defend my approach against it as the more easily recognizable social science, especially in design, organizational science, innovation and entrepreneurship, I'd be able to fund these experimental methods summer camps I'm dreaming about myself!

Angela: Matt raises valid, urgent concerns. But they are not, I think, as simple as anthropology falling behind more action-oriented or communicative disciplines. Influence is never just about who speaks more clearly—it's about who is structurally positioned to be heard. Economics, for example, has long been institutionally tethered to the very structures it claims to analyze. It wasn't formed simply as a descriptive science but as a tool to shape and sustain capitalism. Psychology, meanwhile, has undoubtedly shaped public discourse through accessible studies and pop-science appeal. But the professional demand for that visibility came at a cost—leading to the replication crisis that exposed deep problems in the field's foundations (Hughes 2018).

Job market data also deserves scrutiny. "Anthropologist" is rarely a job title outside of academe. My own career, like many others, has drawn explicitly on anthropological methods and thinking—under titles like "web designer" or "library associate"—yet such roles disappear from most career statistics (VandenBroek 2024). Still, I share your desire for greater impact and visibility. I just don't believe the situation is as dire as it may seem or that the solutions need be as prescriptive. Programs like the one I'm part of at Texas State are growing—not shrinking—because we center applied pathways, career readiness, and public anthropologies without flattening anthropology's diversity of practice. Students aren't only asking for jobs; they value meaningful careers where they can do some good—be that in a board room or picketing in the streets. Each one I see succeed gives me hope despite the challenges we face.

Matt: I appreciate your optimism and commend you on the Texas State program, but that optimism is harder to maintain when I think about the students we've interviewed as part of the Anthropology Career Readiness Network research. I've experienced students and young professionals from programs across the country almost in tears. One student stated: "Even though I have this degree, I don't feel like I can actually use it." (Artz, Briody, Aragon, & Nolan 2024)

Angela: The unevenness between what students learn, what they know how to apply, and what they need to further learn speaks to broader questions about how our discipline approaches emerging technologies like AI. There's that Ada Lovelace quote from our introduction about how we overrate and underrate technology—what do you think anthropology is overrating and undervaluing about AI?

Matt: I really liked that quote, but the thing that came to mind was not what we are overrating and undervaluing about AI; there is quite enough of that in our intro and the broader dialogue. Instead, for me, the question is better framed as: what are we overrating and undervaluing about anthropology itself in relation to AI?

I'd argue we've overrated what we find interesting—our grand problematizing and impenetrable invented jargon—while undervaluing our potential to solve problems and meaningfully address the genuine risks AI poses.

We almost always seem to default to systemic issues of power, understandably so, but there are often complementary, more immediately actionable issues we can simultaneously address while pursuing the larger issues. I personally like to take inspiration from Forsythe, whose feminist analysis was integral to identifying practical knowledge engineering problems that others missed—the kind of granular, situated problems that critical proximity reveals. And so, I think we need to prioritize critical proximity over critical distance in this Techno-Anthropology work we are engaged in (Birkbak, Petersen, and Jensen 2015), especially given the high stakes involved, not to the point of losing sight of the systemic issues, but so that we can reclaim our value by surfacing both the macro-level patterns and the micro-level problems and build alongside the AI we study.

Lora: Well, if we agree that anthropologists are interested in power and find both its workings and the resistance to it remarkable enough to focus on and make the hallmark of our disciplinary architecture, then it should follow that we are collectively overrating its harmful effects, the techno-utopian overreach, and the hegemonic principles and practices which AI organizations, broadly defined, both adopt and promulgate. However, I do not think that is actually the case, much as I am deeply unexcited of the formula "anthro walks in a bar; finds power." I operate and live in Europe, and it is not so strongly felt here (not yet; and whether this is good or bad remains to be seen), but there are other geopolitical contexts in which the changing shifts of power on a global scale are definitely enmeshed, and engendered, with the accelerated advent and deployment of AI—domestically but also in foreign affairs. This, I believe, is yet to play out, and personally, I will admit here to a lot of trepidation about what happens when that does come to pass. And you would not even need to have mechanical bodies—robots—for any of that. In a worst-case scenario, a powerful enough AI can shut everyday life down at scale and quickly. So, I do not think we are overrating AI's power. One topic that looms large that the book was not able to cover but which I should bring up now, also in looking ahead at future trajectories of research and intervention in the realm of anthropology and AI, is dual-use technology in the contemporary global moment. A lot of societally beneficial products that we take for granted today and without which our lives would be very impoverished and greatly inconvenienced come out of dual-use projects in the past. The challenge is to ensure that the benefits of AI are on par with, if not outweigh, its harms and are equitably distributed. That is a challenge that anthropologists share with a range of other disciplines—some, like engineering and finance—far more immediately responsible for how AI takes shape in society. This is why I agree with Matt when he alludes to anthropologists needing to be "in the room" with computational disciplines, as upstream in the process as possible. I think trying to influence it once it's rolling is a lot harder. Sadly, this is our current position—trying to get a word in way after decisions have been made.

As for what we are undervaluing, it's hard for me to say because it's tied to a formulation of a normatively "true state of the case," which I believe our forum here, together with the chapters in the book, show is hard, if not impossible, to posit. When Angela mentioned AI being a massively unstable object, I found myself agreeing but also thinking that is usually the case with most things (and if they appear too stable, anthropologists make it our project to destabilize them), and now I am also starting to think that perhaps AI really is a category of its own in that instability respect. But I also see Matt's point of view on an ostensible underrating of the transformative (and I read Matt's comment as "positive transformation," knowing how upbeat he is on the tech. Matt, you can correct me if I am wrong).

Matt: When I speak of AI's transformative impact, I'm not making a normative claim about whether that transformation is positive or negative. I'm simply pointing to the empirical reality that billions of people now use AI daily—it shapes how we communicate, navigate, discover information, learn, work, and make decisions. This widespread integration represents a significant transformation in society, regardless of how we evaluate its effects.

Lora: Got it. Well, I say ostensibly because right now, it does look like we have not produced many examples of when AI goes right and does good—although Yeager's chapter is one such example in this volume. This, of course, should not happen by forcing it down on colleagues to tell the positive story, but because it is bound to be the case with a technology that is this unstable and multifaceted, as Angela rightly says. Once we balance that deficit in the optics and have the demonstrable ethnographic caseload available that shows the dark side but also the bright side of AI, I think the collective conversation will have reached a level of richness and vibrancy towards which this books makes important steps.

Angela: I absolutely agree with you Lora. Also, your point about geopolitical perspective is important here. I remember at one point, a North American author had included a somewhat off-cuff comment about quadruped robots as "horrific," and you, as a European and entrepreneurial interlocutor in robotics, who gets to engage with them in much more interesting and dynamic ways was a bit caught off by the comment. Meanwhile, as an American, my first instinct, like the author is to see new technologies, especially in AI and robotics, as first "horrific" extensions of militarism, policing, surveillance, and incarceration because these are the primary contexts, histories, and applications most Americans see them in—especially as much of AI is invisible to consumers in other contexts. The horror of that history and entanglement, I think, has a large impact on American anthropology's approach to them—particularly how much we "overvalue" or, more accurately, over-represent these forms and uses of AI. Generally, in the anthropology of technology, I think that we so often over-represent the Silicon Valley military-industrial part of technology—especially its ideological leaders—and thus miss the far more pervasive and complicated spaces of human-technology relations. By not engaging these spaces where AI is caught up in resistance, abolition, care, and more due to our preoccupations with these particular critiques, we risk missing out on the ingenuity, innovation, and creativity of humans elsewhere. That's not to say we ought to pivot away from critiquing these harmful systems and ideologies, but that we again need a "yes…and" approach for a more robust and fruitful anthropology of AI.

Lora: A "yes…and" approach is urgently necessary in addressing AI, especially also as it is inspired by improv theater. As a whole, there is too much "yes…but" around, at least to my taste. It's a blocker, not an enabler attitude. Nothing will move forward if "yes…but" continues.

Matt: Given our experience with this book, what would you like anthropology's relationship with AI to look like in ten years?

Angela: The anthropology of AI ought to be robust and diverse—at once challenging, critiquing, and radically imagining AI futures while also participating in applied, innovative, and entrepreneurial forms of *doing* with, against, and among AI.

Matt: I envision AI Anthropology as a fully established subdiscipline grounded in the AI Anthropology Lifecycle (Artz Forthcoming b)—where practitioners iteratively cycle through anthropology *of* AI to critically examine systems as cultural artifacts, anthropology *by* AI to leverage computational methods for enhanced research capabilities, and anthropology *for* AI to embed human-centered insights directly into development processes—creating a holistic approach that positions anthropologists as indispensable architects of "Good AI," ensuring our discipline's relevance and securing our professional futures rather than allowing AI to displace us from academia and industry.

Lora: In 10 years, I'd like to see a mature anthropological theory of AI, a vibrant range of examples of anthropological AI products, and, by then, robots out into the world, doing good and enabling humans to finally have more time to listen to one another, spend time with one another, and understand one another—an anthropology which will have used AI and robotics to go viral, at scale and become not a popular academic discipline but a popular way of life.

Anthropology's AI Problem Really Ought to Be Its Opportunity: Concluding Thoughts from Lora Koycheva

Whether the reader agrees with Matt or Angela's respective takes on AI Winter in anthropology, through the various contributions in this volume and our editorial forum, what has emerged is that AI spells a problem for anthropology in very immediate ways: a problem right now. That problem is both intellectual and also very practical. For some of our more critical authors, it has spelled out a problem because it tends to be built on divisive tenets that promote racism, ableism, and other forms of inequality. For others, the extreme storytelling surrounding the early lifecycle of AI products—whether one calls it hype or mythology—obscures the realities of what these technologies can and cannot do in terms of cognition. Yet others have seen a potential for building better societies with and through AI—if only the technology is approached from a different angle and perhaps with a different attitude. These intellectual interventions play out against a backdrop of many existential threats facing the discipline as a whole in starkly institutional terms, threats which are perhaps by now best understood as inextricable from the advent of big data computational processes, products, and cultures that have come to dominate contemporary life.

I'd like to leave off this volume with a suggestion that therein, in anthropology's AI problem, lies an opportunity for it to reinvent itself; to reinvent AI; to reinvent the world it is so dedicated to, in all its complexities, paradoxes, contradictions, and incommensurable realities. There is an opportunity to revisit, reinvent, and update our methods and to account for what new technologies enable us to do methodologically that we could not have before, as well as the forms and formats that anthropological and ethnographic knowledge can take, also in the future. There is an opportunity to actively build AI systems based on anthropological principles, backed up with the vast insider knowledge anthropologists have about life and societies all over the world and with anthropological ideals in mind. And there is, still and always, an opportunity to build the worlds which our collective entrenched idealism and humanism has until hitherto found expression in critique and perhaps political activism, but not in building products that directly affect billions of people. In the banality of the dictum "problems are opportunities"—an adage which many anthropologists might sniff at for being part and parcel of the hustle culture built on a very particular brand of American "cruel optimism" (Berlant 2011)—there is however a tried and tested truth that we might want to take at face value for its shrewd pragmatism. Anthropology, of all disciplines, with its pride in seeing in different terms, really ought to apply that to itself—its collective intellectual project and professional arrangements—and see the AI problem as an opportunity. The time is now. And it is a very exciting, if scary, time indeed.

References

Artz, Matt. Forthcoming a. "Artificial Intelligence: The AI Anthropology Lifecycle (of + by + for AI)." In *Practicing Digital Ethnography*, edited by Devin Proctor. New York: Routledge.

Artz, Matt. Forthcoming b. "AI Anthropology: The Future of Applied Anthropological Practice." In *Routledge Handbook of Applied Anthropology*, edited by Christina Wasson, Edward B. Liebow, Karine L. Narahara, Ndukuyakhe Ndlovu, and Alaka Wali. New York: Routledge.

Artz, Matt, and Lora Koycheva. 2024. "Introduction." In *EmTech Anthropology: Careers at the Frontier*, edited by Matt Artz and Lora Koycheva. New York: Routledge. doi:10.4324/9781003458555.

Artz, Matt, Elizabeth K. Briody, Zahira Aragon, and Riall Nolan. 2024. "Anthropology Training and Career Preparation: Key Takeaways from Focus Groups." Anthropology News website, January 17, 2024. https://www.anthropology-news.org/articles/anthropology-training-and-career-preparation-key-takeaways-from-focus-groups/.

Benjamin, Ruha. 2022. *Viral Justice: How We Grow the World We Want*. Princeton University Press.

Berlant, Lauren. 2011. *Cruel Optimism*. Duke University Press.

Birkbak, Andreas, Morten Krogh Petersen, and Torben Elgaard Jensen. 2015. "Critical Proximity as a Methodological Move in Techno-Anthropology." *Techne: Research in Philosophy & Technology* 19 (2).

Briody, Elizabeth K. and Marc S. Robinson. 2020. "Anthropology and Economics in the Public Eye." *Anthropology News* website, July 20, 2020. doi:10.14506/AN.1462.

Dewey, Caitlin. 2012. "Worst College Majors for Your Career." *Kiplinger*, September 6, 2012. https://www.yahoo.com/news/worst-college-majors-for-your-career.html.

Goudreau, Jenna. 2012. "The 10 Worst College Majors." *Forbes*, October 11, 2012. http://www.forbes.com/sites/jennagoudreau/2012/10/11/the-10-worst-college-majors/#5b4e7c6e53c9.

Holmes, Douglas R., and George E. Marcus. 2008. "Collaboration Today and the Re-Imagination of the Classic Scene of Fieldwork Encounter." *Collaborative Anthropologies* 1: 81–101. doi:10.1353/cla.0.0003.

Hughes, Brian. 2018. *Psychology in Crisis*. Palgrave Macmillan UK.

Koycheva, Lora. 2023. "*Ethnography for an Accessible Future: Scaling embodiment as a Paradigm for Anthropology in the Digital World Through Telepresence Robots*." Report for UNESCO and LiiV Center for Innovating Digital Anthropology. Document code SHS/MOST/DA/2023/PI/6. https://unesdoc.unesco.org/ark:/48223/pf0000384899.

Lovelace, Ada Augusta. 1843. "Notes by the Translator of Luigi F. Menabrea's Sketch of the Analytical Engine Invented by Charles Babbage." In *Scientific Memoirs, Selected from the Transactions of Foreign Academies of Science and Learned Societies, and from Foreign Journals*, Vol III, edited by Richard Taylor, translated by Ada Augusta Countess of Lovelace, 691–731. London: Richard and John E. Taylor.

Ortner, Sherry B. 2016. "Dark Anthropology and Its Others: Theory since the Eighties." *HAU: Journal of Ethnographic Theory* 6 (1): 47–73. doi:10.14318/hau6.1.004.

Rabinow, Paul. 2009. *Anthropos today: Reflections on modern equipment*. Princeton University Press.

Rapacon, Cynthia. 2017. "10 Worst College Majors for Your Career." *Kiplinger*, September 7, 2017. http://www.kiplinger.com/slideshow/college/T012-S001-worst-college-majors-for-your-career-2016-2017/index.html.

Santos, Jose Leonardo. 2025a. "Ethnographies of a Dying Discipline: Anthropology in the 21st Century." *American Anthropologist* 127: 365–367. doi:10.1111/aman.28058.

Santos, Jose Leonardo. 2025b. "'Eliminate Anthropology': Attitudes Toward Social Science in the Public Discourse." *American Anthropologist* 127: 278–291. doi:10.1111/aman.28055.

Speakman, Robert J., C. Spencer Hadden, Michael H. Colvin, Justine Cramb, Kelsey C. Jones, T. W. Jones, et al. 2018. "Market Share and Recent Hiring Trends in Anthropology Faculty Positions." *PLOS ONE* 13 (9): e0202528. doi:10.1371/journal.pone.0202528.

Star, Susan Leigh. 2010. "This Is Not a Boundary Object: Reflections on the Origin of a Concept." *Science, Technology & Human Values* 35 (5): 601–17. https://doi.org/10.1177/0162243910377624.

Star, Susan Leigh, and James R. Griesemer. 1989. "Institutional Ecology, 'Translations' and Boundary Objects: Amateurs and Professionals in Berkeley's Museum of Vertebrate Zoology, 1907-39." *Social Studies of Science* 19 (3): 387–420. doi:10.1177/030631289019003001.

U.S. Department of Labor. 2015. "Occupational Outlook Handbook: Anthropologists and Archeologists." Accessed March 1, 2018. https://www.bls.gov/ooh/life-physical-and-social-science/anthropologists-and-archeologists.htm.

VandenBroek, Angela K. 2024. "Tactics for Anthropology + Design beyond the Academic and Applied Binary." In *The Routledge Companion to Practicing Anthropology and Design*, edited by Jenessa Mae Spears and Christine Z. Miller, 101–113. New York: Routledge. doi:10.4324/9781003340188-9.

Winters, Mike. 2024. "The Best—and Worst—Paying College Majors, 5 Years After Graduation." *CNBC*. https://www.cnbc.com/2024/03/24/best-and-worst-paying-college-majors-5-years-after-graduation.html.

INDEX

Note: Locators in *italic* indicate figures.